Words of Praise for *Sacred Ceremony*

"*Sacred Ceremony* is the most thorough, thoughtful, and accessible book on ritual and ceremony that exists today. It is a treasure that can help you connect to the Source of Life, renew in times of transition, find healing and guidance, celebrate the cycles of life, and maintain a vibrant connection to the Sacred every day. Thank you, Steven, for compiling such a meaningful and practical guide."

— **Joan Borysenko, Ph.D.,** author of *Minding the Body, Mending the Mind* and *Inner Peace for Busy People*

"*Sacred Ceremony* is one of those rare books for which we've been searching all of our lives. Steven Farmer is to be commended, as he has created very good medicine indeed—a spiritual feast to nourish our hungry souls in this time of change."

— **Hank Wesselman, Ph.D.,** author of *Spiritwalker, Medicinemaker,* and *Visionseeker*

"During times of change, human beings naturally gravitate to ritual, ceremony, prayers, and realms of the sacred to support significant transitions and rites of passage. Steven Farmer provides an excellent resource guide for individuals, families, and communities who, during times of change, may want to create meaningful ways to mark important events in their lives."

— **Angeles Arrien, Ph.D.,** cultural anthropologist, and author of *The Four-Fold Way* and *Signs of Life*

"Steven Farmer has written an inspiring book that not only offers practical and effective guidelines for creating ceremony, but more important, ways to understand and appreciate both the ancient background and modern meaning of these events. Farmer speaks from the wisdom of generations before us as well as his own personal life and spirit. Here's a book to read carefully and consult again and again as the seasons of the year and one's own life continue to turn."

— **Tom Cowan,** author of *Shamanism as a Spiritual Practice for Daily Life*

"Steven has gifted us with a profoundly personal, wise and well-researched book. It will help readers to reconnect with the sacred, to Mother Earth, and to themselves."

— **Beverly Engel,** author of *Women Circling the Earth: A Guide to Fostering Community, Healing and Empowerment*

"We all need celebration and ceremony in our lives. How does one create meaningful personal ceremonies? Where to start? *Sacred Ceremony* is a comprehensive, perceptive and very accessible guide."

— **Donna Henes,** urban shaman, and the author of *Celestially Auspicious Occasions: Seasons, Cycles and Celebrations*

"As Steven Farmer points out, most of us have 'ordinary' ceremonies that we participate in without realizing their sacred dimension. The special care we give to arranging the top of our desks, our gardens, flowers, or houseplants are often examples of an unseen world that, although not be consciously aware of, we all yearn for. Written from the many years of Dr. Farmer's rich clinical, social, and anthropological study and experience, this book brings to the reader clear reasoning and practical suggestions for each of us to bring forth the sacred dimension toward the many passages in our lives."

— **Peter A. Levine, Ph.D.,** author of *Waking the Tiger: Healing Trauma*

SACRED CEREMONY

Also by Steven D. Farmer, Ph.D.

Power Animals:
How to Connect with Your Animal Spirit Guide

Adult Children of Abusive Parents:
*A Healing Program for Those Who Have Been Physically,
Sexually, or Emotionally Abused*

Animal Spirit Guides:
*An Easy-to-Use Handbook for Identifying and Understanding
Your Power Animals and Animal Spirit Helpers*

The Wounded Male:
*The First Practical, Hands-on Guide
Designed to Help Men Heal Their Lives*

Adult Children as Husbands, Wives, and Lovers:
Solutions for Creating Healthy Intimacy

Healing Words:
Affirmations for Adult Children of Abusive Parents
(with Juliette Anthony)

All of the above are available at your
local bookstore, or may be ordered by visiting:
Hay House USA: **www.hayhouse.com**®
Hay House Australia: **www.hayhouse.com.au**
Hay House UK: **www.hayhouse.co.uk**
Hay House South Africa: **orders@psdprom.co.za**
Hay House India: **www.hayhouseindia.co.in**

SACRED CEREMONY

*How to Create
Ceremonies
for Healing,
Transitions,
and Celebrations*

Steven D. Farmer, Ph.D.

HAY HOUSE, INC.
Carlsbad, California
London • Sydney • Johannesburg
Vancouver • Hong Kong • New Delhi

Published and distributed in the United States by: Hay House, Inc.: www.hayhouse.com • **Published and distributed in Australia by:** Hay House Australia Pty. Ltd.: www.hayhouse.com.au • **Published and distributed in the United Kingdom by:** Hay House UK, Ltd.: www.hayhouse.co.uk • **Published and distributed in the Republic of South Africa by:** Hay House SA (Pty), Ltd.: orders@psdprom.co.za • **Distributed in Canada by:** Raincoast: www.raincoast.com • **Published in India by:** Hay House Publications (India) Pvt. Ltd.: www.hayhouseindia.co.in

Editorial supervision: Jill Kramer • *Design:* Ashley Brown

The author of this book does not dispense medical advice or prescribe the use of any technique as a form of treatment for physical or medical problems without the advice of a physician, either directly or indirectly. The intent of the author is only to offer information of a general nature to help you in your quest for emotional and spiritual well-being. In the event you use any of the information in this book for yourself, which is your constitutional right, the author and the publisher assume no responsibility for your actions.

"The Opening of Eyes," in *Songs for Coming Home* by David Whyte. Copyright © 1984 by David Whyte. Used by permission of Many Rivers Press, Langley, WA.

"I Am Not I," by Juan Ramon Jimenez. Reprinted from *Lorca and Jimenez Selected Poems* chosen and translated by Robert Bly, Beacon Press, Boston, 1995. Copyright © 1995 by Robert Bly. Used with his permission.

Some of the names and identifying characteristics of the individuals in this book have been changed to protect their privacy.

Library of Congress Cataloging-in-Publication Data

Farmer, Steven.
  Sacred ceremony : how to create ceremonies for healing, transitions, and celebrations / Steven D. Farmer.
      p. cm.
  Includes bibliographical references.
  ISBN 1-56170-981-6 (tradepaper)
    1. Rites and ceremonies. 2. Spiritual life. I. Title.
  BL600 .F36 2002
  291.3′8—dc21

                                            2002002579

ISBN 13: 978-1-56170-981-6
ISBN 10: 1-56170-981-6

09 08 07 06   9 8 7 6
1st printing, October 2002
6th printing, September 2006

Printed in the United States of America

To our Earth Mother and all of her children.

The Opening of Eyes

That day I saw beneath dark clouds
the passing light over the water
and I heard the voice of the world speak out,
I knew then, as I had before
life is no passing memory of what has been
nor the remaining pages in a great book
waiting to be read.

It's the opening of eyes long closed.
It's the vision of far off things
seen for the silence they hold.
It's the heart after years
of secret conversing
speaking out loud in the clear air.

It's Moses in the desert
fallen to his knees before the lit bush.
It's the man throwing away his shoes
as if to enter heaven
and finding himself astonished,
opened at last,
fallen in love with solid ground.

— David Whyte, from *Songs for Coming Home*

Contents

Acknowledgments

First and foremost, my deepest gratitude and love to my wife and "twin flame," Doreen. You inspire me simply by your presence and your immense capacity for loving me unconditionally, working alongside me at home and in our travels, waiting patiently or shopping for shoes and scarves while I wrote this book. *Je t'aime.*

To my daughters, Nicole and Catherine, thanks for your unique ways of teaching me, showing me parts of myself, and loving me in spite of my imperfections. I love you always. To my "adopted" sons, Chuck and Grant, thank you for welcoming me into your lives and accepting me wholeheartedly.

To Jade, my friend and mentor. Thanks for your teachings, your contributions to this book, your healing gifts, and most of all, your clear and steadfast friendship.

To Bill and Joanne Hannan, my friends and my adopted mother and father, for your unconditional love and support (plus some editing "opinions").

I'm extremely fortunate and grateful to have had some wise and powerful teachers along the path, including Michael Harner, Angeles Arrien, Tom Cowan, Larry Peters, and Serge King. Thank you for your courage in teaching these ancient ways. Thanks to other teachers and friends who have inspired me, including Peter Levine, Joan Oliver, Robert Bly, Bill Kauth, and Bill Lyon.

To my friends Kevin Buck, Alan Garner, Chris and Becky Prelitz, Susan Clark, BecOhBee, Bronny Daniels, Holmes Bryant, Paul Clark, Gary Miller, Leon Nacson, Mickey and Debbie Griffith, Dan and Linda Clark, Edd Mabrey, and Tim Ramaekers, who encouraged me and in some cases contributed material, thank you.

To others who contributed in their own way, including Karen

Palmer, Bill Christy, Johnna, Julie Fare, Adam and Sam Truesly, thanks for your encouragement.

A special thanks to the president and CEO of Hay House, Reid Tracy, for giving me this opportunity; to my editor, Jill Kramer, for always being there to answer my questions and helping me hone the manuscript; and to Louise Hay, for her generous support of new authors. Thanks to all the other Hay House personnel who have nurtured this book into existence—in particular, Jacqui and Tonya, for their support in the publicity area.

And finally, thanks to my ancestors and spirit guides who inspire me and guide me, and to Mother Earth for her bountiful provisions.

✻ ✻ ✻   ✻ ✻ ✻

Introduction
The Different Ways We Try to Reach God

A few years ago, my friend Laura and I were leaving a midnight Christmas service. Troubled by what I judged as the minister's condescension and arrogance, I was quietly reflecting on the experience, thinking that he spoke as if he were talking to peasants who needed to be force-fed their religion and shamed into believing.

I asked Laura what she thought of the service, and as I turned to her, I noted that her eyes were swollen, and tears were gently trickling down her face. I immediately suspected that she'd had an entirely different experience than I. Commenting that I thought the preacher was far too judgmental, she responded by saying, "Oh, no. I was quite moved. It didn't matter what he said. I'm just fascinated with all the different ways we humans try to reach God."

At first I was mildly surprised that she didn't agree with my assessment, but once I let her words sink in, I could appreciate her perspective. I was able to see beyond my judgments and realize that this minister was trying to "reach God" in his own way— as I and everybody else who attended that service was doing. Then I could look at the underpinnings, the more common foundation for this season we call "Christmas," one that is both a religious and a cultural festival, and more deeply appreciate the richness of symbolism and meaning in these Christmas rituals and ceremonies. They had been carried out in some form or another for nearly 2,000 years, yet had their foundations in even more ancient festivals that had the common theme of celebrating the return of the light.

So I went home, lit some candles and incense, and prayed.

The Bridge Between the Worlds

Yes, we do "try to reach God" in so many different and varied ways. One way we bring the divine closer to home is via rituals. Another universal way is through the enactment of sacred ceremony, which, as you will see, resembles ritual, yet differs in some important ways.

The Christmas Eve incident above happened several years ago, and it was another piece in an ongoing personal inquiry into the various ways that we try to communicate with and honor the divine. Like many of us born during the mid to latter part of the 20th century, I've sampled a variety of religious and spiritual practices. Like a spiritual gourmand, I've feasted on those aspects that fit my tastes.

My spirituality is universal—it encompasses a variety of religious and spiritual pursuits, with shamanic practice being my primary spiritual path. In addition, I incorporate certain aspects of Christianity, as well as Buddhist and Taoist philosophy. Like many of you, I don't fit into any convenient religious or spiritual category, yet have integrated many elements that are common to a number of different ones.

By trade I'm a writer, professional speaker, minister, and former psychotherapist. As I mentioned, for me the most appealing spiritual path has been the shamanic, in part because it has no temples, gurus, or priesthood. Shamans in ancient, indigenous cultures were the tribal doctors, priests, and oracles, all rolled into one. They were the ones who could mediate between the human community and the spirit world. By intentionally sending their soul into non-ordinary reality, and conferring with the spirits there, they provided healing for those who were sick, discovered where the hunters needed to go to find game, and generally helped the community survive by appealing to the spirits for help in times of need.

One of the most powerful aspects of shamanic practice was and is *ceremony*. It can be something as simple as singing and dancing to appeal to the spirits for rain; or as complex as treating a patient for a serious illness with a combination of herbs, incantations, and invocations, thereby removing the spiritual source of the illness through a process called *spiritual extraction*. Some of these ceremonies are designed simply to express gratitude for the abundant provisions that life has to offer.

Ceremony, whether or not it's shamanic, is typically magical, creative, and healing, and provides a bridge between the material and spirit worlds. It's a *felt* demonstration of how the power of the universe works, and it provides an excellent way to honor all those events in our lives that we want to sanctify. Participating in sacred ceremony helps us bring our being into alignment with the natural flow and rhythm of life.

My friend Jade Wah'oo Grigori, a shaman and ceremonialist from Sedona, Arizona, sums it up admirably: "Ceremony is the intentful construction of the bridge which spans the barriers that we've created between our soul and our mundane life. Through the creation of ceremony, we allow the free movement of our soul into the mundane and of our consciousness in the realm of soul. It's a two-way bridge."

The Need for Sacred Ceremony

From weddings to funerals, from fasting to ecstatic dancing, throughout history humankind has attempted to contact the divine via various ceremonies and rituals. When we pay tribute to important life events through ceremony, it reminds us of how intimately connected we are with God and nature, and helps us be at peace with the inevitable changes that life brings. Often, all it takes is a simple ceremony performed with intention and sincerity to appreciate the awesome wonder of being alive.

Among other objectives, sacred ceremony can help us release attachments to people and situations that are no longer purposeful, opening the door to new experiences in our lives. For instance, recently my wife, Doreen, and I drove out along Ortega Highway, a road that winds its way up and over the mountains surrounding Orange County on its way to Lake Elsinore. We went to a favorite spot of mine a couple of miles from the highway, along an old dirt road near some hills covered with California gray sage. Nestled in these hills about 50 yards off the road is a huge, gnarly oak tree that I'd visited a few times, where Doreen and I planned to do a ceremony of release.

I'd recently closed my psychotherapy practice and had some business cards and forms that I'd used for the practice with me. On a sheet of paper, Doreen had written down information about some people and situations that were part of *her* past, but which still had a hold on her. For each of us, these pieces of paper represented what we wanted to release.

After some preparation, we started the ceremony. We took the papers to the small hole I'd dug in the earth near the oak tree and set them in it. I lit the papers, and we watched them burn as we declared aloud our intention to release these aspects of our former lives. Once they were reduced to ashes, we covered them with earth, then offered a prayer of gratitude, thanking God, the oak tree, Mother Earth, and our spirit guides and angels.

By the close of the proceedings, my heart was wide open, and I had a big grin on my face. Everything was perfect and right, and I was sharing this moment with someone I loved. I was filled with vitality, and I felt an all-encompassing gratitude for life. Both Doreen and I were quietly ecstatic as we drummed and rattled to close the ceremony.

By participating in ceremonies such as this one, people often find themselves in a rapturous state, experiencing a profound and ancient knowing at a soul level. Through the *mythos* always present in sacred ceremonies—that vast reservoir of species memory represented in symbols, songs, dances, and stories, all of which have common themes and mythologies cross-culturally—we find a common ground with all of humanity.

All Ceremonies Are Healing

No matter the stated purpose, sacred ceremony inevitably helps heal the fundamental spiritual wound—the illusion of separateness from the Creator and Creation. By our participation, we're reassured that we're not autonomous from that which sustains us materially and spiritually, and reminded of our place within the vast and intricate network of life.

A ceremony may be intended for a specific healing, such as relieving someone of their emotional, physical, or spiritual suffering. Or we may call for spiritual assistance through ceremony to repair relationships or mitigate some situation in the community. Other ceremonies are targeted principally for transitions or celebrations. What better way to commemorate important events such as weddings, personal achievements, and anniversaries than to join with others in joyous and sacred celebration? Natural Earth rhythms and events, such as the change of seasons or the monthly arrival of the full moon can be cause for festivities. Religious, cultural, and national holidays may be celebrated in the usual ways, yet any of these can be augmented with other elements of ceremony to create even greater texture and meaning.

In the hectic and driven pace that has become a part of our modern, technologically dominated lives, it's even more critical that we access the spiritual realm consistently. Ceremonies that convey the substance of spirit into our minds and hearts can and should be a part of everyone's daily menu, no matter what religious creed you follow or spiritual beliefs you hold. Although sacred ceremonies are often clothed in the language and customs of a particular religion, race, or culture, they need not be restricted by convention and tradition. Instead, with open heart and clear intention, you can develop ceremonies for yourself, your family, and your community.

In *Sacred Ceremony*, you'll find ways to create simple ceremonies for the critical events and passages you make in your life's journey. Rather than engaging in preordained rituals or exacting formulas, once you've adopted some basic principles and procedures, you can draw upon the inspiration of Spirit to guide you in the creation of ceremony. By employing these ideas and suggestions, you'll gain greater trust in Spirit's guidance, increased confidence in your ability to facilitate ceremonies, and enhanced cooperation with the powerful and mysterious forces of Life.

❀ ❀ ❀　❀ ❀ ❀

PART I

Purpose,
Preparation,
and Process
of Sacred
Ceremony

Chapter 1

Creating Sacred Ceremony

You have the capacity within you to create sacred ceremony. It requires some dedication, intention, and humility, plus a willingness to listen to Spirit's guidance. Yet, once you get a handle on some of the basics, I urge you to go for it. It doesn't have to be perfect as long as you're sincere with your intention, so don't be overly concerned with "mistakes." Spirit is very forgiving.

One of the privileges of living in a society that supports diversity is that we're not bound by a common religion or spiritual tradition. Instead, we have the opportunity to draw from ceremonies and rituals to which we've been exposed, as well as from life experience. There are commonalities in symbols, stories, and mythologies that cut across all denominations. For instance, lighting a candle is such an elemental aspect of many spiritual traditions that it can hardly be claimed as belonging to any particular one.

In addition, many have tried conventional religions and found that they don't completely satisfy their spiritual hunger. While major religions offer an extensive history and a rich set of traditions, many have become institutionalized. Coupled with an entrenched hierarchical organizational structure, this creates inherent limitations in risk-taking and experimentation. This type of system discourages innovation, and holds on to the status quo at all costs. While this can instill a sense of predictability and security, all too often form takes precedence over substance, and new ideas and creative expression are suppressed.

The New Age has clearly dawned, and with it, many are seeking ways to *experience* God, or Spirit, and discovering new ways to honor and increase awareness of the sacred in everyday life. One of the best ways to do this is to incorporate sacred ceremony as an integral aspect of your life. Once you've gathered a certain amount of experience and have been exposed to some different methods for performing ceremony, then it's time to experiment by creating your own ceremony, and perhaps even facilitating it for others.

With some guidelines, preparation, reverence, and gratitude, you can develop ceremonies that are personally meaningful for any appropriate event. If you're unaccustomed to performing ceremonies, or you're more comfortable with preordained rituals, then like any new skill or craft, your initial efforts may feel a bit awkward. You may find that you're borrowing pieces from other traditions, or you may make mistakes. Again, it's your *intention* and *sincerity* that count. Spirit will listen to you if your heart is in the right place, no matter what alleged "errors" you may make.

Remember, in the eyes of God, there are no mistakes.

Ritual or Ceremony?

Both sacred ceremonies and sacred rituals are an attempt to invoke spiritual presence and blessings through action. However, there are some important differences. One of the main ones is that rituals tend to feature a repetitious sequence of actions that must be carried out in a prescribed manner in order to achieve a desired result. The objective is to receive spiritual intercession and support for this hoped-for outcome—you ask Spirit for something, and the ritual becomes the means to achieving that end. And much of the time, rituals do yield the desired outcome.

The rich tradition that's brought into focus with a sacred ritual typically has a lot of history behind it. In many instances, rituals have been done in the same way for many years, often centuries, without alteration. As a result, they're imbued with the power that comes from this repetitive practice over time.

Also, their predictability conveys a sense of security for both the one performing the ritual as well as the participants. In fact, it can be quite disturbing when someone tinkers with a traditional ritual. In any religious service, for instance, there are certain procedures to follow that invoke the spiritual presence. If things don't go in the expected sequence, it can be quite disconcerting to the participants. If the minister unexpectedly changes the service one day, such as asking for volunteers to speak at the service when this isn't ordinarily done, or asking attendees to dance instead of sing, you can imagine the kind of confusion and discomfort this might bring about.

In personal rituals, the same idea applies. Their consistency gives us a sense of security. Once we've established the ritual, whether sacred or mundane, it's upsetting if it's disrupted or altered. Imagine changing your own morning ritual. If you ordinarily brush your teeth, shower, then shave and make your coffee, try changing the order in which you do these tasks. At minimum, you'll feel a ripple of disturbance. If your bedtime ritual consists of reading, followed by prayers, try skipping both of these one night. It'll probably make it more difficult for you to fall asleep.

As for sacred rituals, there are several books that offer prescriptions for rituals that target a specific outcome, such as attracting a soulmate. Typically, these have very exacting formulas for a particular sequence of behaviors to be carried out, with a list of required materials and ingredients for successful results. As I stated previously, they frequently do achieve the desired results, and there's often a strong sense of spiritual presence, however their success depends largely on following the meticulous and detailed instructions. They leave very little room for spontaneous spiritual expression or inspiration.

Sacred ceremonies, on the other hand, require some structure and follow some guidelines, yet make allowances within their execution for the intuiting of spiritual direction and guidance. Unlike the primary objective of ritual, which is to achieve a desired outcome, with ceremony we seek Spirit's help in creatively aligning with our heart's desire while coordinating this with the desires of Spirit. In ceremony, we trust in the inspiration of the moment within the sacred container that's been established for the enactment of the ceremony. We invite the power of Spirit, but don't demand or expect it to show up in a specified way. Although we may desire certain results, what we achieve is in alignment with the will of Spirit.

My friend Jade Wah'oo Grigori describes it as such:

> Ritual is something that we do in order to call upon or beseech the forces of creation to act on our behalf. Ceremony is the inspired expression of our dance with creation. Even in ritual there are certainly those times when in the performance of [it] the person is inspired, and it shows through because all of a sudden it has that other glow or quality, and so it's actually broached into the ceremonial at that time.
>
> You can do morning ritual, yet you can also do morning ceremony. This would be to take the time to be quiet within, to observe one's experience of this moment, to look into the activities that need to be accomplished for this day, look at the context of the day in which we're going to perform those functions, and express the movement of Spirit's desire in the fulfillment of [Its] need within the functions that must be accomplished.

Rituals certainly serve a purpose, and while most are performed with sincere intention, the substance and meaning is often lost both to the practitioner and the adherents. They risk becoming habitual routines stemming from a sense of obligation and dogged commitment, rather than a heartfelt, embodied sense of spiritual presence.

All sacred rituals started out as ceremony, and some are faint echoes of the original ceremonies from which they stem. People gain a sense of some larger force operating through their engagement with these sanctioned formalities of rituals, yet any sense of awe inspired by their participation is seen as dependent on the replication of these formulas. For example, engaging in a spiritual pursuit on Sundays is a ritual where we feel inspired, yet this emotion may be tied in to the formula of attending church. While the repetitious nature of rituals may instill the aforementioned sense of security, it may unfortunately come at the expense of a more creative dance with the forces of Life.

New Age or Archaic Revival?

We're in an era that has been referred to as the "New Age," although it may be more accurately called an "archaic revival." Much of what we see happening around us and inside us is a revival of spiritual and healing modalities that have been a part of the human race for as long as we can trace our history as a species. So what is called New Age is truly a renaissance of old-age practices cast in the light of contemporary times.

In ancient eras (and in indigenous peoples today), typically one person in the community was primarily responsible for direct access to the spiritual world. This was the shaman, someone who could send their soul or consciousness to the spirit world, just beyond the veil of our usual senses, and there receive guidance from various "spirit guides." By having regular access to what author and shaman Carlos Castaneda called "non-ordinary" reality and forming strong relationships with the spirits that dwell there, shamans would appeal to these spirits for their assistance in various tribal or communal affairs. The shaman was a combination priest, doctor, and magician rolled into one, responsible for leading ceremonies—from those that would help the hunters know where to find the animals, to those that would heal a member of the community.

Although shamans were always the tribal healers, their primary role was much more grand. In *The Spell of the Sensuous*, David Abraham states that the shaman . . .

> . . . acts as an intermediary between the human community and the larger ecological field, ensuring that there is an appropriate flow of nourishment, not just from the landscape to the human inhabitants, but from the human community back to the local earth. By his constant rituals, trances, ecstasies, and "journeys," he ensures that the relation between human society and the larger society of beings is balanced and reciprocal, and that the village never takes more from the living land than it returns to it—not just materially but with prayers, propitiations, and praise.

Because the shaman was considered to have a more direct link to the spirit world and spirit guides, the ceremonies could at times change direction or content. Although there were systematic approaches to these various ceremonies, they were not rigid and fixed. Depending on guidance from their spirit helpers, the shamans could introduce new elements, while older ones could be eliminated over time.

Spiritual Authority

The spiritual leader—priest, minister, or shaman—is often viewed as being somehow closer to God than the ordinary human being. This kind of hierarchical system implies that the rest of us cannot have a direct relationship with Source, that we require a go-between. This type of structure is inherent in most major religions, and while it *does* provide answers to spiritual questions, it places spiritual authority onto someone else. With this comes a tendency to surrender our spiritual authority, as well as our spiritual responsibility, to someone or something external. While this may work for someone who's in "spiritual infancy," no matter what their chronological age, a natural progression would be to eventually seek one's own answers, or at least to ask questions until an answer appears.

I'm not suggesting that we do away with these types of structures and systems, as they can be tremendously valuable, especially as a focal point of spiritual community. Instead, we should nurture a spiritual development that moves toward increasing autonomy from any religious dogma or fundamentalism. Otherwise we risk making the form of our religious or spiritual practice more important than a personal, active, and creative relationship with Spirit.

In these changing times, many of us are awakening to the need for a more personal and intimate relationship with Life and with the Creator. Rather than simply an intellectual and part-time relationship, more people are having direct and embodied experiences of Spirit.

This type of experience crosses religious boundaries, and many are coming to agree with what Aldous Huxley referred to as "The Perennial Philosophy." In his book of the same name, he described it as a . . .

> . . . metaphysic that recognizes a divine Reality substantial to the world of things and lives and minds; the psychology that finds in the soul something similar to, or even identical with, divine

Reality; the ethic that places man's final end in the knowledge of the immanent and transcendent Ground of all being—the thing is immemorial and universal. Rudiments of the Perennial Philosophy may be found among the traditional lore of primitive peoples in every region of the world, and in its fully developed forms it has a place in every one of the higher religions.

Bringing Forth Ceremony

As I've said, with some preparation, a few basic principles, and sincere intent, you can bring forth ceremonies that are personally meaningful. Use the resources available to you, starting with this book, as well as others (see the Recommend Reading section). I also encourage you to explore and experiment, and especially to participate in others' sacred ceremonies. Just remember that one of the most important resources you have is your internal guidance and your relationship with those spiritual beings that can assist you—your spirit guides.

Ceremonies need not be associated with any one religion or spiritual practice, although they certainly may be. Often in ceremony you'll find commonalities in the symbols, stories, and procedures among a number of spiritual disciplines. The uniqueness lies in the creative synthesis of these elements brought forth for the stated intent of the ceremony.

You can start with very simple, personal ceremonies, such as greeting the rising sun on the morning of the winter solstice, or creating a ceremony of release for some emotional blockages. Again, let go of any perfectionistic concerns about doing it "right." As you gather experience and gain confidence, you will naturally get a sense of how to gracefully work between the material world and the spiritual dimensions.

Know that when you create ceremony with your heart open, your faith in place, and with clear intention, you're honoring the Creator and Creation.

※ ※ ※   ※ ※ ※

Chapter 2

Creating a Sacred Altar

During a visit to Bangkok a few years ago, I was impressed by the large number of altars I saw. There was one on virtually every street corner, on major thoroughfares, and on the side streets. On one of those smaller roads, there was a particular altar that caught my attention. It was a small platform affixed to a pole, elevated about six feet off the ground. At the center was a beautiful rendering of the Buddha, and on either side, images of male and female Hindu deities, respectively. This was not surprising, since there's considerable harmony between the two major religions (Hinduism and Buddhism) in Thailand.

The altar stood like a guardian of the street, with the small yet powerful figure of Buddha gazing over his domain. Every morning there were offerings of food left on the altar, placed there as a gift for the spirits. By the end of the day, the food items had mysteriously disappeared. I suppose that bugs may have eaten them or a hungry child may have snatched them. Or, perhaps the spirits *did* receive these offerings, and in exchange were willing to watch over and protect the inhabitants of this neighborhood.

Regardless, I was struck by this representation of a culture that had its spirituality woven so intricately into the fabric of everyday life. Inherent in daily life was an expression of mystical spirituality that had been present since ancient times. I learned that in this country, as in many others, every home has a sacred altar.

An altar can be used for private or shared communion, and you can find one in any place of worship. Creating an altar is a representation of your own personal view of the sacred. It doesn't take anything away from the temple or church, but is an expression of honoring Spirit in a highly personal way.

In our culture, I suspect that each of us already has an altar, even though it may not be designated as such. It may be a desk or the top of a dresser where items from your pocket or purse end up, or perhaps an array of framed family photos on the table in the living room. Some may even keep an altar that's a conscious statement of the sacred, evinced by various symbols, objects, and artifacts that define a unique expression of spirituality. If you don't have an altar, or would like to modify the one you do have, what follows are guidelines for constructing and creating your own. These are suggestions, not formulas, so feel free to change these in ways that feel instinctively correct and which are compatible with your spiritual principles and beliefs.

Choosing a Location

Basically, you'll need a flat surface, one that's free from clutter. It's important to dedicate that space exclusively for the altar. Be careful: It's all too easy for this space to become a catch-all, such as a table in the bedroom where it's convenient to drop car keys, wallets, earrings, and so on. Set a clear intention that this space is to be used exclusively for your altar.

The space can be very small, no bigger than the size of a small bookshelf, or it can be as large as a desktop. This is a matter of personal preference. A friend of mine, Jocelyn, has dedicated an entire spare bedroom to her worship, and she has a beautiful altar taking up one entire wall. She uses the space for her private worship, as well as for practicing yoga. This is certainly exceptional, and most of us can do with one or possibly two smaller altars in our home. Or, as I witnessed in Southeast Asia, you can keep an altar in every room.

I like having altars in various rooms, but particularly in the living room and bedroom. Wherever you decide, what's important is that the placement of your altar *feels* right to you. Some people like it to be more prominently displayed, whereas others like it to be less obvious. If having an altar in your home is new to you, then you may want to keep it in an unobtrusive area, free from the inquiring gaze of guests or skeptical family members.

In spite of my self-consciousness, when I first created an altar, it was in the living room of my home. It was a small one, set up on a table that could be clearly seen from the front door. It was very simple, bearing a candle, a sprig of sage, and some small objects that had special meaning to me. In spite of my apprehension about what people would think when they saw it, I found that all of my friends who visited were either curious about it or said nothing at all. Knowing me, most of them just took it in stride as part of my latest spiritual exploration.

Materials and Construction

Once you've decided on a place to create a dedicated altar, then it's time to put it together. First, cover the tabletop with an attractive cloth—it can be anything from a piece of fabric that's been sitting around for a couple of years, to a sarong you purchased awhile back and never wore. Again, the guideline is that it looks and feels right to you.

For the centerpiece, choose an object that has a particular spiritual or religious meaning. It may be a Christian cross, a Buddha, Shiva, or a photo of any revered religious or spiritual figures. Jocelyn (who has her entire room dedicated as holy space) has half a dozen photos of various spiritual masters on her altar, from Jesus to Yogananda.

At the center of one my altars, which was built on a sofa table, was a Celtic cross, which is a Christian cross with a circle in the middle. The cross symbolizes the masculine, while the circle represents the feminine. When entering my home, one's eyes were greeted by a rather large stained-glass image of a flower in the room directly across from the entrance. This became a natural centerpiece for the altar beneath it.

Some additional items you can place on your altar are representative of the four elements: fire, air, earth, and water (see next chapter). Once you've established the basics, make it a living altar, one that becomes imbued with your essence. Every few weeks, look over the objects, consider their placement, and determine whether they still fit. Add sacred items as they come to you, and remove those that have diminished in meaning. Use the altar for prayer, meditation, and ceremony. It will grow on you, and you will grow with it.

Now for more of the basics: the four elements.

❈ ❈ ❈   ❈ ❈ ❈

Chapter 3

The Four Elements

According to many traditions, there are four major elements: fire, water, air, and earth. They're considered to be the most basic foundations of life on this planet.

Fire—Consider fire. A hearth fire on the coldest of evenings warms our bones. Fire at night, even the electrically induced fires of lamps and flashlights, is what lights our way in the darkness. So, for your altar, at least one candle is essential. Place a decorative candle directly in front of the centerpiece, or make the candle itself the centerpiece. A simple candle on the altar lights the way for the other pieces. When you're using the altar for a specific purpose, such as praying or meditating, the candle can be your focal point. Fire burns away the "negative energy."

Water—Water can be represented by a special vial of water, such as "holy water," received from the healing waters of various rivers, lakes, streams, and oceans. Another symbol is a seashell, which may have some personal significance—for example, it may be a reminder of where it was collected.

I've gathered several shells from one of my favorite beaches near San Felipe, Mexico, a very magical place. Once while taking a very long walk along that stretch of sand, which extended for miles and miles, I experienced an immersion into the timeless. It could just as easily have been 25,000 years ago as much as the present moment. I'd been hoping for a sizable abalone shell to place on my altar at home, and was thinking about it when I noticed a glistening object sticking out of the sand. When I went to dig it out, there was a shell just like I'd been imagining. I gratefully accepted it as a miraculous gift from the spirits of that place. It sits proudly on one of my altars at home.

Air—What symbols come to mind when you think about the element of air? One of the best symbolic representations for air is a feather. Keep your eye out for feathers, and you will undoubtedly be gifted with that special one for your altar. Another possibility is an artistic symbol for air. One friend kept a small bronze image of an eagle on his altar to represent air.

Earth—There are many possibilities for an earth symbol, including an actual piece of earth. One of the most common is a rock or stone, one that's unique and personally meaningful. One of my friends makes it a habit to collect stones from sacred places she visits, so she has stones from Glastonbury, England; the Amazon; Sedona, Arizona; and several places in between. Each one has a special significance, and she has arranged them on her altar accordingly.

El Santuario

On one of my altars is a bag of red earth that comes from a very special place near Santa Fe, New Mexico, a church called El Santuario de Chimayo. El Santuario has been called the "Lourdes of America," a place where people have purportedly been healed from a variety of illnesses. The outside of the church looks like any older, Spanish-style adobe church. As you go inside and approach the central altar, you notice an entryway to a room just to the left. As you enter this room, the wall is adorned with about 20 pairs of crutches. Next you notice an incredible number of altars, most dedicated to deceased loved ones, mixed with other altars that have various purposes.

To the side there's another door, one that requires you to bend down to enter. This takes you into a room about ten feet by ten feet. There in the center of this room is a hole in the ground filled with red earth. Legend has it that centuries ago, before there was a church, a priest found the cross buried in this same spot. A procession transported the cross to the central church many miles away, where it was placed on the altar. Sometime later, the priest found the exact same cross back in the original location. Once more it was carried to the central church, and once more the cross somehow made its way back to that same area where it had been first discovered!

There the cross remained, and it can be seen today on the altar of El Santuario. The earth in this area was deemed holy, and the church was constructed around this sacred spot, with the hole left open in the tiny room. Over the centuries, the red earth has been used for healing purposes, and many people make annual pilgrimages to El Santuario specifically to receive its healing properties. Visitors are welcome to take a small quantity of this dirt for their own purpose. It's rumored that no matter how much of this earth is taken, the hole continues to remain full.

My daughter Catherine (16 at the time) and I visited El Santuario a few years ago. When we first glimpsed this round hole filled with red soil in the middle of that small room, we were awestruck. There was a tangible presence of a powerful healing force. The others in the room were quiet; some were gently weeping, as were Catherine and myself. After praying for several timeless moments, we reverently filled our bags with the sacred earth, then quietly and slowly left El Santuario. We were so deeply affected by this experience that we barely spoke as we made the half-hour drive back to Santa Fe.

When we returned home, I placed some of this earth on my altar, while the rest remains in a bag in my ceremonial kit. On occasion, I've used this earth for healing ceremonies. Whenever I use it, I'm brought back to that day at El Santuario and the magical, mystical legend connected to the church and its sacred earth.

Receiving the Gifts of the Four Elements

Make sure that you're careful when you take things from the earth or sea, whether it's a stone, shell, or a flower. Use your inner guidance and common sense as to the appropriateness of taking one of these objects. When it comes to any gifts from the earth, I close my eyes and quietly meditate for a few moments and ask the spirits if it's okay to accept a piece of that land. Assuming they're in agreement, I can feel that I'm *receiving*, rather than *taking*, and I can express my gratitude for such wonderful gifts.

Once you've established the space for your altar, the cloth covering, a centerpiece, and representations of the four elements, then it's time to consider other sacred objects for your altar.

Bringing in the Sacred Objects

Now that you've set up the basics for your altar, you'll naturally find other items that are significant to you that deserve a place there. Hold the intent to create a meaningful and pleasing altar, and you'll be inspired. Although most altars are quite beautiful to look at, you're not building this altar just for looks. More important is the symbolic and personal meaning contained within each piece on your altar. Take your time in building it. As I've mentioned, let it be a living altar, one that will develop and change over time.

Once you've established the foundation, add other sacred objects. Here's where the fun begins. Remember that beautiful rose your child gave you? Perhaps in its dried state it's an appropriate piece to place there. Other objects can be specifically religious or spiritual symbols. Although I'm not Catholic, I have a rosary draped over one side of one of my altars, and a corresponding set of *mala* beads on the other. Malas are a special string of 108 beads that are used in some Hindu practices for meditation. Another piece is a small statue of a Celtic fairy, a gift from someone at one of my workshops. The list is endless as to what can end up on your altar.

One item I recommend having is an earthen bowl (or a larger seashell) with some sage in it. Sage is considered in many native North American traditions to be one of the oldest plants on Earth. My favorite is white sage, sometimes called California gray sage. You can usually find this in metaphysical bookstores, health-food stores, or other New Age retail establishments, typically in a sage bundle, sometimes called a smudge stick. Or you can gather fresh sage, dry it out, and use some of the leafed branches in the bowl. Sage is burned for the purpose of doing a spiritual clearing, called "smudging"—or as I sometimes call it, "saging" (more on this later).

I'm sure you have many personally significant items that will make your way to your altar. Whatever feels like it belongs probably does; the items need not make any sense to anyone except you. This is *your* altar. Whatever you deem sacred, no matter how ordinary it may seem to others, is sacred to you. Don't deny yourself the immense pleasure of honoring the holiness in this specific way.

❈ ❈ ❈ ❈ ❈ ❈

Chapter 4

The Family Altar

There are two types of family altars: *ancestral* and *household*.

Ancestral Altar—While in Southeast Asia, I noted that nearly every household had an altar with photos or other renderings of deceased loved ones. The age of the beloved who had passed on didn't matter. Whether they died at 13 or 83, they were considered ancestors. In many traditions, the ones who have come before are honored, and one way to do so is via an *ancestral altar*.

In Vietnam, several years after the war, I visited a Buddhist temple in downtown Saigon (now called Ho Chi Minh City). There were at least a dozen large tables, and on each was a collection of various artifacts. Woven in between the artifacts were scores of photos of people, young and old. At some of these altars were Vietnamese families performing rituals. As they prayed, someone in the group would light three sticks of incense, bow three times, then place the incense in a holder directly at the front of the altar. The Roshi (priest) explained to us that the vast majority of these pictures were of relatives whose lives were claimed by the war years earlier. It was quite unnerving to witness the sheer numbers of photos that were on the various altars, and very humbling to see how this culture honored their ancestors.

You can create your own version of an ancestral altar. On a table, place photos of your ancestors and deceased loved ones and friends, along with a candle and representations of the four elements. You need not include everyone (such as Uncle Harry who was mean to you when you were little)—just choose those you feel an affinity toward. Definitely do *not* include pictures of any *living* family members on this particular altar. Put those photos elsewhere.

Household Altar—A *household altar*, on the other hand, is a shrine where everyone in the existing family places at least two or three sacred objects. It can be used as a centerpiece at home for any spiritual activities. Family members can use it for themselves if they want to perform a private ceremony, meditation, or prayer. Another possibility is that friends of the family can be invited to contribute a sacred object, if family members agree. This is a good place for photos of important people in your life who are still alive. It's also a great reminder for everyone to maintain religious and/or spiritual awareness.

Set up this household altar in much the same way you would any other. This one can be located in plain view so that it's accessible. Most of the time this will be the living room, although there may be another room in the house more suitable. It's important that the parents lead the way in creating this altar, whether the children are younger or are already adults on their own. Unless your family is accustomed to such practices, there might be some initial resistance, but as long as you're more inviting than demanding, your children will eventually join in.

Blessing the Altar

This step is done to consecrate the altar, to demarcate its special nature. This can be your initiation into creating sacred ceremony.

Once you've set up the altar, choose a time to do the ceremony. If it's your personal altar, a private ceremony is best. Once you've set aside the place and time, take a seat in front of your altar. Invoke the spiritual guides that are most suitable for the occasion, and say a prayer, preferably one of gratitude.

Some say that *all* prayers should be prayers of gratitude. I do believe that you should start prayers out with specific thanks for what God has done for you, then add any petitions for blessings or healings. In other words, it's okay to ask. I find that starting prayers with thankfulness sets the mood much more effectively. It reminds me that life is a gift, and thanking the Creator for these gifts lifts my heart.

Once you've invoked this spiritual Presence, light the candle, burn some sage, and with your hand or a feather, brush the smoke first across the altar and the sacred objects, then across your own body. Then burn some of your favorite incense. If you choose, drum, rattle, chant, or dance for a few minutes, with the intention of building the power. Once this is complete, take a few moments with each of the items on the altar table and meditate on it. Consider its history, its purpose on the altar. There's no need to have the exact answers; considering the question is what's important.

Next, offer prayers on behalf of anyone in your world who's suffering—friends, family, animals, plants, trees, or a world situation. There have been hundreds of scientific studies on prayer, and the vast majority have shown statistically significant results with regard to the prayed-for outcome. Many involved prayers done on infants, plants, and animals, so this eliminates any placebo effect. Also, researchers have found that no matter what religious denomination someone is, prayer is equally effective, and the most effective means is to pray on behalf of someone else. Finally, slightly better results are achieved when you let go and let God, so I suggest that you always close your prayers with, "Thy will be done."

❋ ❋ ❋

Next, we'll explore the what, when, where, how, and why of ceremonies. Although some of this information may seem complex, it doesn't need to be. The simplest ceremonies are often the most precious and meaningful. What could be more spiritually elegant and satisfying than spending a few moments with a sunset, contemplating one's life, communing with nature, and quietly feeling the Life Force inside you and all around you? That's ceremony.

Let's first look at the three basic types of sacred ceremony.

❋ ❋ ❋ ❋ ❋ ❋

Chapter 5

Three Basic Types
of Ceremony

There are three types of sacred ceremonies: those intended for *healing*, for *transitions*, and for *celebrations*. Although there's typically overlap, these categories provide guidelines for identifying, preparing, and generating your own ceremonies.

As herbalist and ceremonialist Elchai describes it: "My goal is to celebrate the normal, the ordinary, and the everyday events with ceremony, because, in fact, your whole life is one magnificent ceremony, one long dramatic myth with you as its central character."

Ceremony can become such an integral part of life that you begin to *think, feel, and breathe* ceremony. Although this book, as well as other resources, will give you some ideas, when it comes to creating ceremony, I encourage you to take some risks. Many of us are trying to find new and creative ways to honor the sacred in everyday life, to consecrate the various life changes that we go through in our experience of humanness. I'm sure that God and the angels will lovingly smile on you whenever you make any sincere attempt to do so.

With your first attempts, you may even feel a bit awkward and self-conscious, but don't let that stop you. Most of us have not been raised in a strong tradition of ceremony; or have been raised with rigid, empty rituals that didn't convey a deeper, embodied meaning to our relationship with Source. Not that there's anything wrong with these rituals, it's just that when performed without full presence and meaning, they can become routine and obligatory.

We're in a very spiritually creative time in our evolution as a species, and we're being prompted to upgrade our spiritual consciousness. The earth is begging for our assistance, urging us to rediscover our true place in the web of life. Sacred ceremony as an integral part of our life naturally facilitates our opening to Spirit. It's through the enactment of ceremony in a sincere and reverential way that Spirit will come alive and become more than just an intellectual concept.

Healing Ceremonies

Ceremonies performed primarily for healing can be targeted for physical, mental, emotional, or spiritual wounds. When there's healing within one domain, there's always healing in others. If we break an arm, it will affect our emotional disposition, physical sense of well-being, and how we think. As the arm heals and we feel better, this affects our mental and physical state, and our "spirits" pick up.

Healing ceremonies can be for an individual, a family, or an entire community. All of us were deeply affected by the tragedies of September 11, 2001. Many of us came together in healing ceremonies to assuage our anger and our grief, and thousands of people participated in prayer vigils to solicit God's blessings—especially those most directly affected by this catastrophe. Given all the heartache and pain inherent in such an event, it's amazing how it can bring a community together—in this case, an entire nation.

In this book, I'll give you ideas on how to create powerful healing ceremonies—ones that, at minimum, will help to heal the fundamental spiritual wound—the illusion of separation from the Creator. More specifically, these healing ceremonies will help with the healing of physical, mental, and emotional wounds.

Transition Ceremonies

There are points in everyone's life journey where you stand on the threshold of significant change. Ceremony can serve as a bridge to the next phase of your life that's instigated by the event. Once you've gone through this type of ceremony, your life will never be quite the same. Can you recall how your life changed after you went to school for the first time, or after the birth of your first child? I can't think of a more beautiful way to mark such an event than with a simple, sacred ceremony.

Transition ceremonies are those that mark important life passages, such as birth, starting school, the onset of puberty, marriage, divorce, and death. Sometimes these are referred to as rites of passage, and some of these events can rightfully be called initiations into the spiritually based life. Ceremonies of this type may last a couple of hours or go on for days. Many cultures have traditional rituals for such events, and you can draw elements from these rituals that can help you create the appropriate ceremony for the occasion.

As we'll see, there are many transitions we go through in our lives, and we can commemorate any of these passages by creating ceremonies of celebration.

Celebration Ceremonies

In addition to annual ceremonies that commemorate particular transitions, such as birthdays and anniversaries, there are other events that are characterized by their periodic and recurrent nature. These range from traditional holy days to the celebration of celestial events and earth rhythms, such as full moon, new moon, solstice, and equinox cycles, as well as those occasional cosmic events such as solar and lunar eclipses and comets.

Even with our more traditional holidays (holy days), there's room for creativity in the honoring of these special days. How many times have you thought that the Christmas is too rushed and commercial—such that it's become devoid of deeper meaning? I certainly have. Rather than suffering silently and just going along with the repetitious flow, another option is to modify the usual rituals and create sacred ceremony that incorporates some of the most significant elements. No matter what holiday it is, you can enhance the richness, texture, and meaning of these occasions by honoring them in unique ways.

What about tradition? I'm certainly not advocating that you re-create ways to honor these days, but simply to become more creative and *involved* in this honoring. For example, one year some Christian friends of mine decided to honor the holy day of Christmas by buying gifts for orphaned children, as well as helping serve meals to the homeless. This has now become part of their Christmas tradition, resulting from a dissatisfaction with the commercialism of Christmas and a desire and willingness to do something more congruent with Jesus' teachings and life.

Next we'll look at the identifiable stages that all ceremonies go through, whether for healing, transition, or celebration.

※ ※ ※   ※ ※ ※

Chapter 6

The Stages of Ceremony

The three stages of sacred ceremony are *separation, transformation,* and *incorporation*. It's not necessary for each of these to be part of every ceremony, and you'll find that some ceremonies will emphasize one over the other. In a ceremony for someone who's dying, separation is underscored; in puberty rites of passage, the transformation stage is at the forefront; baptismal ceremonies highlight the incorporation stage.

These stages parallel the cyclical nature of life, which has a beginning, middle, and end. You're born into the world, live your life, then you die. Nature's cycles are similar: sunrise, daytime, sunset; and full moon to new moon. With every death, there's a rebirth. Death is simply another stage of the life process; some traditions believe that the soul never dies but merely goes through a transformation called *reincarnation*.

You'll find that as you generate sacred ceremony, these elements are always present to one degree or another. Often this simply happens. When called upon to create ceremony, you can think in terms of these stages and develop the structure in accordance with them. I'm sure you'll see how these stages are represented when you reflect on other ceremonies and rituals that you've participated in.

Separation

This is the start of the ceremony, where what has been up to this point is left behind. It signifies that something new is about to enter your life, but first you must leave the old behind. It's a metaphorical "little death," an end to some phase or aspect of your life.

The separation can be real or symbolic. An example of real separation is found in more traditional wedding ceremonies, where the father walks the bride to the wedding altar and gives her to the groom, signifying the end of a former relationship the woman had with her father. Similarly, both bride and groom may have been living with their parents up to this time. By entering into the marriage, they leave their parents' homes and enter into a new dwelling of their own.

Another example is a birthing ceremony. With more contemporary birthing practices, once the baby exits the mother's body, it's placed upon the mother's belly with the umbilical cord still attached. The cord is then ceremonially cut, which is a dramatic and actual severance or separation from the mother's body, and serves to initiate the infant into the earthly realm.

In other ceremonies, this separation is largely symbolic. The people involved in the ceremony move from one area to another, or pass through a marked area or symbolic gateway that clearly indicates the entry into ceremonial space. Usually, in any release ceremonies that I do with groups, I'll set up a "gateway," which may simply be a line on the ground. Prior to the actual release, the participants will walk up to this symbolic gateway and stand before it for a few moments before stepping across it. Once they cross the line, they've committed themselves completely to the release, and are in full ceremonial space.

Transformation

This is the stage of ceremony where release and renewal occur, where the cycles of death and rebirth collide, and where dramatic change often takes place. It has also been termed the *initiation* or *threshold* stage. The movement or change that occurs is from the old to the new, from the past to a new course into the future, with a living present occurring during this stage. This is the part we usually think of as the actual ceremony. The first stage, separation, is the opening, while the transformation begins once you step through the gateway into the ceremonial space. It's the body of the ceremony.

In a marriage ceremony, all that follows once the couple is together at the altar is the transformation stage. From the point when the bride approaches and joins with the groom, to the minister's welcome, the exchange of vows, the witnessing by family and friends, and the pronouncement, all are steps in the transformation cycle—the shift from the old life to a new one—in this instance, from being single to being married.

In the case of an infant, once the umbilical cord is severed, the infant can be welcomed into the world through a ritual of the chosen faith, or through a ceremony created by the parents and attendees. This transformation, or initiation, may include anointing with oil and water, a hands-on welcome by those in attendance, a reading by the parents, or other actions that signify the infant's (and parents'!) shift into a new future.

Incorporation

Now that the transformation stage of the marriage ceremony and birth is complete, what's next? The return back through the gateway, which can be the most critical part of the ceremony, signals the incorporation stage. The individual, couple, or group is reintroduced back into the community with a new identity, or at least with a significant transformation. *Incorporation* literally means "being brought into the body," or in the case of ceremony, being brought back into the body of the family, village, or community.

In a wedding ceremony, this stage is typically marked by the official who performed the wedding saying to the couple, "I now pronounce you husband and wife," followed by their turning to face their friends and family, saying something such as, "I'm pleased to introduce you to Mr. and Mrs. John Smith!" From this point on, they're no longer bride and groom, but a couple. They now have a different identity and will live in the world and the community with this new distinction.

Once the infant's cord has been cut, it's introduced to the world as an individual. Certainly the child is still totally dependent on the parents, yet the major step of separation from the mother's body has now taken place. Another type of ceremony, a baptismal or christening, will serve to further incorporate the child into the world, family, and community.

For teenagers going through rites of passage, this is the most crucial step. To be considered fully grown, the community must welcome and accept this change in their stature.

Next, we'll take a closer look at some basic principles of ceremony.

✵ ✵ ✵   ✵ ✵ ✵

Chapter 7
The Four Principles of Ceremony

Now that you're ready to plan the ceremony, there are four principles to consider before actually performing the ceremony. If it's possible to give careful thought to these things ahead of time, the ceremony will go smoother. If not, then you get to improvise and really put these ideas to the test!

We'll start with the most critical factor. Even in a spontaneous ceremony, why you're doing what you're doing needs to be clear. This is called *intention*.

Intention

Intention is making a decision about what the ceremony means. What is its purpose? Will it be primarily a ceremony for healing, transition, or celebration? Is it mainly for the individual, family, or community? How do you stay focused on your intention throughout the three stages of ceremony? What's the desired outcome? What do you want to occur as a result of this process?

When a ceremony is devoid of clear intention, it also loses passion, inspiration, and direction. The ceremony may then slip into empty ritual, where form prevails over substance, and structure becomes a priority over heartfelt sacredness. Clear intention is the skeleton that supports the body of the ceremony, giving it backbone.

In some ways, intention is everything. Once we set an intention, then we can act more clearly and with greater certainty. The conscious mind then becomes the instrument to focus our awareness and attention. We build *power*. The ceremony is inspired. Spontaneous healings can occur, and participants often experience an embodied sense of Spirit, an ecstatic state, with insights, revelations, and even visions taking place. This doesn't happen in every ceremony, mind you, but there's a far greater opportunity for this to occur when intention is clear and established before implementation.

Timing and Location

Choosing when and where to hold the ceremony is another important consideration. You can do so the way most of us do these days—by looking at dates on the calendar and the clock on the wall—or you can choose the time the way our ancestors did: by coordinating the event with seasonal and natural cycles. It might be sunrise, sunset, the darkest hour of night, or the brightest point of the day. Also, the ceremony can be timed to coincide with the solstice, equinox, full moon, or new moon.

Choosing the location is equally important. Is it best to hold this particular event inside or outside? What about the size of the space needed? Can everyone fit? Also, if performed outside, is the space accessible to the other participants? Holding the ceremony on a mountaintop has a certain aesthetic and romantic appeal, but obviously it wouldn't be very practical. Whatever choice is made for the space, I encourage you to consider the ramifications carefully.

In addition, do something to make the space different, to make it "extra-ordinary." If the ceremony is taking place outside and at night, perhaps put out tiki torches for illumination and scatter flowers about the ground. If it's in your living room, move the chairs and tables around, open the space up, and bring in appropriate decorations. By making the space distinctive, the message is that something very special is about to take place. It also enhances the sense that when the ceremony is performed, those involved are moving outside of ordinary time and into ceremonial space.

Progression—Beginning, Middle, End

The beginning and end of a ceremony need to be clearly marked. The opening can be characterized by some unique shift that says through this action, "We have begun!" A distinctive sound such as a rattle or drumbeat, a period of silence, a prayer, or the lighting of a candle or incense will work. The start of the proceedings may be signaled by the participants physically moving to the ceremonial area, sometimes through a specified "gateway," such as a constructed or natural arch, or simply a line marking the threshold. Or it may begin with the group engaging in some free-form dancing or movement, as music is played or drums are sounded. Any act that differentiates the usual and ordinary from the sacred territory of ceremony will signal that the proceedings have begun.

It's helpful to let participants know ahead of time what they may expect, as well as the meaning behind what will take place. When I facilitate a ceremony, I describe in advance what will be occurring, being particularly careful to mention if I expect anyone from the group to take part. This lessens any confusion and prevents unexpected occurrences that may distract from the proceedings. Doing so also satisfies people's natural intellectual curiosity.

I can't stress enough how important it is to plan a distinct finale. It gives the message to the participants that they're now re-entering ordinary reality. In a celebration ceremony, an identifiable ending prevents the event from dissolving into a chatty and chaotic party atmosphere. Sure, party on—but not until the ceremonial proceedings have concluded! For example, in a baptismal ceremony, if the finish is clearly underscored, then participants can relax afterwards, breaking up into small groups, perhaps, and sharing in the feast that might follow.

The close of a ceremony is similar to the beginning in that there is a rather obvious signal of some sort that terminates the event. Examples include the playing of a distinct drumbeat or rattle, blowing out a candle that's been burning, chanting, singing a designated song, or saying a closing prayer, usually one of gratitude. Sometimes I'll simply clap my hands and declare, "It is done!" Again, whatever the method, it should be something that clearly says, "This is the conclusion of the ceremony!"

Structured or Free-Form

The degree of structure in a ceremony is negotiable. The rule of thumb is to strike a balance between structure and spontaneity. It helps to create an outline, a plan that says what happens when, who says what, how the physical setting is to be established, and so on. Sticking rigidly to such a plan may feel counterproductive and may actually interfere with the feeling of the holiness of the process, yet without relatively distinct leadership and structure, the ceremony can dissolve into chaos and confusion.

The structure provides the outline, and within this framework, there's room for the creative expression of spirit. In going from point "A" to point "B," it's important to have a map and a direction, yet along the way, any number of things can happen. You can stop along the roadside, explore the nearby meadow, gaze at the stars at night, and generally welcome the unexpected. As part and parcel of the ceremonial process, Spirit is called upon to not only help us get to point "B," but also to inspire the journey itself.

✵ ✵ ✵   ✵ ✵ ✵

PART II

Ceremonial
Tools and
Procedures

Chapter 8
Ingredients for the Ceremony

As I mentioned earlier, I'm not going to offer you precise formulas or exacting recipes, yet you'll find it useful to incorporate some of the following ingredients in most ceremonies. It's not necessary to use each and every one of these in any particular ceremony, and as you explore the use of these tools and procedures, you'll discover which ones work best for the specific ceremony you're performing. Also, I'll let you know later which ones I've found useful for specific types of ceremonies.

We'll start with one that I talked about earlier: altars.

Altars

I've already described how to construct an altar in your home or workplace. This procedure is similar, except it's usually a temporary setup. Designed to be the focal point of the ceremony, this altar is constructed just before its start. If the ceremony is performed in a circle, the altar goes in the middle. In any other arrangement, it should be set in a place that's clearly visible to participants, such as in front of the room if it's a larger group set up theater style. If you're performing the ceremony at home, you can make the already existing altar the focal point.

Set up your altar on a blanket or cloth. I have a special blanket that I use, and a "portable altar," one that contains what I need for the ceremony. In a cloth backpack, I carry such items as a sage bundle, an earthen bowl, a vial for water, a feather, incense, a small cloth place setting, a rattle, a crystal, and a bag of earth from El Santuario. I add things to this as the occasion demands.

In a larger group, everyone can contribute to the construction of the altar. At a recent weeklong Hawaiian healing retreat, on the first day I asked each of the participants to contribute to the altar, so it became a living piece of sacred art over the next several days as things were added, removed, and rearranged according to the visions and promptings of each of us. The altar was on a fairly large table placed in front of the room, clearly the centerpiece for the group meetings.

We started the sessions each day by lighting the candle in the center of the altar. Each day, a small amount of food was placed on the altar to be blessed. This food was then taken outside at the end of each session as an offering to the spirits of the land. It was a remarkable, living shrine, and the pieces that were added throughout the week took on even greater symbolic value to all of us. At the end of the workshop, several of the students graciously and carefully dismantled the altar.

As a rule, keep the altar simple but significant. Ideally, each piece that's placed on it should have some particular significance, and perhaps a story attached to it. You'll find that it's both fun and practical when doing a group ceremony to ask each participant to make a contribution.

Invocation

This takes place just after the signal for the beginning of the ceremony. Through deep prayer, you're asking your spirit guides to be present during the course of the proceedings. It really doesn't matter who or what spirit beings you're calling on. If it's a partisan group, then obviously you'd invoke the names of the deities that this particular group worships. For most groups, there are generic terms that can be used along with any sectarian names. There are a thousand names for the Creator, and probably ten times as many for any lesser deities.

Terms such as *Great Spirit, Creator,* or *God* seem to be universally acceptable. Ancient peoples believed that Spirit expresses itself in many forms, that the world is alive and animated by this

Life Force. Many indigenous peoples don't just *believe* that the world is alive, they *know* it in their heart of hearts, and relate to the world accordingly. Even the pre-Christian Celtic tribes treated the world around them with respect for the Life Force that animated each and every member of the plant, animal, and mineral kingdom.

The invocation can also be made through sound and rhythm, such as rattling, singing, or drumming. I'll often use a rattle accompanied by a song to call upon the spirits of the four directions—east, south, west, and north—as well as the spirits of the heavens and the earth. Other times I may play a "spirit-calling" song, one that I received from my spirit guides, on my wooden flute. Before I begin, I ask all the participants to call in their spirit guides and helpers. By doing so, we build power, so the more help that can be accessed, the more powerful the ceremony is in its execution and impact.

Prayer

The invocation itself can be a simple prayer, and there can also be prayer at other points during the ceremony. Prayer can be carried out in any of the more familiar forms, with hands positioned in any one of the universal and cross-cultural prayer gestures called *mudras,* or it can be expressed through a song or chant. It's useful to have specific prayers in the ceremony, particular near the beginning and end.

As I mentioned previously, there have been hundreds of scientific studies done on prayer that demonstrate how effective it is. It's been found that plants grow faster, heart patients recover faster, and so on. It's also been suggested that when several people pray together for the same purpose, the probability increases that the desired outcome will be achieved.

In a sense, sacred ceremony *is* prayer. Prayer is a way to beseech the Creator for assistance and express gratitude, as well as consecrate the holiness of Earthly events. Ceremony has a similar purpose, yet typically is a more involved and extended process, one that expands on prayer through the manifest expression of intent. My experience is that there's greater opportunity through the mechanisms of ceremony to embody and experience spiritual realities.

Breath

In my research on sacred ceremony, I've noted that conscious breathing is usually overlooked. Yet what can be a more direct embodied experience of the Life Force than breath? When we come into the world through our mother's body, instinct tells us to take that first breath. And it's with that first breath of life that we're *inspired*—we breathe spirit in to start our life on Earth. When we die, the last thing we do is exhale, or *expire*, which means to "breathe spirit out." And then there are the thousands of breaths in between.

We're a culture of shallow breathers. Unless you practice some specific type of meditation that incorporates conscious breathing, it's likely that you neglect to breathe fully and deeply. Plus, we tend to be so caught up in the intensity and pace of contemporary life that we literally forget to breathe, and as a result, we carry around a lot of tension that could be eased by conscious breathing.

In the Hawaiian language, the sound "ha" means *breath, life energy,* or *soul,* depending on the context in which it's used. *Aloha,* the Hawaiian word used both for greetings and farewells, literally translated, means "joyfully sharing life energy." Loosely translated, *aloha* means "go with breath." During their colonization, the Hawaiians came up with another word for the Western Europeans who were steadily emigrating to the islands. The word was *haole* (pronounced HAOW-lee). *Ole* means "without," so literally translated, *haole* means "without breath," and has now taken on a pejorative meaning.

A meditative discipline that has become increasingly popular, and which I highly recommend, is yoga. It's a very ancient spiritual practice that encompasses the mind, body, and spirit, and works with the breath through meditation and various postures, or *asanas*. It's become increasingly recognized in the Western world as a discipline that promotes greater health and well-being. While practicing the various postures, students are coached to continue their breathing throughout, to release muscle tension gradually by letting it go as they exhale, and to gently stretch into the posture.

There are instances of consciously using breath in the ceremonial context: One example is in a ceremony of release, where a stone or other natural object has "agreed" to take with it some characteristic of yours that you no longer wish to have. Let's say that you want to release your fear of public speaking. In the context of ceremony, with your breath, build up the feeling of that fear, holding the stone in your left hand. Then, with that strong breath now filled with the fear, exhale your fear into the stone. The stone, which is now filled with the energy of your fear, is buried in the earth or released into a body of water.

Ceremonial Trance

The poet and storyteller Robert Bly has said that when we enter a ritual, we enter "ritual space." I prefer to call it ceremonial space, and the altered state of consciousness that occurs as *ceremonial trance*. *Trance* describes a phenomenon in which the electrical activity of the brain actually slows down. Just about everyone is familiar with trance states; they show up in a variety of conditions.

You know that sleepy, daydreamy kind of feeling when you're listening to a boring lecture or reading a dry textbook? Or that grogginess you feel when you first wake up, or that relaxed feeling you experience just before going to sleep? All of these are trance states. When meditating, we go into a trance. The main distinctions are the form and the depth.

We associate very profound states of trance with hypnosis, meditation, and deeper forms of relaxation. Ceremonial trance can vary from mild, to a very deep, altered state of consciousness. Participating in a ceremony takes you out of ordinary time and space into what can be called *archaic time*. This is often described as a sense of timelessness. I ask participants in ceremonies to take off their watches to encourage their entry into non-ordinary dimensions of time and space.

Rhythm, movement, chanting, singing, storytelling, praying, and silence can all induce a rather pleasing altered state of consciousness. When all the participants are acting in unison when engaging in any of these activities, it further encourages this ceremonial trance. All the elements and activities that occur within sacred ceremony combine to reach down into a deep race consciousness, a mythological domain that stimulates ceremonial trance. It can literally make you swoon, and often can induce a rapturous, ecstatic state.

Symbols

Symbols are those objects that carry both personal and archetypal meaning. An object becomes a symbol when it's imbued with personal significance. It's not the object itself so much as what it means, or symbolizes, to the individual. For example, when my daughter Nicole was 14 years old, she started rummaging through some boxes in the garage. She came into the house holding a small music box swaddled in a cushiony, yellow, velvet wrapping. It was playing "When You Wish Upon a Star." Tears were streaming down her face as she realized that this was a music box that she'd enjoyed when she was just a baby, and which had provided her with many hours of comfort and joy. It had been put away when she was about five years old during a move, a time filled with uncertainty and turmoil. Discovering the box brought back the original significance and the accompanying emotions.

Another characteristic of symbols is their archetypal significance. *Archetypes* are those prototypical characteristics of a symbol that have universal and cross-cultural meaning. For instance, the archetypes of mother, magician, princess, or king typically have distinctive cultural articulations, yet the fundamental qualities in each of these are in our species-consciousness and are common to all humans. Nicole's music box was not only personally significant, it was also a representation of the archetypes of music and the nursery lullaby. She was experiencing, and for a time reliving, the archetype of the inner child. The beauty of this is that the basic elements in Nicole's story are played out in their own unique ways in other cultures.

Within any personal or cultural symbols, we'll find archetypal meaning. The concrete symbols we use—a stone, a feather, a bowl of water, and a candle—touch an instinctively familiar chord for everyone. These symbols may be used in ceremony for the Four Elements, and you may find some slight variation of each of these whether attending a ceremony in Nepal or in your backyard. As you prepare the ceremony, consider what symbols would be appropriate for the ceremony, in addition to the four elements.

The Four Elements

As described before in the section on altars, the four basic elements of earth, air, fire, and water should be represented in ceremonies. You can use the actual elements, or their symbols. The obvious exception is air, which you can symbolize with a feather. A stone or bit of earth itself can be the element earth. Since the earth from El Santuario has been such a valuable asset in my healing work, I'll often place this on the ceremonial altar. A vial of water or a seashell will do as the representation of water, and most often a candle will represent fire. These powerful and basic symbols are profoundly familiar to everyone present, whether or not they have an awareness of their potent symbology. They're the basic stuff of which all life is made.

The Four Directions

To each of the four directions—east, south, west and north—there are certain characteristics attributed. When you're honoring these directions at the opening of a ceremony, you're also honoring the *spirits* of each direction, as well as perhaps invoking their assistance for some purpose. There are various meanings and qualities attributed to each of these directions, depending on the interpretations of any particular tradition.

In *Quest: Guide for Creating Your Own Vision Quest*, author Denise Linn describes the characteristics of each of these directions from the perspective of a Native American medicine wheel:

	East	South	West	North
Element	air	water	fire	earth
Season	spring	summer	autumn	winter
Animals	eagle/owl	frog/dolphin	phoenix/snake	bear/turtle
Quality	mental	emotional	spiritual	physical
Sun	dawn	noon	sunset	midnight
Moon	waxing moon	full moon	waning moon	new moon
Color	yellow	blue	red	black/white
Human	birth	childhood	young adult	elder
Creativity	activation	nurturance	experimentation	consolidation
Key Word	inspiration	intuition	transformation	introspection

Offerings

An offering is anything that you give up to Spirit. In the feast that often follows a group ceremony, food is first taken outside and offered to the spirits. The food left on the altars in Bangkok that I described earlier was a gift to the gods. In Hawaii, flowers are frequently left on the remaining walls of the temples of the earlier peoples, which are called *heiaus* (pronounced HEY-ows), as a gesture to those spiritual guardians of the temple. During Catholic Lent, a person voluntarily abstains from some habit or addiction as an offering to God. Fasting means that you're surrendering your eating habits to Spirit, usually as a means of developing your compassion and gratitude.

During a ceremony, another type of offering is to place one's sacred objects on the altar. Because the altar holds the spiritual focus and is imbued with power, once these objects are taken back, they're then similarly imbued with this spiritual power. In the Hawaiian healing retreat mentioned earlier, all of us contributed one or two sacred objects to the ceremonial altar, which stayed intact throughout the week. Here was a ring, there a Tibetan bell, and so on. Fresh flowers were placed on the altar each morning, as well as bits of food. Other items included a scarf, a necklace, candles of all shapes and sizes, and toward the end, a beautiful painting someone had purchased.

These aren't hodgepodge items, but very personal, sacred items that are contributed for the duration of the ceremony. While resting on the altar, these objects receive the power of the group consciousness and become saturated with the holy intent of the retreat.

Food as an offering can have two purposes. Placed on the ceremonial altar before the ceremony is initiated, it's then considered to be endowed with the blessings of the gods. When the ceremony is completed, typically the food is then placed somewhere out of doors as an offering to the spirits. Sometimes the remainder of the food is shared among the participants. In one healing ceremony that I'll describe later, the participants fed each other the food (grapes and bread) that had been on the altar since the beginning. Everyone commented on how powerful the symbolic value was.

❋ ❋ ❋   ❋ ❋ ❋

Chapter 9

Musical Expression:
Rhythm, Sound,
and Song

Ah, music! What would life be without it? From the simplest note to the more complex textural interweavings of classical musical, from hymnals to rock and roll, music feeds our soul. In an interview in *New Age* magazine (November/December 2001), the renowned American blues musician and performer Taj Mahal stated, "Music is one of the languages of the universe." He went on to note that in Africa, in contrast to the Western world, music is such an integral part of life that it cannot be separated out as a profession.

"There, music is more like breathing. It's a part of the whole life. When I was in Africa, people would ask me, 'What do you do?' I'd say, 'I'm a musician.' And they'd say, 'Yes, of course, but what do you do?' Playing music as the only thing you do—they couldn't grasp that concept." Whether in the Western world or Africa, music is such an integral part of life that something would be missing if it were not incorporated in some way into sacred ceremony.

Angeles Arrien, anthropologist and author of *The Four-Fold Way*, describes how indigenous healers throughout the world blend music, rhythm, and singing into their healing practices. She mentions that singing is one of the four universal healing salves, along with storytelling, dancing, and silence:

> Healers throughout the world recognize the importance of maintaining or retrieving the four universal healing salves:

storytelling, singing, dancing, and silence. Shamanic societies believe that when we stop singing, stop dancing, are no longer enchanted by stories, or become uncomfortable with silence, we experience soul loss, which opens the door to discomfort and disease. The gifted Healer restores the soul through use of the healing salves.

So we start by exploring one fundamental aspect of these "healing salves": rhythm.

Rhythm

Rhythm is with us all the time, from our mother's steady heartbeat while we're still in the womb, to the rhythm and sound of our own breathing when we're in a still, quiet place. It's second nature to incorporate these elements into ceremony. Mickey Hart (the former drummer for the Grateful Dead) in the opening sentence of his book, *Planet Drum*, wrote, "In the beginning, there was the beat." Rhythm is one of the most basic elements in life.

Nearly anything can be used to create rhythm. You don't even need an instrument; you can use your own body as the instrument. Clapping your hands, snapping your fingers, or slapping your thighs creates a beat. At some workshops where we incorporate rhythm, people have used upside-down wastebaskets or water bottles as drums, and vitamin bottles or beads in an empty plastic water bottle as rattles. All it takes is a little imagination to create your own rhythm instrument.

More commonly, in sacred ceremony, drums or rattles are used. They may be used throughout the ceremony, to open or close it, or at particular points during the ceremonial process.

Anthropologist and author Michael Harner in *Way of the Shaman* notes that in the indigenous shamanic cultures he has studied, often the shaman will induce in themselves the altered state of consciousness (which he terms the "shamanic state of consciousness") through rhythm, usually through drumming or rattling. Typically the rhythm is four to seven beats (or shakes) per second.

Researchers have found that after about 12 minutes of steady drumming, particularly at the rate of four to seven beats per second, an amazing thing happens. Our brain waves begin to synchronize with the drumbeat! Typically, in an awakened state, our brain waves register what is called a *beta* rhythm, which is an oscillation of 14 to 20 cycles per second. This is the normal waking state, when you're alert. The next slower cycle is called the *alpha* rhythm, which is 8 to 13 cycles per second. This is a mild trance state, what you experience when you first awaken from a deep sleep, or that drowsy feeling just before bedtime. Next is the *theta* rhythm, four to seven cycles per second, experienced during sleep as well as during moderate to deeper trance states.

Conclusion: Drumming at the rate of four to seven beats per second will tend to slow down the brain waves to a theta rhythm—a corresponding four to seven cycles per second—thus putting the participants into an altered state of consciousness that's characteristic of many meditative and shamanic disciplines!

Many studies have demonstrated the health benefits of drumming, from slowing our brain waves into more meditative states, increasing immune response, and as a very useful tool in managing stress. A recent article in the *Orange County Register* described how senior citizens at a retirement community have been meeting regularly for drumming circles, and those interviewed described that it made them feel better. Drumming is one of those exceptional ancient tools that has health benefits for those of us in contemporary times.

Drumming also helps unify a group. At a musical festival I attended, I purchased a small drum from a gentleman from Senegal, Africa, which had an elegant carved tree on the side of it. The vendor said it was a peace tree. He described how in his home village in Senegal, participants gather around this tree with their drums, rattles, and other percussion instruments once a week. As people gather gradually, they start playing their instruments. At first there's a cacophony of sound, like a percussion orchestra tuning its instruments.

He went on to say, "Then, something beautiful and mystical begins to happen. Much like the rhythm of crickets at night, everyone starts to synchronize the beat. Rhythms are playing within and around other rhythms, interweaving themselves all within the larger group rhythm. The master beat mysteriously appears out of the chaos of sound. It's when we're synchronized that we're praying with our drums for peace for ourselves, our families, our community, and for the world."

And who says there's only one way to pray?

Sound

Like rhythm, sound is all around us. Even in silence, there's sound, if it's only our own heartbeat and breathing. Then there's the sound and rhythm of the ocean waves, a steady, reassuring sound. As the popular Hawaiian troubadour, Israel Kamakawiwo'ole, sang, "The sound of the ocean/soothes my troubled soul/the sound of the ocean/rocks me all night long." The rustle of the trees, the sound of our child's breathing as they sleep, a lover's sigh; all of these and so much more sing to us of life.

Sound is important in ceremony, whether it be singing and chanting, drumming, or the sound of a musical instrument. As I mentioned, I often use a simple wooden flute to play a spirit-calling song. When I play, often something else is coming through me and through the flute. When I finish, I feel a deep state of peace, often merging into a quietly ecstatic state.

Another instrument that has increasingly found its way into contemporary ceremonies is the *didgeridoo*. This is an Australian Aborigine instrument, formed from tree limbs that have been cored out by termites, leaving a thin shell. The net effect is a long tube, sometimes painted with an elaborate aboriginal design on the outside. It's played by placing the tube over your lips and blowing into it with lips pursed. The result is a low, humming, pulsating vibration. In aboriginal mythology, it's said that this instrument was used to sing the world and all its creatures into existence. When played, you can hear the different creatures birthing through the didgeridoo's rhythmic song.

Often, the lilting, low tonal vibrations of the didgeridoo are accompanied by the steady cadence of click sticks, which are two smaller, handheld hardwood sticks with carvings on them. It's said that listening to these two instruments long enough will take you on a journey into the dreamtime, a place of non-ordinary reality. If you haven't experienced meditating or journeying with a didgeridoo, I highly recommend it.

Other instruments can be used at your discretion. The main idea of incorporating any rhythm makers or musical instruments is that it fits the intention of the ceremony. There are also some powerful CDs that can be used for meditations and journeys (see Appendix). It's nearly impossible to perform sacred ceremony without rhythm and sound, so it's helpful to incorporate it consciously and intentionally.

Another way to do so is through singing and chanting.

Singing and Chanting

All the many ways we can express ourselves through our voice—from words to song, from grunts and groans to wordless expressions of delight—demonstrate the diversity of our vocal instrument. The various melodic possibilities of song and chant can be put to great use in sacred ceremony.

In shamanic cultures, shamans will not only drum or rattle, but also sing themselves into a heightened state of consciousness. Indigenous healers have special songs for particular purposes, often those that have been handed down through the shamanic lineage. These can be songs or chants for healing, celebration, or gratitude. As mentioned previously, singing is one of the universal healing salves, and can be used to heal soul loss. In original Hawaiian and Native American practices, as is true in many indigenous cultures, there was no written language, so the history and lineage was handed down through very complex and lengthy chants, accompanied by drumming and dancing.

Another chant that can be used to open or close ceremonies is a simple word, "Om," or more accurately, "Aum," repeated a few times. It's from the ancient language of Sanskrit, which was created not as a means of communication between people, but between humans and God. It's to be chanted slowly and drawn out, starting with "ah," and closing with "mmm." When performed together with a group and repeated a few times in unison, it can meld the group together into a singular, multitonal voice. When repeated enough, it can induce a trancelike state.

※ ※ ※   ※ ※ ※

Chapter 10

Dance, Movement, and Storytelling

In our culture, we don't tend to associate dance and movement with spiritual expression, yet in many cultures, dance is considered an integral aspect of ceremony and one of the universal healing salves. In Native American gatherings, there are traditional sacred dances, some performed only by specified dancers, others in which the entire community participates, all to the sound of drums and ancient chants. There's dancing in African, Balinese, Indian ceremonies, and in many others. In some ceremonies I've facilitated, movement was one way of invoking the sacred.

I did a spontaneous personal ceremony once that was entirely based on movement. One evening while listening to one of my favorite CDs, I was prompted to dance. The song that was playing, "Night Ride Across the Caucasus," from *The Book of Secrets* by Loreena McKennitt, is a beautiful, rhythmic piece with a haunting melody and lyrics. Without consciously thinking about it, I was up and moving to the music, imagining that I was dancing with this invisible "inner woman" in my arms, loving her and caressing her. This was the woman who was both a part of me and the one who was yet to come into my life.

The movement felt so sweet and tender that I wept with joy and sadness. It felt as if a deep wound in my heart and soul was being cleansed and healed, the wound of lost love mixed with the promise of future love. I had a revelation while I was dancing: By healing this relationship with my "inner woman," I would open the door to having a healthy and mature relationship with a real, live woman. I did this dance twice more during the ensuing months, each with conscious intent to "court" this part of me as well as invite the woman of my dreams into my life. Each time I did so, I felt more complete and whole, as if I were preparing the ground by "owning" this part of myself first, rather than constantly trying to find "her" in the form of another woman.

The good news is that I found the woman of my dreams, and I'm now married to her. And it all started with a spontaneous ceremony, with movement and music as the central features.

There are other ways in which dance and movement can be used for nearly any kind of ceremony. In the upcoming chapters on the different types of ceremony, there will be examples of how movement can be used as an integral ingredient.

Storytelling

"Once upon a time . . ." Our enchantment with the world around us begins with stories, particularly those that are ripe with teachings about our relationship with God, the natural world, and other human beings. Children are easily enthralled by stories— as is the child in each of us—and just about everyone is mesmerized by a tale well told.

When my children were younger, like most kids, they enjoyed a good bedtime tale. I alternated between telling them a drawn-out adventure, each night making up a new chapter, and reading stories from books. One of the works that both girls enjoyed immensely was *The Giving Tree*, by Shel Silverstein, which is the story of a boy and his lifelong relationship with a tree. This simple story conveyed so much meaning about the human life cycle, the value of sacrifice, and the importance of our relationship with trees.

Not only do stories entertain and enlighten us, but they serve to pass along traditions and mythologies, as well as teach us about our "cultural mythos." Unlike previous eras, where our ancestors might huddle around the fire to exchange stories, or where the elders would act out colorful tales with considerable flair for the children and others who would listen, we derive many of our contemporary stories from movies, books, and television.

For instance, the *Star Wars* series of films have woven themselves into our cultural subtext such that it's hard to find anyone who isn't familiar with them. Another tale that has gained renewed popularity (due to the recent release of a film version of the J.R.R. Tolkien book), is *Lord of the Rings*, an epic story that's similar in theme and structure to *Star Wars*. Within these broad, sweeping sagas are symbolic elements that resonate in a strangely familiar way with the collective human psyche.

Star Wars and *Lord of the Rings* represent classic "hero's journeys," where the protagonists—in these cases, Luke Skywalker or Frodo Baggins—are pulled from their rather ordinary, mundane lives, and through a series of unexpected events, are forced to overcome many challenges and defeat the dark forces that threaten to destroy not only them, but their worlds. The beauty of these types of stories, whether conveyed through film, book, or spoken word, is that each and every one of us can find parallels with these types of tales in our own lives.

In addition to your own hero's journey, you have many other life stories. These tales tell others about you, what you believe, what you think of yourself, and your worldview. In any ceremonies you facilitate, it can be useful to recount some of these personal experiences, particularly as it relates to the intention of the ceremony. For instance, if you're performing a ceremony for a life transition that you've already gone through, detailing an incident from your own experience can serve to encourage and support the participants. Plus, many of these personal stories will have a substratum of archetypal and cultural mythos.

For storytelling to be effective, it can be make-believe or based on real events—although storytellers may emblazon their versions with a particular slant or add and subtract details according to their needs or those of the listeners. Like the fish you caught last summer or the incredible adventure you had while vacationing, with each telling, the fish gets a little bigger; the adventure gets a bit more sensational.

As an aspect of ceremony, stories can be interjected as appropriate. When I've performed marriage ceremonies, I'll usually tell a tale about the couple, perhaps about how they met or some unusual and humorous experience they've gone through together. This isn't done to embarrass the couple, but to augment the ceremony with an interesting sidebar that adds both a human and an eternal dimension to the experience.

You need not be a Garrison Keillor to incorporate storytelling into a ceremony. Nor do any of the stories told have to be lengthy or laced with profound meaning. Often the simplest stories are the most effective. For instance, at the beginning of a ceremony, it can help to describe how it came to be, or if it's one drawn from a particular tradition, how it has come to be passed down through the generations. In a baby-blessing ceremony I performed for some friends, I told of how we'd attempted to perform the ceremony a couple of weeks prior, but had been stymied by a number of now-laughable obstructions.

One other truism with storytelling in ceremonies: You don't need to have a *prepared* story. Often a tale will emerge in your consciousness as the ceremony progresses, one that's perfectly suitable for the moment. Take some chances. If the story doesn't go over well, you can always . . . tell a story about the mishap at some later date!

❊ ❊ ❊   ❊ ❊ ❊

Chapter 11

Flavors, Fasting, and Feasting

For the final touches to a ceremony, let's consider the sense of smell and the taste buds, as well as the value of abstaining from any number of activities, including eating and drinking.

Aromas and Herbs

There's a whole science involving scents called *aromatherapy* that links specific types of smells with particular effects on the body, mind, and emotions. Various aromas will stimulate a very primitive part of the brain, influencing your nervous system in a particular direction, whether or not you're aware of these often subtle responses. For instance, lavender and jasmine have been shown to trigger a response of calmness, while cinnamon and peppermint tend to stimulate activation.

Another source for pleasing scents is incense. One that I commonly use is Nag Champa. It has a subtle fragrance, not overpowering, that helps create an appropriate atmosphere for many ceremonies. Another incense that lends itself well to ceremony is sandalwood. Experiment with various incenses to find out which ones are pleasing to you. I'd caution you to stay away from perfumed sticks that are sold as incense. Their scents are too strong and overpowering to use for ceremonies.

In addition, there are herbs that can be used during a ceremony for different purposes. As mentioned previously, sage can be used for burning before and during ceremonies. It helps clear out the "negative energy" in preparation for the proceedings. At the beginning of the ceremony, you can use the smoke from the burning sage to "brush off" or "smudge" the altar and the sacred objects, then the participants. The smoke itself has a rather pleasant, distinct odor that lingers long past when the sage itself has stopped burning. You can also use cedar in a similar fashion for clearing, or you can combine the two. You can find smudge sticks that have both cedar and sage.

Once the clearing is done with sage, cedar, or both, then you can burn some sweetgrass. This is used to call in the "good energy," or invite in the helping spirits. Like its name, it has a very sweet and inviting aroma, one that says "home."

Also, the scent from plants that are brought in for the ceremony can add to the ambiance. Aside from their visual beauty, any plant that emits a pleasant aroma can enhance the ceremonial atmosphere.

Abstinence

There are times when abstinence before a ceremony can increase the meaning. Sacrifice has a long tradition in many religions and spiritual practices, and to abstain for a period of time from the usual activities of life can represent an offering to the Great Spirit. The intent here isn't to martyr yourself for ceremonial purposes, but to use the suffering resulting from abstinence, whether mild or intense, as an offering to solicit blessings from God.

You may choose to abstain from food, water, sex, or any other material comfort. You can even abstain from talking, spending an entire day or several days without verbal communication. When this is done out in nature, the silence becomes filled with sweet sounds all around. When the abstinence is done as an aspect of ceremony, it helps you focus more intently on the holy purpose of the ceremony.

In a vision quest, under the guidance of experienced facilitators, you may go to a secluded spot in the wilderness for anywhere from one to four days. With considerable preparation, you're guided by your own intention and your prayers. Once you've prepared yourself with the help of your guides, your mission is to find a secluded place out in nature, one where you won't be disturbed, and for a period of that time, usually four days, abstain from eating. The fasting not only physiologically prepares you to be more receptive; it's an offering to Spirit.

The Shared Feast

Ah yes, the feast! What more appropriate way to conclude a ceremony than with food and drink—but not necessarily alcoholic drinks, although these may be a part of it. Contemporary wedding practices typically require that the family and the community share together in food and drink at the reception. In a prayer vigil, sharing food with one another following the ceremony or as part of the closing has the symbolic value of nourishing one another.

After a ceremony at a sweat lodge, it's characteristic for the participants to share in the food that each has contributed. Some sweat-lodge ceremonialists suggest that you fast for several hours or even days before the sweat, so food and drink become a very special and very welcome event.

Following a sweat lodge experience I once participated in, we gathered around the table filled with an array of delicious-looking platters, including fresh fruit salad, warm sliced bread with butter, vegetable fried rice, barbecued chicken, and freshly made oatmeal cookies for dessert, to name a few of the items. The first thing we did before diving in, however, was to make an offering of the food to the spirits. The leader asked one of the women to select a small morsel of one of each of the food groups that were so amply represented on this table and carry it outside on a plate. She was instructed to say a prayer of gratitude as she placed the dish outside, and then rejoin us. We all patiently waited, and I'm sure most were beginning to salivate. Then she returned and we ate heartily.

Another time, my wife, Doreen, and I, along with some friends, did a three-day juice fast to coincide with the full moon and which would end on February 1, which in some traditions is considered to be the true beginning of spring. Since we ingested only liquids for three days, on the fourth day we all met for breakfast. Although I'm not sure it technically qualifies as a feast, with even a short period of abstinence, I must say that breakfast was especially delightful and tasty that morning.

�֍ �֍ ✖

Now that you are armed with some of the tools and procedures that can be useful when engaging in a ceremony, let's move on to actually creating ceremonies, starting with those of a healing nature.

✻ ✻ ✻   ✻ ✻ ✻

PART III

Healing

Ceremonies

Chapter 12

Before You Begin . . .

There are some relevant issues to consider prior to conducting any healing ceremonies. In this chapter, I'll address some of these considerations, such as the focus of the healing, ethical considerations, and the transformational impact that a healing ceremony can have on the lingering effects of trauma. This will give you a framework within which to perform any healing ceremony.

Two Types of Injuries

There are two types of conditions that can benefit from healing ceremonies. They are *physical illness* and *trauma.* Although someone with a physical illness can be greatly helped by healing ceremonies, serious illnesses—particular any that are life-threatening— require a more comprehensive treatment plan than can be found in a book alone, and should be tailored to the individual's needs and preferences. Healing ceremonies can certainly be part of that plan, though, and in life-threatening illnesses, they can be extremely beneficial as a way of augmenting any primary treatment modalities, whether conventional or alternative. In this section, you'll find examples of how someone with a physical illness has benefited from a healing ceremony.

As for trauma, it's at the core of any type of injury, even a serious illness. A traumatic response can be triggered by physical, sexual, or emotional abuse; a significant loss; major illness or injury; natural or human-made disasters; and other events. The primary purpose of the healing ceremonies described in this chapter is to alleviate the suffering caused by the trauma associated with any kind of injury, whether physical, sexual, emotional, or spiritual.

Before exploring this topic in more detail, we'll first take a look at some important ethical considerations.

Ethics

If you feel that you're ready to perform ceremonies for someone other than yourself, then it's important to develop a code of ethics. Here are some suggested ethical guidelines.

Similar to the physician's code, the primary ethic in any kind of healing ceremony work is: *First, do no harm*. Very close to this edict is: *Know your strengths and limitations*. If you feel relatively confident in organizing a community healing, then do so. However, if you're asked to perform a physical healing and have little experience in doing so, then politely decline and help the person find someone who is more qualified.

Another consideration is *training*. There's no license or certification given in order to be a ceremonialist, nor do you necessarily need one. Many of us who conduct ceremonies have gradually evolved into it, usually accumulating an assortment of experiences from various teachers and seminars. One of the best training grounds is having participated in various ceremonies throughout the course of your life. To perform more extensive healing ceremonies, it's imperative that you get some formal training. You can do so with a teacher, or someone skilled in a particular healing tradition—whether it's African, Celtic, Native American, Tibetan, Hawaiian, or any other. The advantage of this type of training is that there's a rich history and background that supports the type of ceremonies you'll perform.

Many people intuitively know about ceremonies, whether or not there's been any formal training. I've known a few very powerful healers who received their training directly from spiritual sources. One claims that his Celtic ancestors have come to him in his meditations and instructed him in some ancient ceremonies. Whatever your path has been, *know thyself*—especially your strengths and limitations.

Collaboration with Physicians and Psychotherapists

Should you feel ready to facilitate ceremonies with others, it's important to heed the realities of the culture in which you live. Although alternative methods of healing are becoming more widely accepted and utilized, the dominant paradigm is still the Western medical mode.

If you're dealing with a medical condition, it's important for the patient to be under the supervision of a physician, although ceremonial work may be done to enhance whatever treatment the individual is undergoing, whether contemporary Western medical treatment, alternative medicine, or a combination of the two. With psychological and emotional problems, refer the person to a psychotherapist in addition to whatever ceremonial work you may be conducting with them. Preferably the physician or psychotherapist is one that's willing to incorporate alternative methodologies as an aspect of the treatment.

If you're a psychotherapist, you may find that ceremonies can be included with great effectiveness as an aspect of your overall treatment plan. Milton H. Erickson, a renowned psychiatrist and hypnotherapist, often prescribed ceremonial work to his clients, without necessarily calling it such. When I had my own psychotherapy practice, I'd often prescribe ceremonies as homework, or at times I'd facilitate these with individual clients within the session itself. In the groups I facilitated, often the entire session would be a ceremony.

Justine, a shamanic colleague, performed regular healing ceremonies with Russell, a man diagnosed with pancreatic cancer. This type of cancer has a statistically high morbidity rate, so Russell initially opted for standard radiation and chemotherapy treatments. However, he continued to do healing ceremonies on a regular basis with Justine, and found these very beneficial. Although he had been expected to live only two or three months from the time of diagnosis, he survived more than two years. He attributed his life extension to the ceremonial healing work rather than the conventional treatments, which he discontinued after the first series. Russell died at home, peacefully, feeling very complete with his life. His wife and two children were at his bedside when he released his final breath.

Cured or Healed

Although someone may not be cured of their disease or illness, like Russell, they can still experience profound healing. There have been many instances where people with catastrophic illnesses have died—in other words, haven't been cured—but have been healed in the most profoundly spiritual way possible. They've reconciled their relationships with Life, with God, and with those they love, feeling a deep sense of peace and calm during their final exit. In addition, there's ample anecdotal evidence of people who have been cured of life-threatening illnesses via exclusively alternative medical approaches. Many of these cures not only involved changes in diet, attitude, and health habits, but also included ceremonial work.

Something that can provide public legitimacy for your ceremonial work is to acquire a ministerial license. There are organizations that will readily grant you a license to do ministerial work due to their philosophy that if you're called upon to do this work, that's all it takes (see Resources). Their philosophy is that it's your own inner urging and calling to be a minister that qualifies you, as opposed to being certified by an external religious organization. The organizations that grant such licenses are completely legitimate, and such a license will allow you to do anything that any other type of ordained minister is typically called to do, including performing healing ceremonies.

So once again we circle back to the primary ethical rule: First, do no harm. Taking into account the above considerations and appropriate precautions, you shouldn't have any difficulty. If you're ever in doubt, talk with a colleague or a friend and get some feedback for what you're considering. Ask someone more experienced, and let yourself be mentored or even supervised. One precaution you can use is to have your clients sign a written disclaimer, circumscribing your role as a ceremonialist or minister doing spiritual healing.

The Inevitable Healing

As I've noted previously, the unstated intention in any healing ceremony is always *spiritual* healing, even when the primary target is physical, emotional, or psychological. The very act of determining the intention for healing and then creating and carrying out the ceremony sets the stage for the direct embodiment of a fundamental spiritual reality—the felt experience of Spirit in our lives, accompanied by a deeper sense of connectedness with the invisible forces that shape our daily lives.

Above and beyond intrinsic spiritual healing, this type of ceremony can focus on a range of possibilities. Perhaps a specific illness or injury, a difficult and problematic emotional state, or a personal relationship that has gone awry can benefit from it. A ceremony can be performed to heal land that has been abused by deforestation or to restore a geographic area devastated by a natural disaster. It can be performed individually, as a personal healing in the context of a group, or as a community. The ceremony may be brief, or extend over a period of several hours or days.

The results of these kind of ceremonies aren't necessarily immediate or tangible, nor do they always achieve the hoped-for outcome—that is, some kind of cure. For example, there may still be a need for further medical treatment, the land may not promptly flourish, and a healing ceremony for the community may afford an important, but not necessarily lasting, sense of cohesion and unity.

Stephen and Ondrea Levine, authors of *Who Dies?: An Investigation of Conscious Living and Conscious Dying,* suggest that even though those with catastrophic illnesses may not end up being cured, they can still heal. In any healing ceremony where the intention is clear and the spiritual forces called upon during the ceremony are focused *through* our attention on the particular need at hand, there is inevitably a spiritual healing. We feel at peace with ourselves and our world, with a quiet certainty about the eternal nature of Life, even beyond the point of death.

Next, I'll outline some of the characteristics of trauma, which are at the core of any injury or illness.

Trauma As an Overwhelming Experience

As I've touched on, trauma is at the core of any type of wound. Traumatic events can encompass natural and human created disasters, physical or sexual assault, robbery, war, major illnesses, loss or violence or the threat of such, or even witnessing violent acts. This isn't an exhaustive list, since many other events can trigger a traumatic reaction.

Although there are some situations that will traumatize almost everyone, a key to understanding trauma is that it isn't in the event itself, but in the individual's *perception* of, and *reaction* to, that event. Therefore, much depends on the individual's makeup and on exposure to prior traumatizing events. Anyone who has been traumatized repeatedly, especially as a child, will be more susceptible to posttraumatic reactions and may be easily triggered by any number of things, including seemingly innocuous events.

So what exactly is trauma? Sigmund Freud described it as a "breach in the protective barrier against stimulation, leading to overwhelming feelings of helplessness." Psychiatrist and author Judith Hermann, in *Trauma and Recovery*, states: "Traumatic events are extraordinary, not because they occur rarely, but rather because they overwhelm the ordinary human adaptation to life . . . the common denominator is a feeling of 'intense fear, helplessness, loss of control, and threat of annihilation.'"

The key word in these definitions is *overwhelming*. A traumatic event literally overwhelms the nervous system, flooding it with adrenaline and cortisol, initially resulting in a state of shock and immobility that can last for seconds or days. If this tremendous flood of instinctual energy can be mobilized, focused, and expressed through some physical action of fleeing or fighting that assures your survival, then once the traumatizing event has passed, the nervous system and the emotions settle out through a complimentary process of physical and emotional discharge and release.

This discharge may be experienced as shaking, trembling, flushing, crying, weeping, laughing, and/or deep breathing. All these physical symptoms are a natural response that should be welcomed as an indication that the nervous system is regulating itself, returning to a state of balance.

When the nervous system and emotions are given the chance to self-regulate by releasing this stored-up energy, then we can go about our normal, day-to-day lives. In a more natural state, this is what happens. All animals, including the human animal, can self-regulate through these cycles of activation, mobilization, orientation, and defense, returning to a state of relative calm by discharging this survival energy once the threat has passed.

But for us human beings, that's not typically how it works.

Fear and Control

When the more natural defenses of running or fighting are blocked and there's no opportunity for discharge and release, then this tremendous instinctual energy remains in the nervous system, keeping us on "alert" status long past the actual threat. There are a couple of reasons that we humans don't naturally discharge this built-up energy.

First, we've been trained most of our lives to control our feelings and our behavior. Through childhood conditioning, we've been repeatedly reminded in various ways to get over it, stop crying, grow up, and so on. These messages may have come through physical punishment or the threat of same, through verbal and nonverbal shaming messages, through abandonment or the threat of it, or some combination of all of the above.

Let's say that a seven-year-old child slips and falls on the sidewalk. A parent who's doing a reasonably good job will come to the child's aid, comforting them and sympathizing with them while checking for any obvious signs of injury. Assuming the injury isn't that serious—perhaps a scraped knee or a sore ankle—the child will be ready to play again in a few minutes.

Sometimes, however, the parent will communicate such messages as, "It's okay. Don't cry. You're all right. Be a big boy (or girl)," or do something even more derisive and punitive. What this tells the child is that they should not allow for the natural physiological and emotional discharge. In other words, *control yourself.* With enough of these experiences, by the time we reach adulthood, this message is typically so well ingrained that any emotional or physiological discharges are immediately squelched; or if they're shown, we feel apologetic and shamed.

Another major reason we block the release of this energy is fear. The trapped energy of this incomplete response to trauma can be very intense and therefore very frightening. Coupled with the well-practiced habit of keeping control at all costs, the fear itself can be overwhelming, aside from the impact of the actual trauma or the traumatic memory.

Posttraumatic Stress Disorder and Shamanism

The lifelong conditioning of maintaining control and the seemingly insurmountable fear of the intense energies involved in response to trauma can keep us from naturally discharging this tremendous storehouse of energy. This keeps us in a frozen state of immobility, or what psychologist and author Peter Levine in *Waking the Tiger: Healing Trauma* describes as "an internal straitjacket created when a devastating moment is frozen in time." He goes on to state: "It stifles the unfolding of being, strangling our attempts to move forward with our lives. It disconnects us from our selves, others, nature and spirit. When people are overwhelmed by threat, we are frozen in fear."

The consequences of unhealed trauma are described in the *Diagnostic and Statistical Manual of Mental Disorders* (DSM-IV) as a psychiatric malady termed "Posttraumatic Stress Disorder" (PTSD). The symptoms are described under three major categories: reexperiencing the trauma, psychic numbing, and increased arousal.

Reexperiencing the trauma includes:

- intrusive recollections;
- nightmares;
- flashbacks; and
- distress at symbols of the traumatic event.

Psychic numbing includes:

- avoidance;
- amnesia;
- diminished interests;
- restricted affect; and
- foreshortened future (i.e., does not expect to have marriage, children, normal life-span).

Increased arousal includes:

- sleep disturbances;
- irritability;
- difficulty concentrating;
- hypervigilance;
- exaggerated startle response; and
- excessive physiological reactivity.

It's important to stress that most of these "symptoms" had survival value at the time of the original traumatizing experience, yet because of the fear of losing control and of the seeming enormity and dread of the pent-up energy, this survival energy becomes symptomatic after a time.

There is a parallel between shamanic healing methodologies and the shaking and trembling that accompanies the release of the pent-up energy from the traumatic memory. In shamanic cultures, it's believed that when a person is wounded through a traumatic experience, it results in "soul loss," where a piece of that person's soul leaves his or her body. The symptoms of soul loss can closely resemble those of posttraumatic stress disorder, and even more specifically, dissociation. The shaman's task is to send their soul, or consciousness, into non-ordinary reality, find the ailing person's soul wherever it may be, and return it to the body. This is called "soul retrieval." What's fascinating is that once the shaman has returned the patient's soul into their body, typically the patient shakes and trembles, sometimes for several minutes.

Transforming Trauma Through Ceremony

Again, for serious or life-threatening illnesses, it's important for the recipient to be under a physician's care and supervision. Healing ceremonies aren't intended to be a substitute for proper medical care, yet they can still be extremely useful, especially for the emotional and psychological effects of such an illness.

Don't shy away from performing healing ceremonies; just use good ethical judgment as to whether the recipient requires referrals to appropriate health-care practitioners. If the condition is beyond the scope of your experience and your spiritual power, call on someone more skilled to perform the healing ceremonial, or at least assist you.

The quality and effectiveness of the ceremony isn't contingent upon its complexity or intensity. Sometimes the simplest ceremonies can be the most impactful and instigate a healing process that leads to tremendous relief, as well as a clearer sense of direction as to what may be needed next to treat the particular malady.

As in any healing ceremony, what we aim to do is relieve the suffering of the patient. Within the relative safety and spiritual surround of ceremonial space, there's opportunity to release some of the stored-up "frozen" energy. This may be experienced as shaking, trembling, flushing, crying, weeping, or even exuberant laughter—a natural, rather than induced, catharsis. You can prepare the participant ahead of time by telling them that this may happen, letting them know it as not only normal and natural, but a positive sign that says there's some healing from the traumatic experience.

In the context of ceremony, often following the release the patient feels quiet and serene. They're completely present and full of vitality. There may still be some residual signs of release, such as tears, but now these are experienced as relief and joy. This is the end result of transformation of the trauma—serenity and an opening of the heart. The frozenness has thawed somewhat, and the clouds have parted to let the sun shine through. This is the spiritual healing—to release what's in the way of our natural tendency to love.

"When I am healed, I am not healed alone."
— A Course in Miracles

Chapter 13
Release and Renewal Ceremonies

There are two types of healing ceremonies that can be used for dealing with trauma, and both can often be incorporated into a single ceremony. The first type is a ceremony of *release*, where the individual lets go of the emotional, mental, and physiological grip of the traumatic experience. The second is one where the individual being treated receives something that's missing, called a ceremony of *renewal*. Most healing ceremonies, to some degree, incorporate elements of release and renewal, since when something is released, a person usually experiences a renewal, even though release is the predominant intention.

In ceremonies where release is the primary intent, it can be targeted for the release of an emotional state, such as fear or anger, psychological blockages, intrusive psychic energies, or even an "old self." These ceremonies can be relatively simple, with little in the way of the accoutrements, yet often with powerful healing taking place. Other release ceremonies may require a lengthier and somewhat more complex process, sometimes one that stretches out for several hours or even a few days.

Letting Go

I've led a number of groups in ceremonies of release, and from each come some incredible stories of healing, very often stemming from wounds that have been with the person most of their life. One such ceremony took place at one of my wife Doreen's six-day intensives. After some preparation and instructions, we started the ceremony by drumming and rattling, and before long, nearly every one of the 120 students had spontaneously stood up and was dancing around the room. We were building power that set the stage for the release phase of the ceremony, which was to take place later.

As sometimes happens in a sacred ceremony, there was some unexpected healing that occurred. One of the participants, Paddy Orr, described her experience as she drummed and danced with the group:

> Suddenly, with a quiet firmness, a voice whispered into my consciousness, "Keep moving. It's important that you keep moving." So I moved, feet trying to go in one direction and my drum pulling me in another. It was so much like the battles I'd been waging with depression and my life purpose for many years. I was again instructed, "Concentrate on the beat. Move into the drum beat." I felt no fear whatsoever—a most unusual thing for me—only a very positive energy, as intense as anything I'd ever experienced.
>
> Abruptly, Steven gave the signal to stop drumming. The quiet was palpable. The group had gathered in the center of the room as if following instructions, yet none had been given. Steven said that if anyone felt the need for healing, let someone nearby place their hands on you for support.
>
> Just before he said this, I realized that I'd become very, very hot. I actually felt as though *I* was the fire! I sought someone out and asked them to place their hands on my shoulders.
>
> I lost track of time at this point. My singular focus was to remain standing, which was becoming more and more difficult. "Hold on!" I told myself. I feared that if I didn't hold on for dear life, as I'd done for so many years, I'd lose control.
>
> Suddenly, there were two voices speaking to me. The first one was Steven, who had instinctively come to my side. He assured me that it was all right to fall, that he'd catch me and I would be safe. I hesitated for only a few

moments, desperately trying to discern the diffe
between falling and falling apart.

Then I heard the second voice. Was it Holy Spirit, ...,
ancestors, or my guardian angel? It didn't matter. Filled
with the wisdom and love of the entire universe, it gently
but firmly whispered, "You've been holding on far too
long. What you really need to do is let go."

At this point, I was on the floor.

I have no idea if I was on the floor for two minutes or
two hours. I saw gray, depression-filled clouds leaving my
body, emerging from my head, heart, and solar plexus.
Some of the gray, puffy clouds had pictures in them; one
of the pictures was me when I was three years old. When
this cloud left, I heard my voice saying, "No one should
have done this to a three-year-old child!"

I felt as though I was both above my body and inside
my body as the clouds were leaving. I felt no emotional
attachment to what was happening. It was all so beautiful, peaceful, and divinely orchestrated.

Abruptly, the whole event was over. The clouds disappeared, and I was suddenly aware of many people surrounding me, gently touching me with their hands. For
the rest of eternity, I can close my eyes at any time and
picture those beautiful faces around me and feel the love
that replaced the departed gray energies from my past.

Although I literally lost two pounds of emotional
garbage, I gained my life. I know there are wonderful
things coming to me in my future, since I now have a
very expectant, productive mind-set. I've been happy and
filled with wonderment and awe, as I realize how each of
us is helped in our Earthly journey by the supportive love
of Spirit.

Transference and Relinquishment Ceremony

Typically in a release ceremony, there are two major steps.
First, there is a *symbolic transference;* and second, a *physical act
of relinquishment*. Symbolic transference is when you use some

object (or create one yourself) that symbolizes what you're ready to release. The object becomes something to which you can transfer the "negative energy." The object could be a piece of jewelry, a photograph, a drawing, a written statement, or something from nature that will "take on" what it is you're ready to release. Symbols are uniquely meaningful to the individual and their circumstances, so what you choose is up to you.

Next is the actual act of transference, of somehow putting into the object itself that which you want to release. It may be that the object is already imbued with significance, in which case, simply identifying it as the symbol may be all you need to do. Otherwise, you can infuse the object by transferring the energetic substance of your release into it by holding it, drawing on it, or using your breath to blow into it.

The next step is the physical act of relinquishment. This is done with the cooperation and assistance of one or more of the four major elements: earth, air, fire, or water. You can burn it with fire, throw it into a body of water, release it into the air, or bury it in the earth. Or you may combine a couple of these. I've performed ceremonies at the beach where I've burned a written piece, then thrown the ashes into the ocean. Relinquishment here means that you willingly and gladly *choose* to let go of that which is now contained in the object you're releasing. That object has graciously agreed to be the transporter of whatever pain and suffering you're relinquishing; and the fire, earth, water, or air has agreed to receive it and transform it.

A fellow shamanic practitioner, Debra Dussman, described a beautiful, simple, and effective ceremony of release:

> A personal one that I use has to do with painful
> emotions. When I find myself in a painful emotional sit
> uation, I'll paint a picture to represent it. Psychologi
> cally, this is a technique used to make us feel better, but
> the true power and magic of the ritual is the final act in
> which I physically blow the feeling into the painting to
> rid myself of it, and then burn the painting. Anything
> can be used in place of the painting, but I like the pro
> cess of creating the picture. I discovered that painting it
> or writing it out didn't make me feel much better, but

when I added the shamanic aspect to it by blowing the
bad feeling into the object, the miracle happened, and the
bad feeling would almost miraculously disappear.

Debra made the symbolic transference by using her breath,
blowing into the created symbol of the picture the feelings she
wanted to release, then used fire to transform and release the disturbing emotion.

Pamela Hughes contributes a story of another simple yet very
powerful release ceremony:

As a college professor of English, young women
seemed to gravitate to me as their rape counselor (on a
nonprofessional level). One day about five years ago, after
my students had written an essay interpreting one of their
own dreams according to Freudian dream theory, a small
blonde girl with large, somber, blue eyes raised her hand
and told the class that for the last two years, every night
she dreamed the same dream and always woke up crying.
"What does this mean?" she asked. She had no idea just
how acute her situation was, so I spoke to her after class.

She confirmed my thought that to have such a
painful holding pattern in her dreams, something
extremely traumatic had to have happened to her. She
explained, tears brimming, that two years ago she had
been raped and never told her mother or went to the
authorities. She felt the guilt and self-blame commonly
experienced by rape victims. I gently counseled that she
was not to blame. She also told me that she kept the
clothes that she was wearing when she raped, a sort of
twisted marker of the event. I told her that in keeping the
clothes, she was holding the memory in her subconscious
and consciousness. I suggested that she burn the clothes
in a ceremony, saying aloud as they burned that it was
over, that what occurred was in the past and gone.

After our next class a few days later, she told me that
she had done what I suggested, and to my initial shock,
had done even more. Alone and at night, she took a sharp
knife for protection, lighter fluid, and dragged a large

garbage pail up onto the train tracks where she had been raped. There she burned her clothes. Once she had described the ceremony, she burst out joyfully, "And I haven't had the dream since!"—and to this day she has not had the dream.

I was amazed and overjoyed by the quick release she experienced, but at the same time, I was shocked and concerned that by my suggestion, she had possibly put herself in jeopardy, perhaps of even being raped again. "But Eva," I protested, "that was dangerous going by yourself—and what if you had been arrested or hurt, what would you have done?"

"I would have called you," she said surely.

My only answer was, "And I would have come."

Effigy Ceremony

An especially effective and powerful release ceremony is an *effigy ceremony*. The word *effigy* may conjure up some type of voodoo ritual, but I can guarantee you that this isn't the case. The basic form of this type of healing ceremony is quite commonly found in many indigenous cultures. The effigy is the piece into which the negative energy is transferred. It can be anything that can be burned, buried, thrown into a body of water, or released into the air. The effigy should be something from nature, such as a stone, leaf, small amount of dirt, piece of bark, stick, or just about anything that you can hold in your hand.

In looking for the object of nature to use, be sure to ask if the particular piece you found is willing to be the carrier for the negative energy you're planning to release. You'll feel a definite "yes" or "no" in your belly, or perhaps even "hear" it in your mind.

Once you've found an object that agrees to do so, that night set it on your bedstand near the side of the bed where you sleep. An option is to put it under your pillow. In either case, just before you go to sleep, pray that you dream *into* the object any and all of the negative "stuff" from your subconscious. Solicit help from your spirit guides to accomplish this. The negative energy that you want to release will then move into the object in the dreamtime, while you're sleeping.

When you awaken the next morning, take the object and wrap it in something biodegradable, such as a tissue or cloth. Set it outside, away from your living space, until you're ready to complete the ceremony. The reason for doing so is that it's now infused with what you want to release, so don't take any chances by keeping it around!

When you're ready, establish the ceremonial context in nature, somewhere you can burn, bury, or immerse it. Let's assume you're going to bury it. You prepare the ground and sit or kneel before this hole in the ground. Once you're ready, take the object with its wrapping and hold it in your right hand, close your eyes, and hold in consciousness whatever it is you're releasing.

Now for more of the symbolic transference. Blow into the object three times, letting your breath be the transport for the negative energy. Bury the object, say your prayers of gratitude for all those who have helped you with this, especially Mother Earth, and say good-bye to what you've relinquished.

Burying My Fears

I did a fairly simple effigy ceremony over a year ago (prompted by signing a contract with my publisher, Hay House, to write this book), yet I was having some trepidation about doing a mediocre job, and doubted whether I was even capable of accomplishing the task! Yes, I was a published author—I had written four other books—but it had been several years since my last one. Could I do it?

So I went out to one of my favorite spots in the forest just off Ortega Highway—the same one where Doreen and I later performed the ceremony of release I described in the Introduction—and carried with me a backpack filled with some of my sacred objects, some water, plus pen and paper. Under the familiar oak tree near the hills covered with fresh sage, I drummed, rattled, sang, and called in my spirit helpers, feeling very supported by the oak tree as I pressed my backbone into its trunk. I asked for guidance about these fears, and was told that it was the fear of coming out of the spiritual closet, of publicly declaring my spirituality. Some of this pointed to past-life memories of being burned at the stake, as so many shamans were in Europe during the Dark Ages.

I found a stone that was willing to take on these fears, and also wrote them down on a piece of paper. I didn't take this home with me to work with it in the dreamtime, instead deciding to do a modified effigy ceremony with the paper and the stone right then and there. I wrapped the stone in the paper, dug a hole near the oak tree's massive trunk, and asked tree spirit and Mother Earth if they would be willing to take these fears and transform them. Once I received agreement, I closed my eyes, bringing up the fear in my body as much as possible, while holding the stone in my right hand. I was shaking and weeping. When this surge of energy was at its strongest, I blew into the stone and paper three times. I then placed the paper-wrapped stone in the hole I had dug, sprinkled some crumpled sage over it, and buried it.

I left a little marker on the gravesite, a circle composed of four smaller stones, each one set in one of the four directions. I've visited this sacred spot since, and although covered with oak leaves, the stones remained there both times to remind me that I need no longer fear, and I no longer *need* my fear.

The result is the book you're holding in your hands right now.

✼ ✼ ✼   ✼ ✼ ✼

Chapter 14

Small Group Healing
Ceremonies

In most older and indigenous cultures, healing was always conducted with the benefit of the family or larger group involved. The
following are examples of healing ceremonies involving this kind
of group dynamic.

Phoenix Rising

I had seen Carl in individual therapy for about four months.
One day he walked in and announced, "Well, I got some news that
will probably change the work we're doing here. I was in for my
physical exam last week and found out I have prostate cancer." I
was stunned. Carl didn't tell me at the time, but I learned later that
the cancer was in an advanced stage.

Carl had recently joined one of my men's groups, and was
immediately accepted and well liked by everyone. This was a
unique group. They were all willing to push the edges of their comfort zones, lovingly challenging each other while remaining consistently supportive. We engaged in ceremony periodically, sometimes planned, sometimes emerging spontaneously as part of the
group process.

During our next get-together, Carl announced his condition
and diagnosis, and the group dealt with it compassionately. The men
expressed their fear and sadness, and there was a lot of soul-searching.
It brought up the issue of mortality and planted it squarely in the
middle of the group.

Later we learned that Carl's first doctor had given him only a few months to live. He proved him wrong by living four and a half years following the initial diagnosis. Carl continued to attend the group regularly for the next three years, and sporadically for another year until his failing health caught up with him.

We shared in his disappointments and his triumphs. The cancer advanced and retreated, with no clear causality to these changes. Carl at first tried various alternative therapies with considerable success, and as the disease progressed, he augmented these with contemporary Western medical approaches. He became his own best researcher for prostate cancer and its treatment.

About a year following his diagnosis, Carl confessed to the group that he was feeling very defeated because the PSA reading (a measure of the prostate cancer) had soared after a relatively lengthy period of low readings. After some discussion and processing of our feelings, a spontaneous healing ceremony emerged in response to Carl's feelings of helplessness and defeat.

With Carl's agreement and at my direction, he lay on the floor, facedown. In the group room were several soft pillows, which we gradually began piling on top of Carl as he named each of his fears one at a time, each pillow representing one of those fears. Carl was sobbing deeply with each "fear" that was placed on him. Once we had exhausted all the pillows in the room—there were about 18— I checked in with Carl and asked what he wanted to do. In between his sobs, he continued to state how helpless he felt, saying he wanted to give up.

Then I lay down on top of the pillows, followed by George, then Andrew. The men were shouting at him, reminding him of his love for his wife and children. We repeatedly asked him, "Do you want to live or do you want to die?" For a while he would just weep and say he wanted to give up, and this highly charged and very emotional scenario went on for a few more minutes.

Suddenly we heard a low, steady growl arising from under this pile of pillows and men's bodies, and the energy shifted. We felt Carl's anger, his "warrior" energy beginning to arise, increasing with the force of his growl. With this, we all became cheerleaders as Carl pushed and pushed with the deep force of his warrior spirit. "You gonna choose life or death, Carl?" I yelled. "I want to live! I want to live!" he shouted. This became a repeated mantra as he slowly but steadily surged upward and forward, fighting with the urgency of a man who had been given another chance at life. "Do it for Julia! For Theresa! For Sarah!" another man shouted, invoking the names of Carl's wife and children.

Like that mythical bird rising from the ashes of its own death, Carl pressed, pushed, snarled, and growled, accompanied by the urgent shouts of these men who loved him like a brother. George and Andrew had slid from this symbolic tower, while I remained, much like a living sculpture on top of a skyscraper during a severe earthquake, rocking to and fro with each surge of the Life Force from Carl's urgent fight.

As the tower toppled, so did I, just in time to see Carl emerge from this pile of pillows, panting, red-faced, yet triumphant. Greeted by the cheers of the men, he broke into a breathless grin as we surrounded him with good, strong masculine love. His heart had opened, and the tears were flowing, but this time they were tears of relief and joy rather than sorrow.

His suffering had been transformed, and once more, his spirit triumphed.

Peruvian Healing Ceremony

A very powerful group healing ceremony is a Peruvian method known as *Hampui Naqui,* which translated means, "Come spirit, come." Dr. Karen Palmer, a psychologist and shamanic practitioner, taught me this ceremony. She, in turn, received this from Americo Ybar, a Peruvian shaman. There's a very specific procedure to follow, and can be done by almost any smaller group of people.

In the Peruvian language, *Pachimama* is "Earth Mother," and it's said that she is willing to take on many of our troubles, burdens, and even destructive and negative energies, and in doing so, transforms them. In this ceremony, a small group, from six to eight people, works directly with the individual to be healed. The group transfers the individual's physical, mental, emotional, or spiritual illness to Pachimama.

To start, prepare the sacred space as you would in any other sacred ceremony. Although this can be conducted indoors, it's best done outside, weather and logistics permitting. The person in need of healing, the patient, lies face up on the ground as the group of healers gathers around them, kneeling or sitting. There are three rounds faceup, as explained below, and a repeat of these with the patient facedown. Designate one of the healers as the leader, the one who will provide the cues for each step in the following sequence.

Once the preparation is complete, the patient and the healers then center themselves by closing their eyes and focusing on their breathing, releasing tension with each exhalation. The healers simultaneously raise their arms into the air, palms up, holding them there for a few moments to absorb the vitalizing energy of the sun into their hands. Then in unison, they bring their hands down, first to their heart area, then to the patient, lightly and gently tapping him with their fingers. This is done to open up the energetic or auric field. After a few moments of tapping, at the leader's cue, they place their palms on the ground for a few moments, giving any residual negative energy to Pachimama. She loves this stuff and eats it right up!

Once this is complete, for the second round, the healers raise their hands again into the air, palms up to the sun, and absorb more of the sun's purifying energy. They repeat the step of bringing their hands down in unison, first to their heart area, then to the patient, but this time they gently brush off the person's auric field. There's no physical touch, but instead, their hands are cleaning the energetic field a couple of inches beyond the person's skin. With this accomplished, the healers once again place their palms on the earth or floor and give any of the negative energy to Pachimama.

For the third round, the group raises their palms up to the sun again, then to their hearts. Then the healers place their hands, containing the radiant and healing energy of the sun, wherever they're guided to do so on the person's body. They leave their hands resting in various spots for a few moments, passively focusing the sun's restorative power to the patient, moving their hands to other areas on the person's body as guided. After this, the healers simply relax their hands in their laps, or they may choose to first place their hands over their hearts. There's no need to discharge this restorative energy!

Next, the patient turns facedown, and the process is repeated. The entire procedure can take anywhere from about 30 to 60 minutes, and can be repeated as often as necessary. It's a wonderful experience, and can be coupled with other ceremonies, particularly some of those described in the section on Earth cycles and seasonal celebrations. In addition, music can accompany the process, whether it be drumming, rattling, or singing; or if indoors, you can play recorded music.

✻ ✻ ✻   ✻ ✻ ✻

Chapter 15

A Community Healing Ceremony

Following the devastating and life-changing terrorist attacks of September 11, 2001, I, like many others, was feeling the desperate need to take some sort of action. I realized that most of us who lived here in these United States were emotionally torn apart and dealing with various degrees of posttraumatic stress disorder. Following such massive trauma, one of the most natural urges is to want to do *something—anything*—that will alleviate the incredible level of physiological and emotional stress that follows witnessing, directly or indirectly, a horror of such magnitude.

My initial reaction was shock, followed by fantasies of perpetrating violence upon those who committed these acts. Yet at the same time, I clearly wanted to transmute these instinctual aggressive urges into a more sensible and purposeful response. Not vengeance, but justice. Not war, but peace.

It's not that I was in favor of peace at any costs—a true warrior will defend his home, family, and land when necessary. It's just that I wanted to introduce and maintain a calm, sensible attitude, and not just reflexively react. One cartoon that I came across said it all. It showed a little boy and his father sitting on a couch watching television. The boy turned to his father and said, "Will we hate back?"

I didn't want to hate back, but instead wanted to honor and mourn the victims of this tragedy as well as take some form of positive action.

There were candlelight vigils across the country, and my wife, Doreen; and my daughter Nicole and I attended one at Main Beach in Laguna. Still, I wanted to do something more. A couple of days later, I was inspired to create a healing ceremony. Doreen was all for it, and we arranged with our friend Johnna, the owner of Laguna Yoga, to use her studio to hold a healing ceremony on Sunday night.

Creating the Sacred Container

Our intention was to create a sacred container for people to share their thoughts and feelings about the recent events. We wanted to pray for the souls of those who had lost their lives, and for their families. In addition, we wanted to transform our own anger, fear, and pain into love, peace, and gratitude. Under the circumstances, this seemed like a tall order, as many of us felt that justice had to be served. I believed justice could still be served, *and* it was my desire to maintain a calmness and steadiness during these very disturbing times.

The day came, and we packed up all the items we wanted to use in the ceremony. We arrived early enough to set up the room. Our first order was to set up the altar. We covered a small table with a sarong of muted purples and lavenders and laid this down over a large blanket in the center of the room. We placed a large purple candle in the center, acquired just for this occasion. Around the candle we placed other sacred objects, including representations of the four elements. A few more preparations and everything was set.

We had asked the participants to wait outside until we were ready. Doreen, Johnna, and I, plus our friends Bronny and Glenn, who had assisted us, sat in a circle and prayed for a successful ceremony. We brushed the altar and the sacred objects with smoke from a sage/cedar smudge stick, then did the same with the room, then each other.

Now it was time to let the guests in. We glanced out the window and noticed the crowd of about 50 people standing in a circle holding hands, doing a group prayer—they had started the ceremony already! We opened the door and called them in. The door became the "gate," the entry point into ceremonial space. They came in two at a time. Johnna and Bronny welcomed everyone and "saged" them once they entered through the gate, then instructed them to have a seat in the circle, requesting that they remain silent.

Once gathered in the room, I welcomed everyone and stated the purpose for this gathering and ceremony. We were here to mourn the tremendous losses of September 11, losses that touched everyone who had heard about or witnessed this disaster, but particularly those who had known someone who had perished directly as a result of the event. I then suggested that anyone who had something they wanted to place on the altar do so, to receive blessings.

Then we joined hands and prayed. I opened the prayer, followed by Doreen adding her plea to the angels, and after that, anyone who wanted to offer a prayer was invited to do so. Several did, and many expressed gratitude for the opportunity to come together in community as we were doing, and asked for blessings for those involved in the tragedy.

Next, I went to the center of the room near the altar and rattled to the six directions—east, south, west, north, heaven, and the earth—calling in the spirits of those directions. I suggested that everyone there ask their spirit guides to join us. This was a way to build the power that was needed to do the healing, and in the quiet that followed, you could *feel* the intensity building.

The Talking Stick

Next we used a talking stick, in this case a tree branch about three feet long, sanded smooth, with two strands of bark remaining and a leather thong attached at the top. It was given to me as a gift for a ceremony I had facilitated. I explained the ground rules for use of the talking stick. Whoever held the stick had the floor. The rest of us were obliged to listen without comment. As long as you held the talking stick, you could express whatever you wanted, and no one could interrupt or comment. I began the process by expressing my sadness and anger over this tremendous tragedy, describing my initial reactions to the news, and the strong desire to transform my anger and fear into peace and compassion. Many people were nodding as I talked.

Then, one at a time, others spoke. There were such heartfelt sentiments expressed, truly a compassionate response. Many acknowledged their fears and their anger, yet all had a common desire to clear these more reactive emotions. Most of us wanted to transmute these feelings, to find a center of calmness within. Nearly all agreed with the trite but true idea that "peace begins with me." We laughed at the irony of one man's story of how he had gotten angry with the cars and drivers he encountered on the way, muttering, "I wish these damned cars would get out of the way so I can get to the peace vigil!"

The time with the talking stick came to a natural close after some beautifully tender and powerful comments. Then Doreen offered an expression of hope and a call to continue to return to a peaceful state within, no matter what else occurs externally. She spoke of the angelic presence in the room, and the angelic presence that we can all carry.

Passing the Fire

We had given a candle to everyone when they entered the room, and as Doreen spoke, I lit the first candle, then with my candle lit Doreen's, who then lit the person's on her right, and so on, until every candle in the room was lit. Everyone then placed their lit candles in the center of the room, surrounding the altar. We then transitioned to drumming and dancing, starting out with a slow, dirge-like beat. Gradually others joined in with their percussion instruments, and a few got up and danced to the rhythm. The pace of the drumming picked up, and within a few moments, people were spontaneously chanting, and almost everyone was dancing. With all the candles in the center of the room around this beautiful altar, it looked like an ancient scene of natives dancing around the fire. The drumming and rattling built to a crescendo, and then as if on cue, came to a halt.

For a few moments, everyone stood in silence. The only sound you could hear was people trying to catch their breath. We were all swooning in a ceremonial trance. Through another prayer, we offered up this dynamic energy generated through the drumming and dancing, asking that it be sent out as a healing force to whoever in the world needed it.

Feeding One Another

From here we moved to the feeding. Everyone was asked to take a small paper plate and put a few grapes and some bread on it. Then we circulated around the room, feeding one another. It was an intensely symbolic act of nourishing each other, of a community of people bonding during a time of crisis.

To close the ceremony, we once again gathered in a circle and offered another prayer of gratitude. Following this, I blew out the candle, which gave a clear indication that the formal part of the ceremony was over. The people continued socializing for a while, and the mood was one of good cheer, with an atmosphere distinctly different from when we'd started. Something had moved as a result of this ceremony, something that could only be accomplished through ceremony. There was a distinct sense of camaraderie and community. Everyone left feeling complete—and also very high from the "medicine" served by a shared communal ceremony.

The world, for at least a while, felt a little bit safer.

※ ※ ※ ※ ※ ※

Chapter 16

Home Clearing
and Blessing

The home clearing and blessing is a ceremony to do for your home about once a year. It's essential to do this whenever you move into a new space. Although this ceremony is for clearing a residence, it can also be used for an office or warehouse—any enclosed area that will be used for some particular length of time. It's a version of a release and renewal ceremony specifically for dwellings.

You'll need some crushed cedar, a smudge stick or a branch of white sage, a braid of sweetgrass, an earthen bowl for these herbs, a small charcoal button (to burn the cedar), a large feather, a candle for each room of the house, and a rattle (optional). Once you've gathered the equipment, place the items on your altar, do your invocation, and invite any helping spirits to assist you. Set candles in the center of each room and light them.

This ceremony is performed in four rounds. For the first one, take the earthen bowl and light the charcoal. Once the charcoal is burning well, sprinkle some cedar on it. Start with your living room, stand in the center of the room, and using the feather, sweep some smoke into each of the four directions, starting with the east, and going clockwise until you've returned to the east. Cedar is a very powerful cleanser and helps rid the house of unwanted, negative energy. Repeat this procedure in each room in the house, even smaller closets.

When you've done this for every room in your home, for the second round either sprinkle some crushed sage onto the charcoal or light the smudge stick, and start again with the living room. Using the feather, brush the smoke from the sage in every corner, along the walls, and especially any openings, such as windows and doors. This further clears any negative energy.

Pause for a few moments and see if you can feel a difference. When you're ready for the third round, the blessing (or renewal) round, light the braid of sweetgrass, and move about the home in any fashion that seems to feel right. As you do, sweep the smoke from the sweetgrass throughout the home. Burning this herb invites more positive energy and spiritual presence into your home, and also amplifies the sweetness of home.

The fourth round is optional. If you're so inclined, take the rattle and, starting with the living room, rattle in the helping spirits and positive energy from each of the four directions. Continue on by rattling in the spirits of the sky above and the earth below so that you've called in the spirits of six directions, rather than four. You can repeat this with each room, or you can simply move about your home, rattling and calling in those spiritual beings and positive energies that will help protect your space and bring in greater comfort and joy. Another option is to walk through the home singing or whistling in the helping spirits and positive energy.

Once you're done with the four rounds, return to the living room and say a prayer of thanks. Be sure to put out the candles in each room, and place them on your altar. For three consecutive evenings, burn them for about an hour.

My sister Susan describes a slightly different type of house clearing and blessing:

> When we were having our new home built, I went regularly to the construction site after hours. My intent was to communicate with the spirits and beings who lived there and were being disrupted by our presence. I let them know I wanted to live in harmony, and asked for their permission and help. I routinely brought bread, fruit, water, and other offerings, and left them for the spirits of the land. Over time, the relationship improved, yet was still much more formal than my relationship with the spirits and beings at the home we were leaving.
>
> Simultaneously, I spent time at our existing home, talking with all the spirit-beings, telling them we were moving, thanking them for the wonderful times we

shared, and asking their help in clearing myself from the space.

I knew I needed something physical to take with me, so one day I stood outside and asked nature to provide me with a reminder. The next day, our grass was covered with hundreds of bird feathers from crows, pigeons, sparrows, blue jays, woodpeckers, finches, cowbirds, robins, and more. I thanked them all for their gifts and took them with me to my new house, and today I still have those wonderful, beautiful gifts.

Once the new home was ready for moving in, I convened a group of women, and we conducted a house blessing. We went through each room of the house clapping our hands to dislodge any harmful or negative energy, and then we saged each room and rang bells to clear the space and make it ready for us. When we finished that process, we went to our family room and convened in a circle. Each person brought a blessing that they had written or found that reflected their wishes for us in our new home and dedicated this space to our highest intent and greatest good. It was a beautiful, loving, touching ceremony of prayers, songs, laughter, and tears—a tribute from friends and a very holy time.

Following the ceremony, we had a wonderful potluck meal, and I later planted the blessings in the four directions surrounding our home, asking the spirits of the four directions for their blessings as well. I continue to feel and relish in the energy of that blessing.

Each day I go outside and put snacks out as an offering, in addition to birdseed and water. I thank all the angels, devas, fairies, elves, gnomes, leprechauns, and other spirits and beings for keeping nature in alignment with God.

After the home or space clearing is complete, you then may want to add a finishing touch of a *ceremonial bath*.

Ceremonial Bath

Whether you call this process a ceremony or a ritual doesn't really matter—it's very healing, helps you detoxify your skin, and feels very good. You can do this after your home clearing, after any other ceremony, or anytime you feel the need. The symbolic act of using water to ritually cleanse and purify is in itself powerful. To do this consciously and as a sacred act adds that much more.

Set up as many candles as you would like around the bathtub and in the bathroom. You can use store-bought bath salts, or you can prepare a mixture that suits you. I suggest a cup of Epsom salts and some ginger root. To prepare the ginger root, grate an inch or two of the root into boiling water, let it boil for ten minutes, then strain the water into the bathtub. Fill the tub as full as possible, with the water being as hot as you like, with the Epsom salts and ginger root mixture in it. Put in some of your favorite essential oils as well— such as lavender, jasmine, patchouli, sandalwood, or a combination. Smudge the room and yourself, light some incense and the candles, put some soothing music on, and climb in.

Enjoy!

❀ ❀ ❀   ❀ ❀ ❀

Part IV

Transition

Ceremonies

Chapter 17

Passages, Milestones, and the Life Cycle

All throughout life, we shift from one identity to another as we pass through various milestones. These transitions are critical to our growth, bookmarks that define the end of one chapter in our human development and the emergence into the next. They not only redefine who we are as we negotiate our way through life, but also help determine where we fit into our social structure.

When we're in the process of these profound changes, either dictated by our natural biological maturation or by the circumstances life imposes upon us, there can be a tremendous amount of confusion and uncertainty. Without relevant and meaningful ceremonies to mark these transitions, the confusion and uncertainty can keep us wandering and wondering, adrift in a state of continual low-level anxiety that extends beyond the developmental period or circumstance.

This is why it's important to introduce ceremony during these passages, to highlight and sanctify these profound shifts. Ceremony not only provides a sacred container in which these important life events can be consciously acknowledged and witnessed by members of the individual's family and community, but it also provides answers to questions that would be difficult to answer otherwise.

How do we welcome a child into the world? Where does adolescence end and adulthood begin? What about the union of two people in marriage, where not only the individuals involved form a new entity, but their families and friends come together to weave a new network of community as well? Cultural values, family traditions, and spiritual belief systems provide some of the answers to these and similar questions, while ceremonies provide a context within which the meaning of these life passages can unfold. Other answers to these questions are discovered through the multifaceted *experience* of the ceremony, and often cannot be described simply with words.

Acknowledging these various milestones with a sacred ceremony supplies us with a map of how to navigate through life's changes, from the beginning of life to the end. In fact, all transitions contain within them symbolic representations of birth and death, accentuated and acknowledged by the living metaphor called ceremony. Within the larger life cycle, these passages become experiential reminders of the continuum of life, that with every death there is a birth, and vice versa. So, it's natural to start at the beginning of the life cycle.

Births and Babies

It was New Year's Eve, 1979. My wife at the time, Susan, and I had planned a quiet at home celebration with Bill and Denise, some friends of ours. The doctor had told us earlier that day that the baby could come at any moment, so we stayed close to home. Our friends left shortly after midnight. Susan began cleaning the kitchen, and I retired to the den and flipped on the television. *Saturday Night Fever* was playing. I was just settling into the movie when I heard Susan yell from the living room, "Steven, my water broke!"

The rest of the journey was a blur until early that morning, when the crown of the baby's head began showing. Without much more pushing on Susan's part, the baby's full body appeared. What I remember thinking at that point is: *There really is a God!* That phrase kept repeating itself in my head for the next hour or so.

We commemorated the event the next day when we got home by ceremonially burying the placenta in our backyard, next to a tree. It was a symbolic act of returning that which baby Nicole no longer needed to Mother Earth—from which her body had been formed. It represented the release of the pregnancy, especially for her mother. As for me, the father, it allowed me to drift into that ceremonial space where I knew I was connected as a father to thousands of my ancestors who had probably performed a similar kind of ceremony following the birth of their children. The entire process put me in direct touch with the miraculous, the "wonder-full," the awesomeness of the continuous cycles of birth and death, and the myriad cycles within cycles.

At that time, I only had a vague sense of what sacred ceremony was about, yet in retrospect, the entire process had many of the same qualities. Following this momentous event, I knew that my life would never be the same. This was not only Nicole's entry into the world; it was also a major transition for me into my role as a father.

Honoring New Life

We've come a long way from the rather cold, sterile birth practices of the first half of this century, where the delivery was performed by the doctor, fathers weren't allowed in the delivery room, and the baby was quickly taken from the mother and placed in a nursery for the first few hours of its life.

Now there are many more options available to expectant parents. Fathers are now permitted in the delivery room and are more often involved throughout the entire pregnancy. Infants now commonly stay with their mother immediately after delivery. Home births have risen in popularity, and as in more traditional times, midwives attend to the pregnancy and birth. No matter what the choice of soon-to-be-parents, ceremony can provide a conscious recognition of the presence of Spirit in the process.

There are several things that expectant parents can do to prepare for the new baby. If it's a home birth, prepare the birth room with soft colors, candles, music, and special blankets for mother and child. Whether at home or in a hospital, decide who else besides the father will be invited, such as any grandparents or other elders, or even a minister or ceremonialist. You can even prepare a blessing, something simple such as anointing the child with water and harmless essential oils.

The LeBoyer method involves a birth in a quiet, low-lit room, placing the infant on the mother's abdomen while the umbilical cord is cut, with a soothing, warm bath for the infant after the birth. Cutting the cord can be done with great reverence, usually by the father. As I described in the story of Nicole's birth, we buried the placenta with considerable care, next to a tree, with the idea that this would give something back to Mother Earth, the life-giver. The entire experience of birth is so full of wonder and magic that the process alone has many of the elements of ceremony inherent in it already.

A birth ceremony I heard about many years ago described how the Lakota tribe apparently ceremonially consecrated and welcomed their newborn. When the baby was birthed, the medicine man would first roll the infant on the earth, saying, "Meet your mother!" Then he would hold the infant up to the sun, saying, "Meet your father!" These simple but elegant gestures acknowledged the infant's spiritual parents.

Baby Blessing

Holding a blessing ceremony is traditionally a means of sanctifying the child's soul, welcoming it to life on Earth. In some older traditions, children were not fully accepted into the human community in which they were born until some form of ritual or ceremonial blessing was bestowed.

Truly, the child is already a blessing by the fact of their birth. The intention of this kind of ceremony is instead to honor and recognize the infant's natural state of grace, rather than confer it upon them. It's also to formally welcome the child. The child is born not only unto their parents, but also into a community, so it's important to include family and friends as witnesses and participants in the welcoming. Skylar's blessing ceremony contains all these elements.

Skylar's Blessing Ceremony

The following describes a blessing ceremony that I had the privilege to facilitate. This was with some younger friends, Matty and Melissa, for their first child, Skylar. We designed the ceremony together and decided to hold it at Table Rock beach, one of Matty and Melissa's favorite coves, just before sunset on the night of the full moon. The period of the full moon is considered to be a time of completion. There's a fullness of consciousness, and falsehoods and truths are revealed. It's a time of release, of letting go that which no longer serves.

About 20 people showed up for the ceremony, a combination of family and friends, a nice mix ranging from younger to older. We set up a blanket in what was to be the center of the sacred circle, help-ing to define the ceremonial space and serve as the ceremonial altar. Upon it we placed a vial of ocean water, a small bowl of earth from the grandparent's house, an owl feather, and a candle to rep-resent the four basic elements. These would be available for a sub-sequent part of the ceremony when the parents would baptize their child with each of the four elements. Also, there was a basket for gifts from those in attendance. The mother, Melissa, would preserve these gifts and present them to Skylar, along with the story of his blessing ceremony, when Skylar was old enough to understand and appreciate them and their legacy.

A couple of young men in attendance began to drum as a sig-nal for all of us to gather. The parents and their child took their place in the east, which is the direction of new beginnings. Once every-one had gathered to form the sacred circle, I smudged the sacred objects on the blanket in the center of the circle, then the people themselves. The drumming stopped, and I called in the spirits of the seven directions, using a rattle. First, the east, then south, west, north, the celestial or heavenly spirits, the spirits of the earth, and finally, the seventh direction, the spirit that's inside each of us.

From there, I sat in the center of the circle and took a few moments to describe what the ceremony was about and what was to come. I stressed the fact that those attending were an integral part of the ceremony—not just spectators, but participants. I stated, "You're all important people in this family's community, and by your presence here, you promise to care for and uphold them as they move into the future as a family unit."

Blessing of the Four Elements

Matty and Melissa brought Skylar into the center of the circle. He was wide-eyed and quite intrigued by all that was going on. The

next step was for the parents themselves to baptize him with each
of the four elements, and as they did so, I offered these words as part
of the blessing:

> *From the watery world where you have recently*
> >   *emerged, little one*
> *Let us praise the qualities of water:*
> *May its cleansing heal you*
> *May its currents lead you*
> *May its depths intrigue you*
> *May its buoyancy teach you trust.*
> *Trust the Waters of Life.*
> (The parents sprinkled water on the baby's head and chest.)
> *From the solid Earth upon which we stand*
> >   *holding you, little one*
> *Let us praise the qualities of Earth:*
> *May its great plains give you patience*
> *May its rocky peaks give you longing*
> *May its deep forests give you wisdom*
> *May its cool valleys give you peace.*
> *Trust the Earth.*
> (The parents rubbed some earth on his head and feet.)
> *From the blazing fireball which holds our*
> >   *planet's orbit, little one,*
> *Let us praise the qualities of fire:*
> *May its warmth give you comfort*
> *May its light give you insight*
> *May its creative powers give you hope*
> *May its destructive powers give you discretion.*
> *Trust the Fire.*
> (The parents took some of the ash from the burnt sage and
> anointed the crown of his head, his belly, and his feet.)
> *From the sky above which is a dome for our world*
> *Let us praise the qualities of air:*
> *May its winds enliven you*
> *May its light lengthen your days*
> *May its darkness unfold your own mysteries*
> *May its majesty remind you of yours.*
> *Trust the Air.*

(The parents fanned him with the owl feather.)
Now we praise this planet and all that lives on it.
For we are the stuff the cosmos is made from.
We are born with stardust in our bones.
We breathe the winds of heaven.
We walk on sacred ground.
The rivers of life run in our veins
and in our synapses the sparks of fire fly.
We are of the earth.
We are the eyes and ears of the planet.
We are her heart and mind.
Let us understand this wisdom and live into it
each and every day of our lives —so it is!

Blessings of Family and Friends

Next I asked the friends and family (other than grandparents and godparents) to come into the center of the circle one at a time, greet Skylar, and welcome him into the world. When they did, they each placed their gifts into the basket and spoke from their hearts to this little child. The parents then did the same, followed by the grandparents, who bestowed not only their gifts and blessing, but also a kiss on the child's forehead. I especially acknowledged the elders by saying, "We give thanks to those who brought us life, and thanks to those who pass it on. May the grace, beauty, and power of the ancestors be with you, Skylar, now and in times of need."

At this point, the godparents were called into the center of the circle and asked to stand next to the grandparents. The godparents are in charge of nurturing the child's spiritual development and are expected to maintain close ties to the child and the parents for the rest of their lives. This is why they're often given special consideration in a blessing ceremony, and are asked to make a covenant with God, the parents, and the child. In this instance, friends Catherine and Gabe were asked to be Skylar's godparents. Once they agreed to this responsibility to Skylar, they then placed their sacred gifts on the altar and offered a blessing to the baby.

The closing of the ceremony took place just as the sun was setting, soon to be followed by the full moon rising. We prayed together as I recited the following:

> *We give thanks to the generosity of friends and family*
> *   who make this life rich and precious.*
> *May Skylar's presence among us bring gladness and beauty.*
> *May his life be a blessing to all those he encounters.*
> *May he travel a path with heart,*
> *   and rejoicing, reach the end of his soul's desire.*
> *Amen.*

From here we all turned to Skylar, and I said, "Dear Skylar Joseph Hawk Tustison—welcome to the world!" With that declaration, the two drummers started drumming—this time with a little faster beat. We cheered in unison, and everyone was invited to come forward and honor the parents and welcome Skylar in their own way. By now the sun was tucked away for the evening, and we could see the glimmerings of the full moon rising. The timing could not have been planned any better.

In this ceremony, as in others, when you call upon the creative force of Spirit with the intent of sanctifying a life passage, there isn't just one way or the "right" way to do so. Use the general guidelines for ceremony as a sketch pad, and view the above as only one example of how you can create your own baby blessing ceremony. Let your prayers, meditations, and journeys be the guidelines for creating the basic structure of the ceremony. Once you've devised a structure, have set your intent, and have established the sacred, then show up and let Spirit do the work with you and through you.

❋ ❋ ❋ ❋ ❋ ❋

Chapter 18
Childhood and Adolescent Transitions

The Tooth Fairy

There are other transitions that occur throughout childhood, any of which can be acknowledged and blessed through the creation of a sacred ceremony—for example, being weaned from the breast or bottle, undergoing toilet training, taking that first trip on a train, being left with a baby-sitter for the first time, getting a cat or dog, losing a baby tooth, starting school . . . there are countless other events that mark significant passages in a child's development.

As I mentioned, any of these events is a symbolic death and rebirth, a cycle of an ending and a beginning. In the more dramatic transitions, such as going to school for the first time, the child is dying to an old identity or way of life and entering into another. Even when it comes to an event such as the loss of a first baby tooth, for the child it's a momentous occasion.

It certainly was a big deal to my six-year-old niece, Jordan. She came up to me recently and said, "Uncle Steven, Uncle Steven! Look!" She showed me how one of her front baby teeth was loose, nearly ready to come out, and asked me for an apple so that it would help the tooth along. She'd been told that whenever the tooth came out, she would be graced with a visit from the tooth fairy, which is our cultural way of marking this simple event. Jordan was obviously eager to lose the tooth, but . . . I didn't give her an apple.

I still like the story of the tooth fairy. It's a fun and useful transition story for children going through an inevitable physical change. You can incorporate this cultural myth into your own life

and embellish it in your own way. For example, find a special little box or pouch in which the tooth can be placed. When you look
for one, have your child with you and make it part of the ceremony.
You may find it by rummaging through closets or drawers, or
shopping for it. Let everyone in the family know about this event.
Make a fuss about placing the tooth under the child's pillow. Tell
the child the story of the tooth fairy, or make up your own.
Although tooth fairies traditionally leave money in exchange for
teeth, they have the option of putting something besides money
in its place; something more enduring that symbolizes the "first-
ness" of the event. Perhaps a ring, necklace, or other appropriate
item will magically "show up" under the pillow.

Use your imagination and trust your inspiration. Enter the
world of the child for a few moments, and see if you can get a
sense of anything else that might be appropriate for the particular
transition the child is facing. I encourage you to engage Spirit in
bringing forth such a ceremony. But you don't need drums, rattles,
sage, or anything else to create such a ceremony, unless, of course,
these fit. It's all up to you.

Adolescent Rites of Passage

Although all major transitions are worthy of being honored
with a ceremony, one that deserves particular attention is the adolescent's passage into adulthood. Throughout our lives, we're faced
with other passages that are rightly deserving of ceremonial recognition, with some of the more common ones being covered in this
section. However, due to the dramatic growth and expansion that
occurs during puberty, it's critical to demarcate this natural process
with some type of ceremony through which the adolescent can
emerge into a more clearly defined stage of man- or womanhood.

In ancient and indigenous cultures, the very fabric of the society was dependent on the performance of these sacred ceremonies
of transition, or rites of passage. They were defined by traditions
that had taken place over centuries, guided by the elders who were
the keepers of the wisdom, the ancient sacred secrets that explained
the mysteries of life. These rites of passage assured that the ancient
knowledge and tribal customs would be passed on, providing a deep

sense of continuity for the entire community. As author and activist Dadisi Sanyika suggests in "Gang Rites and Rituals of Initiation," from *Crossroads: The Quest for Contemporary Rites of Passage*:

> The basic social strategy in traditional, indigenous culture was that the elders of the community maintained the cohesion and health of the collective by the systematic transmission of the values and knowledge of the group to the next generation through a system of initiation. They combined this function of initiation with the need to mark puberty as a period of rebirth. Puberty is the developmental period where young people experience major biochemical, physiological, anatomical, and psychological changes. In the natural wisdom of primal societies this was seen as a period that necessitates a ritualized process that reenacts the sacred process of creation.

Sadly, this critical type of ceremony that links the present and future with the ancient past is sorely lacking. Kathleen Wall and Gary Ferguson, in *Rites of Passage: Celebrating Life's Changes*, say:

> Of the few childhood and adolescent rites still found in this culture—confirmation, bat mitzvah, sweet sixteenth, graduation—many have become empty and meaningless. Although they call attention to an event, they do little to foster a clearer sense, either for children or their parents, of its meaning, of what the creation of new roles in life is all about. A girl who graduates from junior high school, for example, may receive cards, gifts, and congratulations. But the event itself does little to help drive home the point that she is passing into a new relationship with the world or to help her understand that, through the gains and losses of this transition, she will become a new and potentially more powerful person.

The Elder's Role

There's no societal structure for our elders to pass along their wisdom. Instead, they tend to be shuffled into "retirement communities," and there slide into old age without the benefit of performing such an important role. Young people who don't have some form of communal and familial guidance through this passage are more likely to drift into adulthood, finding their way through trial and error, looking for guidelines from older peers and from media portrayals of adult values and behavior.

Dadisi Sanyika goes on to say:

> When there is no formal initiation process, an unconscious enactment of a rite of passage will occur. This unconscious initiation will often be antisocial rather than a systematic transmission of values and knowledge. Initiation into urban street gangs is a case in point, where the aspects of initiation appear in a process that does not renew the community or its values.

In other words, there seems to be an innate process at work, a natural seeking on the part of adolescents for such guidelines. In the inner city, often these come from older gang members, who will then promote the youngster to adulthood through a ceremonial initiation process that is often violent and destructive.

Television, movies, and music are other sources of information for adolescents, passing along the entertainment industry's version of guidelines for adult behavior. Watch television regularly for a couple of weeks and observe the kinds of values teenagers are inundated with. Girls are prompted by various advertisements to become fully sexual beings long before they're emotionally and spiritually ready to accommodate this natural urging. And what about models for adult masculinity? Sports figures that take drugs and demand millions of dollars? "Gangsta" rappers? Children wanting to understand and define this passage into adulthood will look for guidance and models from the most accessible sources. It just happens that the media usually provides the most immediately available sources for this type of information.

The good news is that in the past few years, we've witnessed more interest in creating rites of passage for adolescents. Since we're such a diverse culture without a singular religion or spiritual practice that can necessarily meet the needs of all teenagers in these times, we have to look to the more fundamental principles underlying any rite of passage and dress it up in the cultural and spiritual clothing that's most compatible with the child's needs and upbringing. A ceremony that may be right for a boy or girl from the inner city may not work as well for someone from the Pacific

Northwest. Nor is it necessary to emulate indigenous practices, in which the ordeal was in some cases so challenging that an initiate didn't always survive.

Creating Rites of Passage

In present-day society, a transition ceremony for teenagers will ideally have two basic functions: *preservation* and *creativity*. The first function, preservation, draws those characteristics from the wisdom of ancient traditions that are effective and powerful, ones well worth preserving and rediscovering. For instance, in most of these practices, there was always a challenge for the adolescent to overcome, such as enduring a few days in the wilderness without food or companionship, or engaging in a physically demanding task. Another characteristic that is critical to preserve is the presence of elders to guide and instruct the adolescent throughout the process. These, along with other elements of ancient customs, can be incorporated into contemporary rites of passage.

Given our society's diversity and the vast number of choices available to anyone on the threshold of adulthood, the second function must be introduced—that of *creativity*. To try and replicate these ancient initiations would be a foolish effort, and wouldn't work for the vast majority of teenagers. Instead, we can draw from the teachings of those who have come before us and combine them with imagination and creativity. By doing so, we can develop initiation ceremonies that more appropriately fit modern-day youth. For example, the adolescent may face some challenges in the wilderness for several days, but instead of being alone and without food, they may be in a group of peers, with meals provided and some guidance from nearby elders. Whatever that blend of ancient and new, what's important is to provide some direction for these children who are struggling to find an appropriate and meaningful adult identity.

Ideally, a transition ceremony for adolescents will still contain all of the stages of any ceremony—separation, transformation, and incorporation—to some degree. Seasoned adults, or elders, should be present to provide guidance, and should continue to provide mentoring past the actual ceremony. The boy or girl must first separate in some fashion from the usual world, and then be guided through the transformation stage (sometimes called *the threshold stage*), typically by facing some ordeal. This can be some physical or emotional challenge, whether climbing a mountain or sitting in stillness and darkness for several hours. Incorporation occurs when the initiate is welcomed back into the family and community as a man or a woman, with increased privileges and responsibilities.

Traditional ceremonies of initiation practiced in ancient cultures were quite intense. They would typically take place during the early stages of puberty, and could last for days, weeks, or several months. These rites of passage would prepare the boy or girl for all the privileges and responsibilities of adult life in the community, and prepared the adolescent for leaving the family home, getting married, having children, and earning a living. This type of transition ceremony would happen only once in a person's lifetime.

Three Phases of an Adolescent's Passage

Unlike traditional cultures, most children in contemporary cultures are simply not ready by the age of 14 to take on these kinds of responsibilities. Instead, it's more realistic to think of three phases of passages into adulthood, each one demarcating a crossing into another identity:

Phase 1—This would be puberty, the passage from childhood into adolescence, where there are distinct physical signs of maturation, such as vocal changes and facial hair for boys, and the menarche for girls.

Phase 2—The high school years, roughly ages 15 to 18, especially when kids enter high school, start driving, and graduate. This would be a good time for a more intense ceremony of transition, such as a vision quest (see below).

Phase 3—This phase, during the late teens, is when the young adults prepare to leave home. This may involve going to college, moving out on their own, and joining the military. This is the transition that helps them become financially independent and autonomous from their families of origin.

These guidelines, as described by Shelley Kessler in *Crossroads*, give us some road markers for the path to adulthood, and will more likely be a better fit for our cultural realities than one comprehensive ceremony. Of course, this is an ideal format for initiation ceremonies, and as mentioned, there may be various "mini-initiations" along the way. There is such an innate, almost instinctual urge on the part of the child growing up to seek guidance in how to become a healthy, fully functional adult, that unless adults provide that direction, they will seek it and find it in other sources.

Vision Quest

Some of the most powerful experiences for adolescent rites of passage stem from the vision quest. This is a process facilitated and guided by experienced "elders," adults who not only have gone through this sort of ordeal, but also appreciate its spiritual context. The guides for this quest should adequately prepare their participants for what they're to embark upon, have contingencies for emergencies, and provide a degree of relative safety. Since this type of initiation experience can be done at almost any age, it's also important that the organization or individuals who run the quest are able to address some of the developmental considerations for this age group. This kind of experience isn't advisable for younger adolescents. I've noted one of the more commonly recommended companies who offer this sort of experience in the Resources.

The model for vision quests often follows a Native American ceremony, one that has been used for centuries by many tribes, as well as by others throughout history. Jesus' and Moses' wanderings in the desert were a form of vision quest. The intention of such an adventure is to discover your vision, or purpose in life, through being alone in the outdoors for up to four days. This may take place in the desert or forest— anywhere you'll be undisturbed by civilization for the duration of the experience.

During this time, the individual will fast for the entire four days but have a limited amount of water available. Organizations that sponsor such events meet with the initiates several times prior to the actual quest, and during this time give considerable instruction, and also address any concerns on the part of those preparing to embark on the vision quest. In addition, following their individual quests, the group stays together for a couple more days, sharing their experiences and exploring the meaning of their vision.

Once the initiate is ready for the vision quest, having already chosen their place and marked it in some fashion, they set out to stay in their spot for three days and three nights. Fasting helps the initiate be open and available for the spiritual experience. It's an integral part of the quest. Participants are instructed to particularly be on the lookout for messages from nature, and the vision may come in any form at any time.

Taking Flight

For a number of years, Adele Getty, ceremonialist and author of *A Sense of the Sacred: Finding Our Spiritual Lives Through Ceremony,* led vision quests in Death Valley, an ominously and appropriately named desert in California. In her book, she describes the experience of a teenager named Philip, a 15-year-old boy from northern California who had been raised by a single mother, and had agreed to the quest mainly to escape from school and family for a week. He had a hard edge, and although he cared about the planet and humanity, he held a particularly dismal view of the future. After three days of preparation, it was time for him and the others in his group to go to their chosen places in the desert.

> When the morning arrived, Philip was up and ready to go. The day was beautiful, and this particular trip was blessed with glorious weather—everything was perfect. On the fourth morning, as the participants returned to base camp, Philip came in looking radiant. He said that when he returned to his place of power, he set up his camp and was lying around almost asleep when he heard a strange and frightening sound. He jumped up and noticed that in the rocks above him, about 20 feet away, there was a prairie falcon nest, and the birds had come soaring in to roost, only to discover an intruder. He admitted to being rather scared, but decided to stay and work it out with the birds.
>
> They would screech and fly around him, and he would make bird noises and be still. By the second day, they had accepted him and he them. He felt this was a message to him to be strong and

have faith. He watched the pair care for their young and stand guard over them, and he found himself longing for his family. In our welcoming circle, he cried for his mother and sister and said that he had always been mean to his little sister because he had been jealous of her from the time she was born. However, by watching the falcons with their family, he realized that his family needed "to stick together and take care of each other." Philip said his sister was really "okay," and that she obviously liked him in spite of the bad time he gave her. He showed the others in the group a collection of feathers he had gathered from the birds and said that he could not wait to get home and give his mother and sister each a feather.

In his journal, Philip wrote:

> "*My life is ending now, I cry for myself and my boyhood dreams. Father, where are you? Bird, will you be my Father? I must father myself now and share in the responsibilities of life. I miss my sister and my mother. Please forgive me for being unkind. I feel like a bird hatching out of an egg and taking flight. My new name is Eyes That See.*"

※ ※ ※

Applying the guidelines that have been described here, it is hoped that you will be able to facilitate a guided initiation that clarifies the adolescent's entry into the adult stage. The intention guiding such a process would be to embrace the sacred as a fundamental aspect of this type of transition ceremony, and to help the young boy or girl get in touch with the profound, spiritual significance governing such a momentous life change.

Next we'll look at ways in which the adolescent can go through an initiation that's specific to their gender, thus helping the young boy or girl establish a clearer identity of themselves—not just as an adult, but as a man or woman.

※ ※ ※   ※ ※ ※

Chapter 19

Initiations for Males

In John Boorman's excellent film *The Emerald Forest*, based on a true story, a five-year-old Caucasian boy named Tommy is kidnapped by members of an indigenous tribe called the Invisible People in the rain forests of South America. The boy's father is a supervisor for a company hired to clear trees in the jungles of the Amazon basin. The boy had been playing near the edge of the clearing, close to the forested jungle, when he saw dark people hiding behind the trees in the jungle. He ran and told his father. Although his dad was skeptical, he went with his son to check this out. Of course, he doesn't see anyone. They play for a while together, and his father turns to go back to the clearing, thinking his son is following him. When he turns around to call his son, he's gone.

The Invisible People kidnap the child and take him to their home deep into the jungle. When his father discovers his son's absence, he immediately sends out a search party, but to no avail. He continues to make various forays into the jungle over the next ten years, searching for his boy. The only clue he has is the feather from an arrow that had been shot into a tree next to him immediately after he noticed his son was missing.

"Must He Die?"

In the next scene, we see Tommy, now about 15 years old, with blazing blue eyes, light skin, and golden hair, living with the tribe of these dark-eyed, dark-skinned, and dark-haired natives of the forest. He has been adopted by one of the women of the tribe, one he calls "Mother."

As the scene opens, Tommy is innocently playing with other youngsters in a natural swimming hole near a waterfall. Suddenly, several men of the tribe slowly swagger toward him, strutting in unison, rhythmically pounding their spears on the rocks, chanting in their deep, male voices some ancient incantation. Led by his adoptive father, they stop a few feet from Tommy. By now he has halted his play, obviously stunned and terrified by the sight of this imposing group of men dressed in their warrior paints and feathers.

His tribal father looks directly at the boy and says in their native language, "Tommy, you think you're a man! I see only a stupid boy! Your time has come to die!"

From nowhere, his adoptive mother steps forward next to the man who has just spoken, looks directly at her boy, and says to her husband with great solemnity, "Must he die?" The leader replies, "Yes!" at which point, his mother says, "I will never see my boy again!" and fades back beyond the group of men and out of sight of her boy. The men then take Tommy far into the jungle, away from the village, and proceed with his initiation.

Like most of these types of initiations, the boy must go through various ordeals, some of them quite tortuous, as a test of his worthiness to be called a man. After a very intense process where he must endure the biting stings of several fire ants, his father dips him into the stream in a ceremonial baptism while proclaiming, "The boy is dead!" As he emerges from the water, his father declares, "The man is born!" to signal that the initiation ceremony is complete. The boy is now fully accorded the role of manhood. He then returns to his community, now acknowledged fully as a man, with all the privileges and responsibilities of manhood. Very soon afterward, Tommy takes a wife for himself, a former childhood friend named Kachiri, who is now fully a woman herself.

※ ※ ※

The scenario in that film certainly differs from the typical initiation experience for males in our culture. Drinking oneself into a stupor, reckless car racing, attending a military boot camp, or even brutal situations such as being jumped and beaten by fellow gang members—all lack one or more of the necessary ingredients for what is true male initiation. In the story above, though, they're all there.

The men from the tribe (the elders) lead the way, providing the con-tinuity of ancient traditions; they define manhood through an ordeal; and have the boy return to the community with a new iden-tity after being separated from his mother.

First and Second Birth

The male has two births: first, the birth from his mother's body; and second, the birth *into* the world of men. This second birth is the substance and purpose of any male initiation, and instigates the separation stage of initiation ceremony. The boy *must* leave his mother, and go with the men of the tribe or village or community. They take him into their world and show him what it means to be a man in accordance with their tribal traditions and norms.

A man's physicality—his strength, durability, and overall har-diness—is valued in most cultures, and men relate to the world more often through physical action. So an important piece in a young male's initiation is to be put through some sort of physical ordeal, one that "tests his mettle" in some way and helps prepare him for his role as an adult. Generally, the more rugged, demanding, and sparse the environment, the more intense and physically grueling the initiation rites for males are.

Another important ingredient in this second birth is the pres-ence of elders. These are the gray-hairs of the tribe, the grandfathers, the ones who carry the spiritual wisdom and the tribal legacies. They're the true spiritual fathers who oversee the young man's ini-tiation. They provide an important link to the ancestors, and speak for the lineage of the family or tribe. Often one of the elders is the tribal shaman, and he's quite active in coordinating the ceremony. In contemporary rites of passage, elders may or may not have gray hair, yet the presence of older, seasoned males to provide guidance is essential.

You can devise appropriate initiatory experiences for males that include all the necessary elements. As I stated earlier, in our culture, it's more often a *series* of initiatory experiences than one lengthy and dramatic rite-of-passage ceremony that moves a boy into manhood. Physical adventures that may be suitable are activities such as lengthy backtracking trips or long bicycling treks. The challenges presented in a vision quest, where the boy is alone in the wilderness for four days with only water, will certainly be a key step toward manhood. And life itself has a knack for giving all of us its version of an initiation!

Kyle's Journey

When the adolescent boy goes through his transition, so do his parents. An example of a physical ordeal that functions as a large part of an initiation, as well as a way for a boy's parents to consecrate their son's transition from boyhood to manhood is shown through Kyle and his mom and dad. Kyle loved cycling, so his parents, Robert and Anne Riggins, gifted him with a weeklong group bicycle excursion for his 16th birthday. He had gone away for weeklong trips before, but these had revolved around forays to summer camp or to the homes of his relatives. On this trip, sponsored and supervised by his church's youth ministry, Kyle was taking on a more physically challenging journey. These physical challenges became his ordeal, and the youth ministers became his guides/facilitators/elders. He was to travel with a group of other boys a considerable distance up the coast of California, at times through formidable terrain, and then camp at designated campsites with the others.

Prior to Kyle's excursion, his parents prepared a special dinner, with cloth napkins, the good china, and Kyle's favorite foods. For the first time at a family meal, Kyle was asked to lead the blessing—up until now, this was a prayer that his father had always led. Wine was poured with great flair into the wine glasses, and for another first, into Kyle's.

First Robert, then Anne, offered a toast, acknowledging their son's achievements, their pride in him for going out on his bicycle excursion, and the fact that he was rapidly becoming a man. Prior to Kyle's departure, his father gave him a pocket watch that had belonged to his grandfather, while his mother provided a small dark blue satchel in which to hold the timepiece. His 14-year-old sister Kelsea gave him one of her amulets, a small cross with a green emerald in the center, which Kyle placed in the blue satchel with the watch.

Parents' Release

Once Robert and Anne saw Kyle ride off with the rest of the group, they got back into their car and later drove to their favorite beach, a small cove where they had spent time both as a couple and a family. Here they had watched many sunsets, but today's was going to be imbued with a different kind of meaning. They took out a picture, one that Kyle had drawn when he was about three years old. It was a drawing he had made of his toy wagon and a favorite stuffed teddy bear sitting in it—an appropriate symbol of a time that was to be no more.

As the sun got closer to the horizon, Robert and Anne dug a hole in the sand, set the picture in it, and lit it on fire. Both became teary-eyed as they watched the picture burn. Through this symbolic act, they were releasing a deep internal hold on their son as a little boy, leaving room for them to welcome him as a man. Once the paper had burned down, they took the ashes, and with a prayer of gratitude, released them into the ocean as the sun was just touching the horizon. Both felt a surge of emotions as they watched the great ocean swallow up the ashes. Robert and Anne returned to the sand where the ashes had burned and sat quietly, holding each other in silence for several minutes until the night had begun to wrap its arms around them, signaling a natural completion to this part of the ceremony.

The Return

Upon Kyle's return the next week, Robert and Anne held a gathering where family and friends came to welcome their son home. They feasted, laughed, and everyone gathered in the living room after dinner listening to Kyle recount the details of his adventure.

Later that evening, Robert and Anne talked to Kyle about recognizing his new status as a young man. They discussed extending his curfew and increasing his responsibilities. Since he would be getting a license now and on occasion be driving the family car until he could buy his own, Kyle had to contribute some money to help pay for the increased cost of insurance. They made him promise that anyone under the influence of drugs or alcohol would not be allowed in the car.

Just as Robert, Anne, and Kyle created this rite of passage from a seemingly ordinary bike trip, so can other parents and elders apply the principles of ceremony to other kinds of activities, such as rock climbing or backpacking, which can then serve as an initiation for adolescent males.

Next, we'll look at how the transition girls make to become women can be greatly enhanced and consecrated through ceremonies.

✳ ✳ ✳   ✳ ✳ ✳

Chapter 20

Initiations for Females

Unlike boys, who require a more clearly demarcated ceremony, girls will naturally move into the first phase of adulthood via the very visible changes in their bodies. A girl's first menstruation, or menarche, is a clear indication that her body is now preparing itself for womanhood, and potentially for pregnancy and childbirth. So although a girl in our culture may find it useful to engage in other types of initiatory experiences, the menarche is the initial signal for the start of womanhood, and can be celebrated ceremonially.

In ceremonies for female rites of passage in indigenous cultures, often the beginning of "moontime" heralded the hour when the girl would go into a form of hibernation, spending the time in a darkened shelter for several days. She was cared for by the women of the tribe or village, and in a complimentary process to male initiations, the older females taught her what it meant to be a woman in her particular culture. She learned to value her role as a significant counterpart to a man's, and began to define her contributions to the community. At some point, she grandly emerged back into the community, now truly a woman.

In "Reenactment of Traditional Rites of Passage," from *Crossroads*, Edith Turner describes a complex female initiation rite among the Ndembu of Zambia:

> The ritual consists of laying the girl initiate under a milk tree in the woods, a tree that represents the matrilineage of the tribe. For a whole day, the village women dance around her as she lies covered with a blanket. At evening she is picked up by her "midwife" instructress (for she is like a baby about to be born) and

carried pick-a-back with a dancing step, amid a bunched crowd of women, around the village plaza, and into her seclusion hut. After three months of training in dance and sexual proficiency, she makes her debut as a grown woman—even as a being greater than that, for she is decorated with many beads and an earthen crown, feasted and led like a spirit into the crowd from an unexpected direction. Her dance before them all is the great moment of her life.

What's important in any transitional ceremony for female adolescents is that the young woman come to know her tremendous creative and nurturing power as a woman and value that power. Validation by older women is an essential ingredient in this passage, as well as learning appreciation for the sacred aspect of the feminine. Whatever the type of initiation ceremony you may create, these are the critical values that should be transmitted.

The Dark Red Pouch

My oldest daughter, Nicole, started her menses at age 12, while she was living with me. I was a single father at the time, and although we had a fairly open relationship, when it came to such matters as the start of her "periods," I knew it was more appropriate for her to have a discussion with, and instruction from, her mother or perhaps another woman, or both. When I spoke with Nicole about it, the seeds of an idea began to surface. Perhaps a ceremony would be an appropriate way to mark this momentous life transition. At that time I was writing *The Wounded Male* and understood a fair amount about male initiations, but I knew that it wasn't my place to be directly involved in my daughter's initiation ceremony. Yet I did know it was important to somehow provide a way to commemorate my daughter's passage into womanhood.

After further discussion with Nicole and her mother, Susan, we agreed to ask a good friend of ours, Donna, if she would be willing to prepare a ceremony. Susan felt that it would be much better if someone other than herself were to perform the ceremony. Donna was the perfect choice, as she was Nicole's godmother and had known Nicole since early childhood. Also, Nicole loved and respected her immensely. When I spoke to Donna about our idea, she was delighted to perform the ceremony. We set the date and time, and agreed that it would be performed at our home.

Nicole was surprisingly enthusiastic and open to participating in this ceremony. I initially thought she might be somewhat reluctant or perhaps even decline. Looking back, I think she was so receptive because she was included in the planning and preparation, and also trusted Donna. She knew that I often did "weird" things, as she had participated in some of my shamanic ceremonials, so the idea of a ceremony for herself was not too bizarre.

The day finally arrived. Nicole bathed and dressed herself in a long flowing gown, did her hair up, and looked absolutely gorgeous. I could see the woman in her emerging more clearly than ever. Donna showed up in a deep purple, velvety gown, her hair up and sprinkled with tiny flowers. We located a spot near the altar in the living room. Donna laid out a beautiful embroidered rug upon which both of them could sit, and placed floor pillows on either side of a low-to-the-ground table. She and Nicole chatted as Donna pulled some objects from a rather large handbag.

I brought out some flowers that I had procured especially for this purpose, put them in a vase, and gave them to Nicole to set on the table. Then I made myself scarce, knowing that it was necessary for the two of them to be alone together—to afford some privacy, and perhaps even secrecy, in sharing the mysteries of being a woman.

I do know that Donna had brought with her a dark red pouch containing some sacred objects. She told me later that the pouch represented the womb; and the red, the blood time. Donna later intimated that she and Nicole prayed together, and mostly talked, with Donna giving her some of her insights on womanhood. Susan gave Nicole a pendant that her grandmother had given to her mother, who then passed it along to Susan when she'd entered high school.

Donna gifted Nicole with a ring that she had found in Nepal while traveling there some years ago. Donna told her, "The ring protected me, I'm sure of it. I had a few close encounters, but was always safe. The man who sold it to me said it had been a gift from an Indian guru, a powerful woman who blessed the ring with the power of love."

Other things took place to which I'm not privy—nor should I be. Some mysteries of womanhood should remain mysteries to men, just as some mysteries of manhood should remain mysteries to women.

After Nicole and Donna had completed the more formal part of the ceremony, the three of us went to dinner together. I was pleased to observe the slight but noticeable shift in Nicole's demeanor. It's as if she was somehow . . . taller. During the entire dinner, I felt a strange mixture of joy and sadness. There was a new type of presence expressing itself through Nicole. She was my daughter, my first child and first girl, yet before me I was witnessing the woman she was to become, emerging from the little girl I had known.

Into the World

There comes a time in every young person's life when they must make their way out into the world. Sometimes this happens as a singular movement, sometimes gradually and in stages. College students often return home for the summer, until graduation signals a time for a change. An adolescent or young adult may make take an extended journey as an important stage in their progress toward becoming an autonomous adult. Any or all of these transitional stages can be marked with ceremony. Remember, ceremonies don't have to be elaborate and extensive. Something simple can serve the purpose, such as a special family dinner to acknowledge the transition. When they're ready to make a major transition, such as moving out, you can create a more comprehensive ceremony.

We marked one such experience with Nicole when she was 18. She was preparing to make an extended journey to Europe, having dreamed of returning there ever since she had gone to England at the invitation of a friend when she was 16. At that time, she had stayed with her friend's family in the countryside of England—just enough to whet her appetite for more. She'd been visualizing and affirming the trip, and had even put together a "storyboard," a collage of magazine photos and captions that was a daily reminder of her dream. So for her 18th birthday, her mother and I were able to arrange another voyage to Europe. This journey signified a transition for her, and after some brainstorming, we agreed that a going-away party was in order.

I suggested that she ask certain of her friends and family to bring a totem of some sort, something small that she could place in a leather pouch, or medicine bag, to take with her on her journey. This medicine bag would be filled with these totems, or symbols to remind her of her friends and family, and could afford her comfort and solace if and whenever her travels invoked any fear or homesickness.

The day came, and as the guests began to arrive, many brought presents, as is often done in more traditional going-away parties. Those who had brought items for the medicine bag placed their objects on a table set off to the side, covered with a lavender silk scarf with a lit candle in the middle. Some friends gave Nicole money for the trip—which she gratefully received—while others brought various small treasures, and still others brought their love and blessings. Everyone had a great time at the party. There was laughter, singing, and conversation, and then gradually, most of the guests departed.

The few who stayed were the friends and family members who had been asked to participate in a separate ceremony. Nicole's mother, Susan; her sisters Catherine and Elizabeth; her stepfather, Tom; and about half a dozen close friends all gathered in a circle. Each of us had brought along something for the medicine bag, and most of these items had already been placed on the altar in the corner of the living room. We took all of these items, plus the cloth and candle, and placed it in the middle of the circle. I described the purpose of the ceremony to everyone, then began the ceremony by rattling and singing a spirit-calling song. Then we prayed, asking for Spirit's blessing for this event and for Nicole's safety while traveling.

I brought out a leather pouch that I had constructed specifically for this purpose. Passing the pouch to the left, one at a time, each of us took the particular object, described its meaning, then carefully placed it into the pouch. The bag filled up with tiny animal totems, rocks, and pendants. One gift in particular brought tears to her eyes. Her stepfather, Tom, gave her a personal treasure—the ticket stub he had saved from a Beatles concert he'd attended over 30 years ago. Nicole had grown up with Beatles music from the time she was very young, and loved their songs. Knowing her stepfather's avid love of music and concerts, she knew that this was a very special gift.

Once we had gone around, I then suggested a second round

where each person chose one positive trait or characteristic they saw in themselves. For instance, if someone saw themselves as courageous, this might be the trait they would identify. Once they named the trait and described it, they were to think of it, feel it, then take the medicine bag in hand and with one breath, breathe it into the bag. Various traits, such as faith, courage, and patience, were breathed or blown into the pouch. When this was complete, the bag was returned to me.

I asked Nicole to hold her hands out, and I placed the medicine bag, now imbued with tremendous power, into her keeping, saying, "Everyone has placed something very special in here for you, Nicole. Keep this nearby at all times. When you feel alone, hold the bag closely as a reminder of those who love you. When you get scared, hold it close by to inspire you with whatever is necessary to deal with that fear. When you sleep, do so with this bag close by, so you can dream good dreams. Know that there's an incredible power contained within, and use it whenever you need to feel strength and fortitude." With this, she accepted the bag, as we all broke out into spontaneous cheering and laughter. I blew the candle out, signifying the completion of the ceremony.

Nicole was away for two months, and by all reports had a wonderful adventure. When I asked her about the medicine bag, she reported that it had come in handy at least a couple of times, especially when she was missing her home, her family, or her friends.

She moved out on her own recently, and I asked her if she had taken the medicine bag with her, and she had. She said, "I found the snake ring that you gave me, and I'm wearing it right now. It's a good idea to go through it every once in a while and take things out that don't fit and add things that do." Funny. I suggested she do that when we created the bag, and she remembered to do so. I'm glad she wears the snake ring. It has special meaning for both of us.

�֍ ✖ ✖   ✖ ✖ ✖

Chapter 21
Adult Transitions

If you bring forth that which is within you,
Then that which is within you
Will be your salvation.
If you do not bring forth that which is within you,
Then that which is within you
Will destroy you.

— Jesus, from the *Gnostic Gospel of Thomas*

Passage into Midlife

S omeone once defined "middle age" as ten years older than the age you are now. It's true that we often don't want to face this particular milestone, but I can guarantee you that if you don't squarely confront this passage and deal with it, it's going to jump out someday and bite you in the behind.

If you do not tackle the challenges presented during the 35- to 55-year-old time period and make a conscious effort to "bring forth that which is within," you can find yourself discounting your natural internal pressures, trying to cover them up through a variety of addictions or escapades. If that's the case, you may try to continue with habits and behaviors that were more appropriate when you were younger. In our youth-obsessed culture, it's no surprise that we attempt to defer and deny the aging process by holding on to whatever representations of our youth we can. Plastic surgeons make lots of money as a result of this kind of obsession.

During this midlife transition, those parts of you that have been submerged begin to call for your attention. If you're a family man and have dedicated much of your life up until now to your career and family, the call to adventure beckons more strongly. If you're a mother who has devoted much of your early adulthood to raising a family, you may feel an increasingly strong urge to go out and meet the world, return to school, or start a new career.

For some, this natural developmental pressure is so great as to cause a major disruption in your life. A divorce or other major loss, or else a sudden career transition, knocks you on the head and says it's time to make some changes. That's how it's happened for many people I know, as well as myself.

What I've found, though, is that an excellent way to deal with all these changes and challenges is to mark them with an appropriate ceremony—perhaps more than one—to provide some soulful and spiritual attunement.

From Material to Spiritual

It's also during the midlife passage that we begin to question our philosophy and approach to life. Generally, our attention turns away from material concerns toward spiritual values and ethical considerations. It can be a very difficult adjustment, and often takes a span of a few years for this shift to occur and for someone to assimilate this revised outlook on life. It generally requires a major overhaul of your entire life, and there are points along the way that are perfect for creating ceremony to mark this passage.

During my early 30s, I was faced with being a new father and felt totally incapable of handling the responsibilities required to be a family man. I felt terrified and overwhelmed and wanted to escape. I'm sure my wife was also feeling this way and didn't know what to do either. So when I was 36 years old, we separated and soon followed that with a divorce. The rumblings of change were in full force by then. I stumbled and crawled along for a few years before I began to focus more on my work and career. Eventually I finished my first book, *Adult Children of Abusive Parents*, and went on to write three more shortly after that.

Although I now look at this time as a period of dramatic change and spiritual awakening, it was years later before I could grasp the implications of these changes. Through these various experiences, some of which were initiatory by nature, my spirituality was evolving.

Although there were certainly meaningful events along the way, one of the most life-changing events during this time was the death of my parents—first my mother, then my father 18 months later. I grieved my mother's passing, yet felt the loss of my father even more profoundly. Something about his passing signaled the need for me to step up to the plate, to really embrace the reality of my age—45 at the time. After we buried my dad's ashes next to my mother's grave, I went home and immediately performed a simple ceremony to honor his passing.

The Spirit of My Father and Grandfather

Yet after a few months, I knew that there was something more I needed to do—I felt that a personal ceremony was in order, one to acknowledge this passage I was going through, which was leading to the next era in my life. And I knew I had to perform the ceremony outdoors, somewhere in the woods. So I headed out to a place relatively close to home to find the perfect spot.

I gathered together some of what I would need for the ceremony and headed out. After about two hours, I turned off the main highway onto a road that led slowly into a deep canyon. This soon turned into a narrow dirt road, dusty and bumpy. I asked my spirit guides to help me find the right place. About 200 yards away, there was a grove of trees that paralleled the road, evidently tracking the stream I'd seen earlier when the road was closer to it.

Heeding my own instincts, I suddenly stopped. This was the place.

I got out of my car and looked around, figuring I would have to hike down the short distance to where the trees and the stream were. Then I looked closely, and there it was—a narrow, barely distinguishable path, wide enough for a car but strewn with a lot of sizable boulders. Somewhat nervously I got back into my car and headed down this path, navigating slowly, grateful for my trusty four-wheel-drive vehicle. Bumpy, but worth it.

I came to a clearing surrounded by a small forest of magnificent oak trees, a bed of their leaves strewn about the floor of the clearing. These stately beings left plenty of room between one other, but they were close enough to remain as kin. The sunlight scooted through the openings in their branches, and the stream whispered its persistent melody. I got out of the car and wandered around, and eventually sat on a log near the water. I had found the perfect place. Other than the sound of the stream and the occasional breeze rustling the leaves, it was very quiet. I knew that there would be no intrusions, and that I would be perfectly safe to camp here.

After exploring the area, I found a spot where I would spend the night. I pulled my bag of sacred objects from the car, along with two quarts of water and a small tarp to lay on the ground. There was no need for food, as I was fasting for the ceremony. I came to the spot, put everything down, took a stick, and drew a circle in the dirt about eight feet in diameter. I was committed to staying within the circle until the next morning.

I rattled in the seven directions, and thanked the spirits of the land for allowing me to be there as a guest. I expressed gratitude to the helping spirits for bringing me to this area, and asked them to remain with me. Setting the tarp on the ground, I constructed the ceremonial altar. I placed it at one end of the tarp, facing the east.

Clearing the debris from the flat rock that was there, I set out a small tapestry, and on it I placed a rabbit fur given to me by a friend. There I set down a candle, a Celtic cross, a bowl with sage and sweetgrass in it, an owl feather, a small vial of ocean water, and one of my favorite photos. It's a picture of my father as young man, in his military uniform, leaning against my grandfather. My dad has a big grin on his face, a cigarette dangling from his lips, looking very cocky. My grandfather is smiling as well, with a proud look on his face. It's a sweet photo, taken sometime shortly after World War II, and had been on my altar at home since my father's death a few months earlier.

I also took my two-sided drum out of its bag, along with my flute. I had gathered several small stones from the nearby stream, and placed those in a semicircle in front of the altar. I saged all of these sacred objects, the circle, then myself, and sat down in the center of the circle to consider what I was doing. I didn't have a complete plan for the ceremony, but more of an idea of where I wanted to go and a commitment to stay within this sacred circle until morning. I felt guided, trusting that inspiration would direct me to do what I needed to do.

I took the flute and played a simple tune, my spirit-calling song. As I played, I went into a mild trance, where the song was playing itself through me. The song of the flute gently harmonized with the running water dancing along the stream, and with the breeze breathing through the trees. Once I finished playing, the melody continued, now accompanied solely by the sound of my breath and my heartbeat. This wonderful symphony continued as I sat there in peaceful bliss. No watches, no time, no worries—just the moment!

After enjoying this setting for what could have been minutes or hours, I picked up the drum and began playing a slow, steady rhythm. After a few moments of drumming, I slipped into a shamanic journey, asking my spirit guides what to do next. They told me, and the remainder of the ceremony became clear.

As the day subsided, I prayed, asking for blessings for all those whom I knew and loved, as well as for what I was about to do. I thought a lot about my life up to that time, and the changes that had occurred and continued to occur. I wept for my mother and my father, and I called upon my ancestors, especially my grandfather and father. I could feel them with me.

I picked up one of the stones near the altar. I asked the stone to carry away any and all grievances, hurts, and transgressions that I may have committed with respect to my father. I cupped the stone in my hand, and as I held in thought these transgressions, both those of which I was aware and those of which I was not, I blew them into the stone with my breath, then tossed the stone into the stream. Next, I did the same with respect to my mother. I continued in this manner with my daughters, their mother, a former lover, an old friend, and any others I could think of. In all, I covered about a dozen people, clearing as much as I could, and in the process, forgave myself (with the help of Spirit), for any "sins" I'd committed with these significant people in my life.

I shed some tears while doing so, and felt cleansed by the time I finished with everyone. Interestingly enough, although I didn't know at the beginning how many stones I would need, by this time there was one left. Wham! It occurred to me to clear and forgive myself for any hurts and self-sabotage I may have perpetrated upon myself. Thus, the 13th stone was for me, and it carried forth its mission admirably! I was trembling as I took the stone into my right hand, tears streaming down my face. How harsh I could be with myself! I allowed the shaking, then blew into the stone three times and tossed it in to the water, which willingly received it. Once I'd released this stone, a wave of joy rippled through my body, and my eyes were brimming with tears of great relief.

The next step was to write. I journaled for some time, mostly reviewing my life, writing whatever came to mind. Then I wrote about my father, receiving some insights into his life. This naturally led to writing out what I wanted for my life in the future. One revelation during this process was that this ceremony truly did signify the end of one cycle and the start of another. In retrospect, it was a midlife rite of passage, a settling into my age, letting go of a few layers of attachment to habits and behaviors that no longer served a purpose for myself at 45 years old.

As darkness settled, the frogs started singing. All I had for light was the candle and a small penlight by my side in case I needed it. Although I was restless at times and wanted to wander about, I kept my commitment and stayed within the circle. After some time, I laid down on the tarp, covered myself with my jacket, and the chorus of frogs sang me to sleep.

"I'm with You"

Awakening with a start, it took me a few moments to realize where I was. The candle was out, so it was very dark. Through the branches, I saw a very faint, shimmering movement. I blinked several times. What was that? It was scary, but strangely familiar.

For a brief moment, I saw my grandfather's spirit—pale and translucent, but clear enough to make out some of his features! And just as quickly, the image faded into the night.

Then I heard his voice inside my head saying, "I'm with you," slowly and repetitively. Soon another voice joined in, which I recognized as that of my father, saying, "I'm so proud of you, my son. Thank you for honoring me in this way." I was stunned, not being entirely sure if I were making this up or not. As if responding to my question on cue, my main spirit guide told me, "You're not making this up. This is for you to hear. You're not alone in your mission. You're a healer and a teacher. Know that the spirit of your father and your grandfather, and many of the men before them, join with you and support you."

Then, darkness and quiet. Even the frogs had ceased their accompaniment during this time.

Slowly, as if by a chain of command, the frogs started singing again. I was wide-eyed, looking here and there for any further signs. Nothing. Right about then it started to lightly rain. I wasn't prepared for this, so I pulled part of the tarp over me and continued with my vigil. It took a while, but eventually I fell asleep once again.

The next day, it was still sprinkling. I was cold and hungry, but satisfied with my experience. Not knowing what time it was, but sensing that the ceremony was complete, I prayed with gratitude for the entire experience. Drumming once more, then rattling while singing a closing song of thanks, I completed the ceremony. As I gathered my belongings, I noticed a hawk feather at the edge of the circle that hadn't been there the day before. I took it as a sign, a "thank you," from Spirit. I trudged to the car, pleased that I had gone through this experience, and also glad that it was over. I felt tired but renewed, as if I'd been on a longer journey.

To this day, I can feel my father's and his grandfather's presence in my life, and I know that they're watching over me. I also knew at that point that I was clearly entering into a different stage of adulthood, of manhood, that I could no longer maintain some of the habits and preferences that I'd had as a younger man. Now that both my parents were gone, I was becoming an elder. When I'd first had that thought, I'd felt intimidated. Following this ceremony, I welcomed the new role.

Taking a New Name

One of the ways to mark the midlife passage is to take on a new name, or a derivative of your present one. In some indigenous peoples, including Native American tribes, adults can acquire a new name in their mature years. It reflects the new identity that has evolved as they have matured. This can be done ceremonially.

Authors Carl Hammerschlag and Howard Silverman, in *Healing Ceremonies*, describe a story of just such a ceremony for a name change. On a hike that Carl took with his longtime friend Chip, now called Charles, his friend disclosed to him some childhood experiences that he had put aside until recently. Charles went on to describe how his mother, a skid-row alcoholic, had given him up for adoption just before her death, when Charles was nine years old. Further, Charles told Carl how his mother would fondle his genitals, talk to them, and even kiss them. She called him "Chipper," because she said that's how he made her feel. His friends shortened his name to "Chip."

Chip's biological father, whom he never knew, had died in World War II. His name was Charles. Raised from age nine by his adoptive parents, they continued to call him Chip. At age 40, he decided to give up his old name and all of the old associations with it, and began to see more and more clearly how this distorted relationship with his mother had messed up his relationships with women. After two failed marriages, he realized that he was terrified of intimacy, so he'd married very obedient, subservient women. Once he was firmly in control, he got bored with them. He related to Carl his awareness that this was a way to avoid a woman's violence. Carl relates the story of how they developed the ceremony on the hike, then performed it later:

> I told him about the Hopi naming ceremony, and Charles immediately asked if he could adapt it. He beamed at the idea. We crafted the ceremony right there in the meadow. He made a list of friends, some of whom lived quite a distance from him. We created an invitation, picked some dates. I agreed to help run the event. We asked people not to bring gifts; instead, their gift would be to come with a name that truly reflected how they saw themselves at this time in their lives.
>
> Eighteen people sat in a circle on Charles's living room floor. In the middle of the circle was a small Indian blanket atop which rested an abalone shell filled with cedar, a burning candle, and a pair of epaulets—the last remnants from his father's military uniform and the only thing of his father's that Charles had. Charles first told the Utah mountain meadow story and how he had shared with me a long-repressed event. He told the story of his childhood and ended by saying he wanted to take his father's name.
>
> Then he said, "These shoulder boards will come to each of you, and while you're holding them, I'd like you to share the gift you brought me today. Tell me the name you choose for yourself. Nobody will ask why or interpret, each of us will get a turn."
>
> He handed the epaulets to me, and I said a little about the

Talking Circle, about creating a sacred space. I lit the sage, saying it gave color and smell so we could see our words rise to touch the ear of the Creator. I told about my grandson's naming and thought about my father, about great-grandchildren, and about dying. I am Abraham, the son of Aaron. My grandson is Aaron, and one day, I hope, someone will carry my name, too. . . .

When I finished, I passed the epaulets on. Some chose names with colors, others with animals. There was one historical figure, and one said she just wanted to be called Mom.

I've known a few people who have changed their names after a certain age, typically sometime during their midlife passage. Eddie to Edd, Chris to Christopher, Liz to Elizabeth, and even Cindy to Sue. The change isn't just in form, but typically reflects a sense of a new and different identity, one that (hopefully) embraces the maturation of the individual into the cycle of midlife. What a beautiful gift to give yourself, a ceremony to more consciously introduce your new name and thus your new identity!

What name would you choose?

❈ ❈ ❈   ❈ ❈ ❈

Chapter 22

Late Adulthood Transitions

Ah yes, in our youth-obsessed culture, the advancing specter of growing old becomes something to be tirelessly avoided. Perhaps because we're that much closer to the final passage, the fear and denial of death causes us to try to maintain the facade of youth in the face of the inevitable and gradual diminishment of our capacities. What's usually overlooked is the tremendous storehouse of knowledge and wisdom that we've accumulated, the gifts we can give to subsequent generations.

As previously noted, our society's beliefs about growing old don't honor the eldership status of our seniors. These beliefs become part of a person's indoctrination, so they may slip into a sense of powerlessness and resignation. Challenging these beliefs by remaining active and curious about the world, making learning and education a top priority, and staying involved in family and community can help someone approach this transition and era with greater enthusiasm and acceptance.

Darrel is a good example. He was a student in a class I taught at Saddleback College in Southern California, and he was pursuing his third college degree. I was struck by his attentiveness and eagerness to learn. He always had something to say in our class discussions. Saddleback College has an "emeritus" program, meaning that there a number of courses and programs for senior citizens, so it was not unusual for a few gray-haired students to be mixed with older teens and young adults. I assumed Darrel to be about 65 or 70. One day after class, he and I struck up a conversation, and I asked him how old he was. I made no attempt to hide my astonishment and admiration when he told me he was 83! He said, "I reckon I'll never stop learning." What a great attitude—and education—he gave my students and me.

Three Major Tasks of Late Adulthood

In this passage into the later stage of life, we're faced with three major tasks. These are *managing loss, recapturing innocence,* and *fostering generativity.* How we approach and deal with these tasks will help determine our well-being and vitality.

Managing loss—As we enter the twilight phase, one of the main tasks we're confronted with is learning to manage loss. Some of the challenges we must face are retirement from a career, with its ensuing loss of status and power, as well as the loss of a nearly lifelong identity with work. Another marker of this era is the lessening of vitality and stamina, as well as for some, a decline in health and the ability to recuperate from illness. Also, this is the time when we're more likely to lose friends and relatives to death.

The good news from is that we *must* somehow challenge the illusion of permanence, to stop identifying so strongly with the material world and deeply explore the mysteries of the eternal, in order to find our true identity in Spirit. This is one of the keys to successfully dealing with loss, as well as gaining in wisdom.

Recapturing innocence—Time to play, time to learn, time to take long walks on the beach or just be—once a person has traversed this late-adulthood passage, they've typically given up a number of responsibilities and obligations and have more choices as to how to spend their time. There's now time to enjoy life, to travel, to involve themselves in creative and novel pursuits, and to enjoy their family, particularly their grandchildren. As an older friend once said to me, "Being older, you can get away with just being yourself, without having to make excuses."

For women in particular, going through menopause can mean an opportunity to come forward as one of the wise grandmothers of the community. This is a time when a woman can regain, or perhaps achieve for the first time, the sense that her life is her own. She can truly be herself without having to compromise, or be beholden to others' demands.

Fostering generativity—Psychologist Erik Erickson, who defined the tasks of various developmental stages from birth to old age, suggests that this is the primary task for this period of life. If a person isn't "generative"—isn't involved in promoting something larger than themselves, something that will benefit future generations—then they face the risk of a tailspin into feelings of helplessness and despair.

Sometimes we're so impacted by personal, community, or world events that it prompts us to reevaluate our priorities, to take a direction that more fully incorporates new ethical and spiritual values that foster generativity. Such was the case with Gerald Levin, 62, CEO of AOL Time Warner. An article in *Newsweek* (December 17, 2001) described an epiphany he experienced following a visit to Ground Zero after the devastation of September 11, 2001. The article by Johnnie L. Roberts describes how Levin arrived at the decision to retire and pursue a different direction:

> AOL Time Warner CEO Gerald Levin returned with his trusted deputy Richard Parsons from a tour of Ground Zero, devastated. Not since the 1997 murder of his son had Levin appeared as shattered as he did looking over the wreckage that September morning. "He seemed to almost cry when he talked about 9-11," says Sandi Reisenbach, a Warner Bros. studio executive. . . . But the devastation also seemed to infuse Levin with a new sense of purpose for his media empire. "Our commitment not to just build our business but to make a difference" is among the company's "unique resources," he proclaimed in a companywide e-mail on Sept. 14. By early November, Levin was telling a gathering of investors that AOL Time Warner would spend heavily on its mission as a "public trust," even if that lowered profits. "I'm the CEO, and this is what I'm going to do," Levin also reportedly said. "I don't care what anyone else says."
>
> But the real stunner came last week when Levin abruptly announced that he will retire next year . . . the sudden resignation was neatly explained as the climax of Levin's recent spiritual metamorphosis. "My true DNA" is to serve "a passionate, philosophical, moralistic purpose," says Levin.

Levin's story—and his "passionate, philosophical, moralistic purpose"—captures the essence of one of the tasks of later adulthood.

Facing Your Mortality

This era also requires that we squarely face our own mortality. This doesn't have to be morbid or depressing, although it will certainly trigger some feelings and create an opportunity for deeper introspection. There's a type of Buddhism where a common practice is to meditate upon one's own death. Practitioners say that doing so makes you appreciate life that much more fully.

Robert Fulghum, in *From Beginning to End: The Rituals of Our Lives*, describes a ceremony in which he faced his eventual death in a poetic and elegant manner. On the opening page of one of the chapters is a black-and-white photograph of a man sitting in a chair in a cemetery, gazing out into the sky. It turns out that this is a picture of the author, although he initially describes what's going on in the third person, saying:

> He is sitting on his own grave. Not because his death is imminent—he's in pretty good shape, actually. And not because he was in a morbid state of mind—he was in a fine mood when the picture was taken. In fact, he has had one of the most affirmative afternoons in his life.
>
> Sitting for an afternoon on his own grave, he has had one of those potent experiences when the large pattern of his life has been unexpectedly reviewed: the past, birth, childhood, adolescence, marriage, career, the present, and the future. He has confronted finitude—the limits of life. The fact of his own death lies before him and beneath him—raising the questions of the when and the where and the how of it. What shall he do with his life between now and then?

Fulghum went on to describe how he'd discussed the considerations with his family, wrote out a will, detailed the funeral instructions, and filled out any forms that were necessary. I have found this sort of confrontation with mortality to be a courageous and perhaps even necessary encounter as a person moves into this later stage of adulthood.

An alternative ceremony to Fulghum's inspired piece would be to create a sacred space, preferably somewhere outdoors, away from your familiar environment. I suggest doing it outside, because that's where your remains will ultimately recycle. If you desire, follow Fulghum's model of doing this near where your body is to be buried or your ashes are to be scattered, but that's not necessary.

Take with you any sacred objects that seem appropriate, and a pen and some paper, then sage the area, if possible. Say a prayer to consecrate the space, asking for a blessing for what you're about to do. Set up your altar, even if it's only a couple of objects sitting on a rock.

Sit down and take a few minutes to quietly meditate on your life. Then, using your journal, write a life review. Take your time. In fact, if you don't finish during the actual ceremony, complete your review soon after. It's important. What have been the significant events that have shaped your life? Who have been the most influential people? Whom have you loved? How have you changed over time? Any regrets? Are there any people with whom you're still carrying a grudge? Write down the answers to these and any other questions until you've exhausted whatever you have to report.

Next, set this down and spend some quiet time letting what you wrote settle in. When that feels complete, write out your instructions in detail for your funeral and memorial, including what you would like the inscription on your gravestone to say. Let your feelings move through you as you write. Tears make for a good "soul cleansing," so if this happens, don't hold back.

Again, once you've completed this task, let your feelings settle. For many, this is one of the most powerful exercises you can do.

And last but not least, assume that you have at least 20 or 30 years remaining. In your journal, write down what you want to do with the rest of your life. What is your mission? Is there a service you want to provide, or one that you're doing that you want to continue? What kind of contribution do you want to make, especially one that will benefit future generations? Like Gerald Levin, perhaps you'll want to serve with "a passionate, philosophical, moralistic purpose." If so, what would that be like?

Close the ceremony by drumming, rattling, and/or singing, followed by a prayer of gratitude for what you *do* have in your life. Make copies of your life review for your descendants, to be given to them after your passing. Go for it. Know that this will be a very healing ceremony.

Another option for leaving a legacy, one that can be introduced in a ceremony, is to do your life review on videotape. You can ask someone to help you with this, perhaps a friend to serve as an interviewer. Once you've done so, you can edit this into a one-hour "special." Similar to the written piece on your life review, you can give it to your children or make arrangements to leave it for them following your final passage.

There are myriad ways to create a ceremony for this passage, and it may be that you perform ceremonies intermittently throughout as a means of honoring this transition. This initiation into later adulthood can hold special meaning for a woman.

A Woman's Passage

For a woman, this passage can be difficult. Similar to the time when she first gets her menses, now her body is telling her that she's in the transitional phase of menopause. Once she crosses this passage, she can now be considered to be a woman of experience and wisdom. In many indigenous tribes, a woman of this age is considered to be an elder, a grandmother, and is highly respected and revered. She's past the age to bear and raise children, and instead, provides counsel and wisdom to the community.

Increasingly, more and more women are ceremonializing this passage with a redefined version of an ancient ceremony called *croning*. For many centuries, the term *crone* has meant "withered old hag," but ancient beliefs considered the crone to be a goddess who took back all life into her womb to be birthed anew. It's refreshing to see how more women are identifying with this profound symbol of the life-and-death forces of creation, proudly proclaiming themselves to be "crones" as they enter through the portals of this passage into later adulthood.

As is the case with other transitions, there are no established ceremonies for this transition. Although it means the loss of opportunity to bear children, it's balanced with the freedom that comes from completing this task. It's a signal for reevaluating priorities, a time for a woman to cleanse herself of unwanted and unneeded responsibilities. Her influence now extends beyond the family into the larger community. She becomes both elder and teacher.

In prior generations, women rarely discussed or ac
this passage. It was kept hidden, often showing up as ɪ
swings, depression, and treated as a pathological condition requir-
ing the woman to receive treatment and medication. Now it's
increasingly seen as a time when a woman is in another phase of fer-
tile and creative power.

A Croning Ceremony

Any ceremonial marking of this transition is best done with
other women. It should contain elements that involve the symbolic
release of the old, and ways to welcome the new. Validation and
recognition by other women at such a ceremony is necessary, and it
would be useful to include at least one or two women who are older
than the one to be honored in the ceremony. Finding an object that
represents this new stage, and asking the other women to bless such
an object will emphasize the importance of this passage.

In *Rites of Passage,* authors Kathleen Wall and Gary Ferguson
share Carolyn's story of how Carolyn's friend Alta facilitated Carolyn's
croning ceremony. They prepared for it by inviting two of Carolyn's
closest women friends, Mary and Joanne. Carolyn dressed in a black
kimono, the color not only representing the death of an old way of
life, but also the "betwixt and between," that dark area between
spiritual and material realities. The kimono, being garb that isn't of
Carolyn's culture, made a statement that she was releasing certain
societal constrictions.

To start the ceremony, Carolyn sat in the middle while the other
three formed a circle enclosing her. After a few moments of quiet
meditation, each of the women, in turn, offered what they considered to be an insight or important truth about growing into later life.
Afterward, they turned to gift-giving. Wall and Ferguson described
what happened for Carolyn from that point on:

> After the women shared their thoughts about life, each pre-
> sented Carolyn with a gift to mark the occasion. Mary gave a
> journal with an insightful inscription, and Joanne, a collection of
> poetry. Alta's gift was to play two haunting melodies on her flute.
> Finally, Carolyn told the women how it felt to be entering the last

portion of her life. She told them what she hoped to accomplish in the years ahead, what new perspectives she wanted to gain. After this, she opened a small leather purse, where, as instructed by Alta, she'd placed personal tokens representing the three stages of a woman through midlife: maidenhood, loverhood, and mother-hood. (Motherhood, by the way, refers not only to the actual bear-ing of children, but also to the fact that over the course of their first 40 to 50 years, women will mother bodies of work, art, relation-ship, etc.)

As she removed each of these tokens, Carolyn told her friends what she hoped to retain from that time of her life—what would be useful for her in her upcoming journey—as well as what she wished to leave behind. For example, when talking about loverhood (her symbol was a wedding ring), Carolyn told about wanting to retain the deep sharing of an intimate relationship but to free herself from the need she felt to take responsibility for her part-ner's sense of well-being. As she finished explaining each object, she carefully placed it in the center of the circle.

As the final part of the ceremony, Alta opened a blanket to reveal a maple staff that a neighbor had carved for her. The wooden staff, she explained to Carolyn, is an ancient symbol of the wise woman. "We offer it to remind you that there is much love to lean on in the years ahead. You won't be walking alone. We'll be with you. And the lives of countless women, over countless years, will be with you, too."

Afterward, the women returned to Alta's house to dine from a table overflowing with food and drink. The food and wine were superb, and the conversation flowed well into the night. "I can't begin to share the deep sense of kinship I had with those women," says Carolyn. "I felt that I was walking down a comfortable, well-worn path. I thought at the time that none of us needed to grunt and groan so much, that the best parts of our lives would live *us*, if only we would let it happen."

Even a simple ceremony where a woman is acknowledged by other women can suffice to mark this momentous life transition. It gives new meaning to the more typical associations with menopause, and honoring this through ceremony within a spiritual context recognizes the significant changes this passage entails.

Chapter 23

Marriage Ceremonies

There are several good books about marriage ceremonies (see the Recommended Reading section at the back of the book), so I won't attempt to provide detailed information on logistics and procedures. Instead, I want to encourage you to create something that's personally meaningful and filled with vitality, a ceremony in which you can include some traditional elements if you so choose.

To become legally married, all it takes is a signed marriage license and an officiant, be it a minister or a justice of the peace. That's it. The next most important element is the vows the couple make to one another. The way this is done ceremonially is up to the two people involved. They can draw from cultural customs, advice from others, and their own creativity when designing the ceremony.

Any marriage ceremony clearly follows the three stages of sacred ceremony—separation, transformation, and incorporation—although there will be elements that are unique to this type of ceremony. For the first stage, the individuals to be married separate from their usual relationship with their parents—perhaps most commonly portrayed in a traditional ceremony where the father gives away the bride, the groom escorts his mother to the front row of seats, and then he moves from his mother to the altar to await his bride.

The second stage, transformation, is the body of the ceremony. The individuals to be married start out single and are transformed into a unit, a married couple.

The stage of incorporation begins when the two people now enter into the community as a singular entity, a married couple. This is represented when the couple turns to face their guests and are introduced as the "newly wedded couple."

Seven Steps of a Marriage Ceremony

A wedding typically follows a pattern that contains some or all of the following seven steps:

1. **Procession and welcome**—"Here comes the bride . . ." Or the couple may enter together. Witnesses and guests are welcomed, with the acknowledgment that the guests aren't just bystanders, but an essential ingredient to connecting the new couple to the community.

2. **Invocation**—Calling upon God to bless the proceedings.

3. **Address**—Usually a reading from a spiritual text, a poem, or some other meaningful work, followed by a brief discourse regarding purpose, community, and faith.

4. **Vows of intent**—The couple makes public their intentions to be married and details some of the values they want to adhere to, followed by their vows to each other.

5. **Blessing and exchange of rings**—As the couple exchanges their rings, a blessing is spoken by the officiant.

6. **Pronouncement and the kiss**—Perhaps the most famous part of a traditional ceremony. Need I say more? Following the kiss, the newly transformed couple is introduced to the community of witnesses.

7. **The benediction and recession**—A sort of "go forth" blessing, read or spoken, followed by the completion of the ceremony.

At this point, a celebration ceremony often takes place, which can be a small, quiet affair; or a large, loud party. Either way, it now becomes a different type of ceremony, one of celebration.

What follows is a relatively traditional type of wedding ceremony that I performed. The bride and groom chose most of the words, and the three of us worked together to design the actual ceremony.

Thomas and Allison's Wedding

The processional started with music, as the participants in the ceremony entered and took their place near the altar. The groom entered, then the bride, accompanied by her father. I welcomed everyone, then offered some introductory words:

> *Love is the substance of the soul. It's the glue of the universe, the harmonizing element that creates and expresses through all forms. Today is a very special day. It's the day we are brought together in love to celebrate and witness the holy union of Thomas and Allison.*
>
> *This simple ceremony is the outward manifestation of a sacred and internal union of hearts and of souls, a union created by loving purpose and maintained by abiding will . . .*
>
> *Who presents this woman to be married to this man?*

Allison's father, of course, said, "I do," then sat down. I continued:

> *Thomas and Allison, I welcome you to this very special event, the culmination of your four-year courtship. I offer you this Celtic blessing:*
>
> **May your souls always bathe in the truth and light of understanding.**
>
> **May your love always lift your head to the heavens, while your feet remain deeply rooted in the earth.**
>
> **May your love be not only of your minds but of your hearts, and may your hearts always be open to one another.**
>
> **May your love be a sanctuary for one another and all you hold sacred.**
>
> **May your love always honor the One who first loved you and inspired you to love another—the One who brought you together—Creator of us all.**
>
> *Now please feel free to offer your blessings for Thomas and Allison by silently praying.*

I then read a passage from Kahlil Gibran's *The Prophet*, after which came the public statement of intent. Thomas and Allison both agreed that they were ready to marry. Now, the publicly witnessed agreement:

> *Do you, Allison, choose Thomas as your lifelong partner? Do you seek to love him with all your heart and soul and mind and body? Will you be a loyal, trustworthy and faithful partner? Will you risk vulnerability to love him as his best self? Will you give your whole true self to this relationship, that it may become a growing, healthy, and expansive source of love for yourselves and all who know you?*

In turn, each said, "I do" to these questions.

Now comes the meat of the ceremony, the vows. Each, in turn, repeated these to one another:

> *I promise to work, to play, to dream with you and to do my best to make those dreams come true. I promise to share your tears and your laughter and to allow you to share mine. I promise to respect the need of both of us to have separate space and to come back to you, as I trust you will come back to me. I promise to respect you and to celebrate the ways you are different from me. I promise to be forgiving and patient as we grow in our lives and in our love together.*

We moved directly from there to the ring ceremony. One at a time, with hands trembling a bit and tears welling in their eyes, each placed on their partner's hand this exquisite universal symbol of unity, and, repeating after me, said the following to one another:

> *Of all the people I have known on my journey, it's with you I choose to share the rest of this journey. With you and your life I choose to weave the strands of my life. I celebrate the gift of this relationship and the work of receiving that gift.*

For my favorite part of my role as minister, I declared, "I now pronounce you husband and wife. You may now kiss each other!"

Next, the benediction, the blessing that sends the couple on their way. This is one of my favorite wedding poems. It's an Apache blessing.

> *Now you will feel no rain,*
> *for each of you will be shelter to the other.*
> *Now you will feel no cold,*
> *for each of you will be warmth to the other.*
> *Now there is no loneliness for you,*
> *now there is no more loneliness.*
> *Now you are two persons*
> *but there is one life before you.*
> *Go now to your dwelling-place to enter into the days of your*
> *togetherness,*
> *And may your days be good and long upon the earth.*

I then asked the couple to turn and face the crowd. Everyone in the audience applauded and cheered, as I introduced them as "Thomas and Allison Hansen, husband and wife!" The music started, and the wedding party exited.

A Nontraditional Marriage Ceremony

A marriage ceremony that I especially enjoyed was my own, to Doreen, on September 20, 2001. This was marriage number three for each of us, so we not only wanted to do something different, but to keep the ceremony quite small. We decided on performing the ceremony at Pearl Street beach near our home in Laguna Beach, with Doreen's sons, Chuck, 23, and Grant, 20; and my daughters, Nicole, 21, and Catherine, 19, present. Also, Doreen asked her friend Johnna to be her attendant, while I asked my friend Alan to be mine. In addition, our close friends Chris and Becky agreed to participate, not only as witnesses and representatives of our community, but also to serve as official photographers for the event.

We recruited Jade, whom I've mentioned before, to minister our ceremony. Knowing Jade as a friend and minister/healer/shaman, we knew he would help us develop something memorable and unique. We also agreed to hold the ceremony on or near the autumn equinox, so we set the date for September 20. Everything was set.

The day arrived! All of us, except the bride and her two attendants, Johnna and Becky, gathered at Pearl Street beach and prepared the area for the ceremony. It's near an outcropping of stone that intersects the beach—big enough so that you would ordinarily have to climb over it if it weren't for the "Eye of the Needle." The Eye of the Needle is a natural archway in the stone, large enough to provide a passage to the next beach over.

Near this natural archway, Jade drew a large circle in the sand, which we marked with stones from the ocean, and placed one of three tiki torches in the center of the sacred circle. The other two were placed at the outer edge of the circle, forming a gateway to go through in order to enter the circle, as well as forming a triangle with the middle torch in the circle.

Once all the preparations were in place, we awaited the bride. Before long, I saw her approaching. The steps to this beach are about 100 yards away and descend from about a 100-foot cliff. One of the most memorable parts of the wedding is when I saw Doreen at the top of the stairs, led by Becky, with Johnna at her side. Even from this distance, although I couldn't see her clearly, she took my breath away. It was like watching an angel descend from a heaven called Pearl Street.

She and the other women joined us, and we all stood at the entrance to the circle. I stood with my daughters near the torch on the right outside of the circle, along with Alan and Chris, while Doreen stood with her sons, Johnna, and Becky by the other torch at the perimeter of the circle. I felt surprisingly relaxed, and absolutely joyful—quietly giddy.

The Family Fires

Jade saged the circle, the sacred objects, the four directions, and then the participants. At his signal, Doreen's boys lit their torch, representing their family fire, as my girls lit the torch near us, representing our family fire. Doreen and I then walked from our respective family fires to meet at the gateway between the two, paused together, then proceeded toward the center of the circle, facing Jade. Walking through the gateway together meant separating ourselves from our previous identities and entering into a new one, by choice, together.

Once Doreen and I met Jade at the center of the sacred circle, her sons and my daughters carried the fire from our individual family fires, walked into the circle, and simultaneously lit the center torch, which became the symbol of the union of our family fires.

Jade performed an invocation and a welcome, then proceeded to address us and the group as to the meaning of marriage. Afterward, we turned to our sons and daughters, and each offered a blessing. The boys wished us well, and Nicole and Catherine each read poems. Doreen and I then offered our blessing to each of the children, our own as well as our soon-to-be stepchildren. I gave both Chuck and Grant a gift, and Doreen did the same with Nicole and Catherine.

Public Vows

From here we read our personal vows to each other. The ones I read to Doreen were:

> *I promise to love you—all of you—like you've never been loved before, through all the changes our life together will bring. I will cherish you, respect you, and be as strong a man as I possibly can for you. You're my woman, my friend, my lover, and now my wife, and will be so for the rest of my life. I promise to treat you with honor and remain faithful to you.*
>
> *I will do whatever I have to do to create and maintain our passion. I promise to be the best friend I possibly can, and to let go of any defensiveness and judgments as soon as I am able, so that love, peace, and the Holy Spirit will guide the way. I will enjoin with you in the sensual appreciation of one another and share with you laughter, stillness, enchantment, and the awesomeness of the world around us. I promise to always seek and find my faith in the Great Spirit and my faith in you, and should I forget, to remember who I am and who*

*you are. I will love you always, and I am with you, now
and always, in heart, mind, and soul.*

The most difficult part of reading these vows to my beautiful
bride was getting through them without blubbering like a fool, as
I was brimming over with such happiness. Doreen then proceeded
to speak her vows. She did not contain her tears or her love as she
looked at me.

*When I was a little girl, I was mesmerized by your
personal power as I watched you on your Craner Avenue
stage. Even then, you glowed brightly as you captured me,
and the audience members, with your presence. I watched
you often, although you did not see me. I was the little
girl who was a faceless, nameless child in the group of
kids who lived down the block.*

*But I grew up. And although I never forgot you, and
often recalled my memory of you standing in front of your
apartment, facing away from me in a dreamlike trance, I
never imagined that I would once again meet you, let
alone have the opportunity to love you. To me, you were
the magnificent wild mustang who ran freely on the
plains, never to be with a companion. You were a beautiful mirage that could never be experienced in reality.*

*But then I prayed. My heart, aching with loneliness
for true love, true partnership, and true companionship,
cried out to God and begged, commanded, and prayed to
be with my one true soulmate. I sat on the quartz crystal
rocks of Sleepy Hollow, sending my message to heaven
every day after my jog upon the beach.*

*But I could not find you. And then I heard an inner
voice whisper incessantly: "Go to yoga, go to yoga." And
I listened. And there you were! I was so happy when I
met you, as your presence literally moved my soul and
opened my heart. You made me laugh, and you made me
smile from head to toe.*

*But you weren't ready for me. And so I waited, with-
out ever forgetting you. Daily, I thought of you and spoke
of you. I tried to be busy with other activities, but I realize*

now that I was simply biding time, waiting for you, waiting for you, waiting for you.

And then you called me. You asked me to go for a walk with you, along our beloved Laguna Beach shoreline. And we stayed for a while right here, on this beach where we now stand before each other. I wanted so badly to tell you my feelings, right then, right there. But I was frightened.

So I waited and prayed. And you called me again. That was the night when I discovered, "You're the guy!" You're him, Steven. My one true love from childhood, from all of my past lives, from my heavenly soul group, reunited once again.

Love can never be kept apart, and we had so many times when we COULD have met one another. Not only in childhood, but in the many times when we lived near each other, when we were with the same publishers, and at the same university.

We're meant to be together—it's so perfectly clear. And today, I am honored to become your wife, your life partner, your soulmate, your twin flame. My intention is that our souls will never again be apart. My prayer is that we have learned any lessons that we needed to learn apart from one another, so that we may now be joined eternally.

Steven, my beloved partner, I promise to always be honest with you, to be kind and thoughtful, and to be loving in all ways. I vow to be your best friend, your companion, your confidante, your lover, and your spiritual sister.

I will do anything for you, anything so that we never again have to be apart from one another. I love you so much, and I always want to be together for the rest of our lives, and into heaven, where we'll watch over our children together.

Everyone was deeply moved by these heartfelt expressions. After a brief pause and shared laughter, we moved next to the exchange of rings. The anointing followed. Jade took out an eagle feather, dipped it into a bowl of ocean water that we had earlier collected, and anointed Doreen with the water by shaking the moistened feather at her, sprinkling her with the blessed water. Then he handed the feather to Doreen as I held the bowl. She dipped it into the bowl, anointed me in similar fashion, then proceeded to anoint everyone else in attendance.

The Wedding Blanket

For the "kiss the bride" part, our two assistants, Alan and Johnna, retrieved the "wedding blanket." Jade explained how this was a traditional matrimonial ceremony. As we stood in the center of the circle embracing, Alan and Johnna covered us with our wedding blanket. Jade commented that while the couple was under the blanket, they could do anything they wanted to, and the community of witnesses couldn't comment or tease in any way. The implication was that while under the blanket, *anything goes.* What we did while under the blanket will remain private, but suffice it to say that we were on a public beach with our children and friends watching.

After several minutes, Alan and Johnna lifted the blanket, and we were presented to the world as a married couple. Jade explained that throughout our marriage, whenever one or the other needed comfort, we were to snuggle with each other under the blanket, and in that womblike experience, to seek comfort from one another.

It's interesting to note how in sacred ceremony, often the elements and other beings cooperate so exquisitely. In this ceremony, although we had scheduled it to start at 5:00 P.M., it was quite a bit later when we got started. As we came out from under the wedding blanket, the sun was just setting on the horizon, with its accompanying array of glorious colors. At 7:07 P.M. on that Thursday, just at the beginning of sunset, at the autumn equinox, we were officially declared husband and wife.

❈ ❈ ❈

With birth and weddings being ceremonies that initiate a new cycle, we now turn to ceremonies that consecrate endings.

❈ ❈ ❈   ❈ ❈ ❈

Chapter 24

Farewells

I've moved a fair amount—something to do with contemporary mobility, or the Southern California lifestyle, or both—so I've always made it a point to say good-bye to the house or apartment I was leaving. When my daughters were younger, whenever we moved I would take them back to their former home after it was empty and cleaned up. We'd go from room to room, taking our time, reflecting on some of the memories the former household contained.

I described some "Letting Go" ceremonies in the section on Healing Ceremonies. Another type of letting-go ceremony relates to the ending of a relationship. When a marriage ends, the closest thing we have to a ceremony are the divorce proceedings, which hardly qualifies as sacred ceremony.

When the two people involved in the breakup are getting along reasonably well and have agreed on the dissolution, the ceremony can be done together. It need not be complex for it to be meaningful. The two people involved can write good-bye letters to each other, set aside a sacred space, and read the letters to each other as one part of the ceremony. Exchanging tokens of remembrance can be included.

Ending a Relationship

My relationship with Cindy, my partner of about four years, was slowly unraveling. We had moved in together rather quickly and impulsively, shortly after starting our relationship. Several things happened in relatively quick succession. My daughter Nicole, who was 13 at the time and had been living with me, joined us in our new home. Within a few months, Cindy's oldest daughter, Mimi, who was the same age as Nicole, came to live with us. In succession, my daughter Catherine and Cindy's oldest daughter moved in with us, with our consent. We went from a household of three to a household of six in just a few months, with the added challenge of step-parenting one another's daughters.

In addition to my private psychotherapy practice, we decided to start another enterprise. Rather impulsively and naively, we opened a specialty retail store that carried environmentally friendly products. Cindy was the manager, and I was the owner and the money man. The stress level of all this happening wore us both out. I retreated from the relationship, and generally withdrew into a manageable depression, feeling lost and helpless, but trying to keep the ship afloat. Both of us knew that we were nearing the end of our time together, but neither of us spoke about it, other than occasional oblique references.

It was in the heat of summer that we took a trip to Joshua Tree, a high desert two hours from Orange County. It was in the 90s, dry, and as is typical in the summer, almost no one was camped there. We found a spot where there was some cooler shade, and exhausted, fell asleep on a tarp I had laid out alongside the car.

We awakened as it was approaching sunset. It had cooled down to a more moderate temperature. We had brought with us some sage, candles, and a few other sacred objects. The first thing we did was talk. Separately we had prepared ourselves for this moment—now it was out in the open. Each of us took a few minutes to write a good-bye letter to one another, especially stating our gratitude to the other.

After a calm and rational discussion, we wandered a ways into the desert and found a spot near a rocky hill not far from our campsite. It was a flat rock, perfect for the two of us to sit. I consecrated the space by saging it, then brushing the smoke across the few sacred objects we had each brought with us, and finally cleared each other with the smoke. We sat on the rock facing each other, aligned with the east-west axis, and set up a small, improvised altar just to the side. It had some artifacts from our days together, plus two stones. The stones were ones we had each found near the area where we now sat. They were to be taken with us following the ceremony as a commemoration of this letting-go.

We took turns reading our good-bye letters. It was difficult at times to get through each of them; however, we made it through, and after each of us finished, we hugged each other for one last time.

Then, we both turned our backs on each other, with backbone against backbone. I faced the setting sun, the west, the direction of completions, while Cindy faced the fading light of the east, the direction of newness and rebirth. After a few moments, almost as if on cue, we switched places so that each could meditate on both aspects of this cycle. After a few moments, we climbed from the rock, then faced the setting sun together, although we stood just a few feet apart.

It was this simple yet meaningful ceremony that carried us through the initial stages of our breakup rather smoothly. Although there were still some difficult moments in later stages, recalling the ceremony and our intention helped us grapple with these challenges more effectively.

Letting Go of Your Partner

If your partner isn't amenable to a mutual ceremony, then a personal ceremony can help accomplish the aim of letting go. In *A Healing Divorce*, authors Phil and Barbara Penningroth relate the story of a ceremony for a woman named Jessie, who was ending a four-year relationship with a man she had hoped to marry:

> When we parted, at his choosing, I had a lot of anger toward him. After much thought, I created a ceremony that I shared with a close girlfriend. I gathered mementos of the relationship—photographs of us together, small gifts he had given me. I also wrote a list of each instance in which I was harboring resentment toward him, being as specific as possible. The emphasis was on my need to forgive myself for my part in each situation. . . .
>
> The list was extensive because I had a lot of blame toward him that I wanted to dissolve, and I wanted to consciously release the hold self-anger and self-hate had on my life.
>
> My girlfriend and I took the mementos and the list up to a large ceremonial plateau that we have on our mountainside. We built a large fire, and I burned the mementos while reading the list. I then tossed the list into the fire.

The most powerful part of the ceremony was when I released my anger over an abortion that I had had with this man. He wanted it but I did not. I went ahead and had the abortion to "save" my relationship with him. I needed to forgive myself for compromising what I desperately had wanted to keep—the baby—for the sake of keeping the relationship with him. As I read this portion of the list, I burned a small rag doll as the symbol of the unborn child. This was an important statement for me because, as it turned out, I will never be able to have another child. It was my way of making amends to myself for my responsibility at the loss of motherhood.

Very shortly after our relationship dissolved, my ex-boyfriend fell madly in love with a mutual acquaintance. They married and had a child a year later. I was privileged to hold their newborn son a week after his birth and, two years later, held their second son a week after his birth. I believe that the ceremony I performed played an essential part in the genuine joy I felt when holding those babies.

It's also ironic that, while watching the challenges of their new parenthood, I thought, *Boy, better her than me.* This was especially true for me after they had the second child. My ex-boyfriend's wife—now a friend of mine—was trying to manage a two-year-old who was screaming and throwing food around the kitchen while my ex-boyfriend, a somewhat inept father, was trying to manage a squalling newborn in a toy-strewn apartment. I would not have traded places with his wife for anything, and I uttered a prayer of thanksgiving to God for the circumstances of my life, just as they were.

Whatever the circumstances of your separation/divorce, taking the time to acknowledge the major shift instigated by such a process with awareness, compassion, and strength can reap tremendous healing and useful insights, such as in Jessie's experience. Articulating the mythos involved in such a separation through sacred ceremony will help you to remember your partner with gratitude and find a place in your heart for him or her.

Now we move on to the ultimate separation, the one in which we shed the last vestiges of any attachments to the material world: *death.*

✾ ✾ ✾　✾ ✾ ✾

Chapter 25

Passing Through the Veil

When natural human attachments are severed through death—whether it happens abruptly and unexpectedly, or gradually over time—anger follows the shock of the loss as we question God's authority in these matters. *How could You? Why them? Why now? Who is to blame for this tragedy?* As we struggle to find some meaning in death, inevitably the disheartening sadness creeps in, leaving a trail of tears on the way to the altar of acceptance.

Inevitably, we must come to the only conclusion that makes any sense: It just "is."

The grieving process is like a thread woven throughout the fabric of the reality of loss, especially a loss of a loved one through death. It doesn't matter whether that loved one is human or animal. Creating a ceremony to honor the beloved soul also helps to circumscribe the grief, to provide a vehicle of spiritual reconciliation that can transform the anger and sadness into appreciation, gratitude, and peaceful resolution.

Gianni Is Doing All Right

With ceremony, often small miracles happen, as in the following story offered by Ronny Ruhlmann, of Sydney, Australia, about the passing of his beloved cat, Gianni:

It was a cool but pleasant April evening in Sydney. My girlfriend, Tina, and I had returned home after an uneventful dinner out, and we'd gone upstairs to go to bed. I was about to turn off the light when I heard my cat, Gianni, calling from out front. I raced downstairs and opened the door, expecting see his black, fluffy tail high in the air, but he wasn't there.

A man suddenly appeared and asked, "Are you looking for your cat? I think he's been hit by a car." I raced outside to find Gianni lying in the gutter next to my car, clearly having been seriously injured. His eyes were wide with fear, yet my brave little guy still kept talking to me. Although my heart was in my throat, I knew I needed to remain composed. With the help of the stranger, I managed to slide Gianni onto a piece of cardboard and got him into the car. He didn't complain, although he must have been in terrible pain.

When we got to the vet, she prepared an intravenous drip to partially sedate him as well as help stabilize him. His x-rays revealed that he'd suffered a broken pelvis. I sat with my hand on him, continually giving him Reiki, while quietly asking God to help me. I told the vet that I didn't want to leave him, but she said that it wasn't possible for me to stay. Since I was so distraught, I didn't have the sense to insist on staying. I went home, feeling sick about leaving my beloved cat.

I received the dreaded phone call around 1:00 A.M.— Gianni was dead.

I drove back to the vet to bring him home. When I got home, I carefully cleaned his fur. His elegant, black, plumed tail lay motionless. I set him on my best towel and took him upstairs to my bed. I lay alongside him, as we had done so many times before, and sent him love, telling him I would always be there for him. I wanted to reassure his spirit and assist him in his passage.

By now the tears were flooding, along with the memories. In particular, I recalled the time he had saved my life. I was going through a divorce and was in a lot of pain, each day vacillating between bearable and unbearable. One particular day I ran a bath, lit as many candles as I had, put on Pachelbel's *Canon in D*, and situated myself in the tub. I sank deeper and deeper into the pain, in the hopes of releasing it. I went into a trance, feeling more and more tortured. I thought I was going to die.

I had a constant dialogue with God at this stage, pleading with him to stop the pain and to show me how to heal in another way. I concluded that perhaps it was my time, so I kept going under, seeking the refuge of the warmth and the silence of the bathwater.

Then I had an idea—I'd put my faith to the ultimate test. I said, "God, if it's my time and my divine destiny, then I am ready and I will not resurface. If it's not, then show me why I should keep going." I sank into the water. The moments that followed were timeless. I felt no fear, no need to even breathe.

Suddenly, I popped up to the surface, as though I were being pulled up by my hair! There was Gianni, standing on his hind legs with both front paws on the edge of the bathtub! He had a very knowing look in his eye, which simply said, "No!" It was the purest and clearest of messages from God, and Gianni was the messenger! He was the representative of the animal kingdom, and at that instant, I knew what my purpose was—that I was in some way to champion the animal kingdom.

I sat in the bathtub, exhausted and slightly bewildered, but quiet. The storm had ended abruptly. The water was cold. How long had I been in that trancelike state? It didn't matter. It was a profound and defining moment in my life—I knew what I was about.

As I grieved and reminisced, with Gianni's still body next to me on the bed, I realized that I wanted to commemorate and honor his short life by creating a ceremony for him. As I lived in a rented house, I asked my parents if I could bury him on their property, to which they agreed. After all, it was his birthplace.

That afternoon, Tina and I drove to the house. My folks were away, so it was private and perfect. I chose a spot between two large pine trees that felt like the right place. I dug a small hole, blessed the spot with incense and candles, and then read aloud a thank-you note I'd written earlier that morning. I asked God for a good passage, and asked Gianni to give me a sign someday that he was okay. I asked specifically for a yellow balloon, since it was relatively uncommon, yet quite noticeable.

When I finished, I laid him in the hole, wrapped in my favorite towel. To complete the ceremony, I burned the note I'd written in his honor. I thanked God for bringing him to me and knelt before Gianni's grave, bowing my forehead to the ground in respect and love for my friend.

About six weeks later, I visited my regular veterinarian to buy some food for my other cats. It was a sunny Saturday morning, and as I walked to my car, I stopped in my tracks. There beneath a small shrub by the footpath was a yellow balloon, swaying in the breeze!

Gianni is doing all right.

✼ ✼ ✼

Usually death makes no sense at first. In some instances, it never does and it never will. As we wind our way through the grieving process, dipping in and out of it, with gradually increasing spaces between the intense emotional forays, our sorrow gives way to cherished memories and, hopefully, to a greater appreciation and gratitude for life and for the living. In our effort to find meaning in this grand finale, we must inevitably turn to our spirituality, and reach deep into our faith in the Great Spirit, acknowledging the serious limitations of any rational understanding of the great mystery of death. It's with Spirit that we will ultimately find the comfort and solace that transcends any fear or confusion. There we will find the peace and Presence that allows us let go and move ahead with our lives.

"To Be Continued . . ."

We all know *intuitively* that there's something beyond the veil of our ordinary senses, something that happens to the life essence of all beings once they depart from the physical realm. Sometimes we receive communications from beyond the veil, like the yellow balloon in Gianni's story. Some have actually gone through the veil and returned, in a so-called near-death experience, giving us some clues as to what this transition entails.

Death persuades us to face these ultimate questions and considerations. It's through the enacted mythos inherent in ceremony, through participating in the symbolic and communal rendering of this rite of passage—one that always contains elements intimately familiar to the collective human psyche—that we find the peace of *knowing* that death isn't some ultimate end. The process of ceremony speaks to our soul's knowlege that it's merely a transition in the continuum of life.

In this vein, a friend of mine wanted her epitaph to read simply, "To be continued . . ."

With someone who is on the immediate threshold of death, ceremony provides a way of consecrating this most powerful transition. They may have struggled with a debilitating illness or condition for a length of time when it becomes increasingly apparent that they're ready to surrender. In some cases, the individual consciously says, "No more!" This was the case with Carl, the subject of a healing ceremony performed with the men's group I mentioned previously.

A Warrior's Final Battle

I earlier described a powerful healing ceremony that we did in a men's group with Carl where he rediscovered his will to live, rather than giving up early in his battle with cancer. Through his growing faith, a holistic approach, and a determined attitude, Carl had lived four years beyond the initial prognosis he'd been given, of just a few months to live. He didn't get cured of cancer—his chances for beating it were slim since it was such an advanced stage—but I know he was healed. He was doing well for the first few years, then he took a downturn, and his health deteriorated over the last several months of his life.

There came a time when Carl could no longer attend the men's group as regularly. The cancer was winning, even though it had been beaten back long enough to afford Carl a few more years of life. As many who have gone through this experience have reported, so it was with Carl: His love and appreciation for life, his family, and friends increased dramatically during this warrior's final battle. There were several weeks when Carl would call and say he was going to try to make the group, only to cancel due to depleted energy or another health crisis.

During the last few months of Carl's life, he attended only one more group. Many of us made it a point to visit him either at home or during his increasingly frequent stays in the hospital. By then, he'd turned almost exclusively to Western medical treatments, including chemotherapy and radiation therapy, to sustain his life as long as he could. He was still putting up a valiant fight.

I visited Carl one day after he had been on one of these many trips to the hospital. He'd had a stroke and was partially paralyzed. Now in a wheelchair, he commented several times that his thinking was "weird," as he put it. Although otherwise articulate and coherent, he would forget names for common items, and he'd also gone blind in one eye. In spite of these challenges, he'd kept his sense of humor and was amazingly cheerful and at peace.

We spent a wonderful two hours together talking, laughing and praying. I led him in a guided meditation that proved to be very calming. At this point, being around Carl was a spiritual experience in and of itself. It was amazing to witness how his strong spirit came through so resoundingly, even though his body was steadily and increasingly deteriorating. To say he was an inspiration is an understatement.

The next day, his wife, Julia, called. Carl had been taken to the hospital once more, this time with some extensive internal bleeding. She related how Carl told her that he wanted no more treatment.

He was ready to die.

That same evening, the men's group of which Carl had been a member for several years, met. After a number of years as a group, that night we were having our final meeting. It was a very natural closing. There were only five men left, and three had given notice that they were quitting the group for various reasons. The reality of Carl's dying and the end of the group was one of those remarkable synchronicities.

The Medicine Bag

It was a very somber and sad group that night. I'd called every-one, told them of the situation with Carl, and asked them to bring something to contribute to a medicine bag for him. The medicine in this case was any object that symbolized a member's gift to Carl, and in some way contained an essence of that particular man.

As we gathered for the group that evening, we saged each other and the room. Sitting in a circle, each man checked in, describing his feelings about these completions that were taking place, with both the group and, even more dramatically, with Carl. We agreed to meet the next evening at the hospital where Carl's wife and two daughters were keeping a death vigil.

Then, each of the group members took out our symbolic objects. I placed a simple, handmade leather bag in the middle of our circle next to the candle. Each man placed his piece in the center of the circle around the candle and leather bag. I then placed some crushed sage and cedar into the bag to sanctify and clear it.

One at a time, each man took his contribution into his hands and declared what it was and what it symbolized. George brought out a stone that had found him while on a challenging trek to Mt. Whitney. He spoke of how it represented his determination and sense of adventure. He also noted that it was very smooth, saying that this smoothness represented another side of the stone's hardness. Andrew contributed a small cross, telling how it represented his love of God. The other men each contributed their particular gift, commenting upon the meaning and why they wanted to give it to Carl upon his final passage.

At this point, all of the objects were placed into the leather pouch and passed around the group. With three breaths, each man then blew into the medicine bag one or two attributes that he saw in himself that he would like to give to Carl. The bag was now filled with power transmitted by the blessings of each of the men in the group.

We Bring the Group to Our Brother

The next day, we all met at the hospital at the agreed-upon time. There was George, Andrew, Darrel, Martin, James, and myself.

Carl's wife, Julia, and their daughters, Theresa and Sarah, graciously departed and let us be alone with Carl, knowing that our purpose was to say farewell to our brother.

Carl was bedridden, half-lidded, and didn't even try to speak. I leaned down to him, whispered in his ear that all of the men from the group were here to bid him farewell, and that instead of his trying to get to the group—which, as I mentioned, he'd attempted several times in the past few months—we brought the group to him. When I asked if he could understand, he squeezed my hand to indicate the affirmative. We brushed each other with smoke from burning sage, then formed a circle around Carl. As we held hands, I rattled and sang a spirit-calling song as an invocation, then invited each man to speak their blessing to Carl. Everyone knew that this was our friend's final journey, and each man spoke his blessing with strength and sincerity.

Safe Travels

We were bidding a fellow warrior a farewell on his final expedition in this world. Each time one of the men had said his piece, Carl squeezed my hand, as if to say thank you. Everyone was weeping by the time we'd finished, and some broke into sobs.

Then I presented Carl with the medicine bag, telling the story of how it had been created, and that he was to keep this by his side throughout the time he remained in his body. I described what each of us had contributed, and noted that it was medicine that would help him with the journey ahead. I explained that when he had passed on through the veil, his wife would then be keeper of this medicine bag, and she would in turn pass it along to his daughters.

When I'd finished, Carl squeezed my hand harder than he ever had, and although there was little expression in his face, a tear fell from his eye. I gently wiped the tear and anointed the medicine bag with it.

Each of us then spent a few moments of one-to-one time with Carl, saying our private good-byes. I invited Carl's wife and daughters back into the room and explained the purpose of the medicine bag to them. His wife received it into her care on our behalf. Each of us said our condolences to Julia, Theresa, and Sarah, then departed.

As we left the room, we were silent for several moments as we walked through the hospital to the parking garage. There we said our good-byes to each other. I knew that each of us had been profoundly impacted by this very powerful and loving ceremony.

My final thought that I want to leave you with is: You never know whether this might be the last time you look in your loved one's eyes, so appreciate every moment of every day.

✻ ✻ ✻   ✻ ✻ ✻

Chapter 26
Funerals and Memorials

Any memorial gives us a container in which to honor our loved ones, whether human or animal, who have passed on, and to express our love and grief. Traditional funeral rites dictate how we handle this final transition from body to spirit. The body, or in some cases, the ashes, become the focal point for this process. "Ashes to ashes, dust to dust," a simple invocation, tells us where our bodies came from and where they now go.

Any funeral will usually follow the sequence of a typical ceremony. The lifeless body, or the urn filled with ashes, becomes the evidence that the person is truly deceased. I recall seeing my father's still body, as they say, "resting in state," and watching to see if he was going to breathe. I touched his cold hand, just one more piece of evidence that his spirit, his life essence, no longer inhabited this shell that for 44 years I had known as my father.

My daughter Catherine, ten at the time, had approached his body with me. She was very quiet. After a few moments, she very slowly and carefully reached out to touch his hand lying upon his chest. "Stiller than still," was all I said to her. It's all I could say at that point, so in awe of this miracle of death, that somehow the body had released its source of animation.

Catherine was no stranger to death. It was a few years earlier that a wonderful opportunity appeared to create a ceremony for a pet that had died. I know that by engaging our children in ceremony, we instill and encourage their acceptance of their grief, and teach them that death is an inherent part of the life cycle.

Ranger's Funeral

When Catherine was six years old, living with her mother, she called me one day in tears. She was so upset that I could barely make out what she was saying. It turns out that her pet lizard, Ranger, had died, after being in her care for only a couple of weeks. Although from my adult frame of reference, it was "only a lizard," I knew that for a child, as well as most adults, losing a pet is a very big deal. Also, I saw this as a teaching opportunity for all of us.

I was to set to pick up both of my girls in a couple of hours, so I assured Catherine that I would take care of the body. Offering some words of consolation, I told her that we'd have a proper funeral for Ranger, and told her to write a good-bye note that she could read at the ceremony.

When I arrived, I wrapped Ranger's body in a tissue, then placed the body in a small cardboard box that was just the right size. Once we got to my apartment and settled in a bit, we prepared for the funeral. Nicole had brought a friend, Katie, and all three girls were willing and eager to participate. As we were getting everything ready, we talked a bit about death and what it meant.

At that time, I lived in a fairly small two-bedroom apartment, with a tiny patio in the back. Off the patio was a patch of ground about eight feet long and three feet wide, surrounded on both sides by brick walls. Mostly weeds grew there, although later, following the death of another pet, a guinea pig, it became the burial ground for pets by default. Here is where the girls dug the hole in the ground that would become Ranger's resting place.

"Thank You for Being with Me . . ."

We gathered in a circle, holding hands around the burial site. We burned some incense, and I said a prayer. I noticed Catherine holding a piece of paper, and I asked her to read her eulogy for Ranger. With tears in her eyes but with a clear, strong voice, my child-with-the-ancient-soul slowly and deliberately read what she had written: "Dear Ranger: You were a good lizard. Thank you for being with me as long as you were. I will miss you. I love you. Good-bye."

Following those beautiful words from Catherine's heart, we then proceeded to put Ranger's body in the grave and cover it. Nicole had designed a cross of sticks tied together with string, which we placed on the grave. Once more we bowed our heads in prayer, then closed this simple but meaningful ceremony.

The Exchange

An addendum to this story: I had decided to move after being in this apartment for four years, and was in the process of cleaning up the back patio and yard. I rarely used the patio, and hadn't been in the yard for over a year. It was overgrown with weeds. Or so I thought. We had not only buried Ranger there, but also the aforementioned guinea pig and a small bird whose body we'd found.

When I went to pull these weeds, to my surprise there was a flourishing tomato plant with what turned out to be a bounty of delicious tomatoes. Apparently someone had thrown the remains of a tomato out there sometime ago, and the seeds had germinated and sprouted, unbeknownst to us! I brought Nicole and Catherine out to see this miracle, and exclaimed, "Look what the bodies of the animals we buried have given us!" I explained how these were a magical gift from these animals, perhaps in exchange for taking such care in honoring their lives and giving them a decent funeral. Maybe this was their way of saying thanks.

They both accepted this explanation, as children do, with a depth of understanding that comes from their unique combination of innocence and agelessness. It left me with a feeling of gratitude for this profound yet simple lesson about the cycles of life.

Not only does ceremony satisfy our craving for understanding and completion, providing a container for the grief we feel, but it also helps carry the deceased person's or animal's soul-essence across the veil into the Light. Thus, by creating and executing ceremony, we're doing our friend—whether that friend be human or animal—a big favor.

So, perform such a ceremony with an attitude of service. That's the best way for the richness and magic of ceremony to be called into play, and one of the best ways to honor your loved one.

"And behold, I am with you always, until the end of age."
— Matthew 28:20

Part V

Celebration

Ceremonies

Chapter 27

The Nature of
Celebration
Ceremonies

A ny event that's deserving of honor and recognition can be commemorated through sacred ceremony. It's most often a joyous occasion, and just as in other types of sacred ceremonies, Spirit is the "glue" as well as the foundation for the event. Although healing and transition ceremonies can feature celebrations as a part of them, there are identifying characteristics that make this type of ceremony unique.

Also, not every celebration needs to be recognized through a sacred ceremony. Getting a raise at work might be acknowledged by going out for a drink with your co-workers and friends. Handing out cigars following the birth of a baby is a familiar practice by fathers, and though it's a completely legitimate way to honor this event, it's more of a cultural ritual than a ceremony. And a prayer of gratitude for receiving an acceptance notice from one's college of choice is a sacred act, but by itself isn't a sacred ceremony.

Sacred celebrations may deviate somewhat from the typical structure and content of a ceremony, yet contain many of the ceremonial tools and instruments as described previously. The stages in a sacred celebration will follow the stages of any ceremony, yet they may not be as distinct as they are in a ceremony of transition. Generally, they're a bit looser, with lots of opportunity for spontaneity.

The intention here is just as it sounds: to celebrate; and to do so exuberantly, joyously, and gratefully.

Two Types of Celebrations

Here, we'll be concentrating on two types of celebration: *personal-social celebrations* and those related to *Earth seasons and celestial cycles.* Both comprise distinct elements, yet they have similarities that overlap.

Personal-social celebrations include events such as birthdays, anniversaries, engagements, pregnancies, and graduations; and occasions such as a raise or promotion, winning an award, completing a major project, paying off a large debt, or recovering from an illness. Some national holidays would be included in this category, also.

Earth seasons and celestial cycles include those seasonal celebrations with which we're so familiar, such as Christmas, New Year's, Easter, Halloween, and others, but with greater emphasis on the seasons and cycles that are the original foundations for these ceremonial holidays. In addition to exploring possibilities for creative celebrations to honor the solstice and equinox, I'll have suggestions for what we can call the *other* four seasonal celebrations, as well as some information on the lunar cycles and their meanings.

Three Characteristics of Sacred Celebration

There are three characteristics that differentiate sacred celebration from other kinds of ceremonies and celebrations. These are *gratitude, expressiveness,* and *enthusiasm* (or just for fun, G.E.E.). You'll find these in other types of ceremonies and certainly in other celebratory gestures and festivities, but in sacred celebration these will be even more prominent.

1. Gratitude—This is what makes the celebration sacred. Maintain an attitude of gratitude for yourself, for family and friends who are participating, and especially for the blessings of Spirit that are invoked and that are present for the event. This gratitude can be expressed frequently and in many ways throughout the ceremony. For example, the couple that is honored at a wedding reception goes around the tables and thanks the guests, and toasts are made to honor them.

When celebrating Earth seasons and celestial cycles, gratitude for the Creator and all of Creation is inherent in the honoring of these seasons and cycles.

2. Expressiveness—Within the sacred context established, there's considerable room for expressiveness—specifically, music, song, and dance. What would a celebration be without these elements? As described in the section on ceremonial tools and instruments, music can mean anything from drumming to chanting.

3. Enthusiasm—Passionate and heartfelt expressions of love, affection, and goodwill are abundant in this type of affair, whether for individual(s) who are the focal point of the event, or for the season that's being honored. Small wonder that another word for *enthusiastic* is "spirited," for the embrace of Spirit is felt throughout the process, whether consciously or not. Feelings are expressed enthusiastically, through words, music, singing, chanting, or dancing, and although we usually associate happiness and laughter with most celebrations, they can cover a broad range—from grief to joy to laughter. Whatever the emotions expressed in this type of ceremony, they're put forth enthusiastically and passionately.

From here we move to the first type of sacred celebration, and arguably the most common: personal-social celebrations.

❁ ❁ ❁   ❁ ❁ ❁

Chapter 28

Personal-Social Celebrations

When you think about it, there are so many opportunities to celebrate. Every new day could be cause for celebration.

A friend of mine who had recently moved to the Vancouver, British Columbia, area was fortunate enough to find a place near the ocean. She described how she watched the sun rise every morning, shortly after she had awakened and spent some time reading spiritual writings. She said she was so filled with gratitude at the dawning of the new day that she quietly wept as she sat nestled in the peace and comfort of her bedroom.

Suggestions for personal-social celebrations in the context of the sacred would fill a book by themselves. I invite you to be as creative as possible in developing ceremonies for honoring personal-social events, and to use the guidelines for sacred ceremony outlined previously. Your imagination, coupled with your sincerity and intention, is the key to creating a remarkable and memorable ceremony.

I'll give you some examples of celebration ceremonies I've participated in, and some that others have done. While they don't cover all possibilities, they will illustrate some of the creative possibilities for celebrations that can be generated within a spiritual context.

Birthdays

In reality, this is an anniversary of the day that you arrived here on the planet. Of course, there were many months prior to that during which time you were gestating and forming, but this calendar day marks the momentous event of your full emergence into the material world. This day should be commemorated in some fashion, whether quietly or in some boisterous manner. For children, I'd suggest that you honor them with the culture's more traditional way of celebrating birthdays, aside from whatever else you may do to commemorate the event.

As we mature, however, many people find that traditional birthday celebrations become less satisfying. As someone once suggested, after 11 years old, birthdays shouldn't be such a big deal that you get upset if someone doesn't remember. Yet whether alone or with family and friends, as an adult you can mark your birthday anniversary in your own unique way.

Susan Clark described how she celebrates her birthday in a meaningful way, both alone and with others.

> Near the time of my birthday, I go for an astrological reading, and then the night before my birthday, I do a ceremony that helps me bring the last year to a close by reflecting on the teachings and challenges—identifying all the gifts of the year and giving thanks for them. I light candles, play favorite music, burn incense, take a peaceful bath, and in deep gratitude, go to sleep. On my birthday, I have some completely quiet time while I contemplate the year ahead and what I want out of it and want to bring to it. I use [Doreen Virtue's] angel and fairy cards to get their blessings, and I journal my thoughts and plans. Then I celebrate with family and friends.

� ✥ ✥

At the time of this writing, I'm about to celebrate a birthday. A few weeks ago, I was asked to participate in an evening of meditation and music, with the theme being supporting peace on the planet. The person organizing this affair asked what date in January might work best. After some consideration, I suggested my birthday, January 11, to which he agreed. This is an unusual way to celebrate my birthday, but it feels absolutely right to do so. In light of the turmoil on the planet, dedicating my birthday anniversary to offering a meditation for peace seems like a more appropriate and meaningful gesture than blowing out the candles on a birthday cake.

Anniversaries

Any sacred celebration that commemorates an event of the past is an anniversary. Just like what we usually call birthdays are really anniversaries of an individual's birth, so any significant event can be honored in subsequent years with a celebration.

The first thing that usually comes to mind when someone thinks of an anniversary is a marriage or wedding anniversary, and there are many ways to celebrate these types of occasions. For example, you might choose to annually revisit the place where you honeymooned. However, no matter where you celebrate, you can exchange meaningful gifts, such as a poem written to each other.

There are many other options to honor this type of annual celebration, such as replaying your wedding video or looking through photo albums. If there are children in your family, include them in the ceremony by telling them about your courtship and marriage, as well as relating the story of their birth. Invite friends over for the celebration, and ask them to bring a dish for a shared feast. One couple took the week before their actual anniversary to spend some time reviewing the previous 12 months in depth, and setting goals for the coming year.

Create a release-and-renewal aspect of the ceremony, where you ceremonially let go of any memories, conflicts, and/or challenging characteristics that you no longer wish to have in your life, and affirm those qualities that you do want for yourself and for your relationship.

Periodically create a renewal ceremony, perhaps every five or ten years, that freshens up your memories and your vows and reaffirms your commitment to each other and to the marriage. Any of the elements mentioned above can be incorporated, plus actually writing new vows to take into account your personal development and the maturation of the relationship. Use your imagination, and if useful, check out the books in the Recommended

Reading section at the back of the book on weddings, as most include ideas for renewal ceremonies.

What follows is an example of a renewal ceremony I officiated with some good friends.

Marriage Renewal Ceremony

A few years ago I had the honor to minister a ten-year renewal ceremony with my longtime friends Bruce and Vicki. It started at their home in Flagstaff, Arizona. A mountainous area, their extensive backyard butts up against a national forest, such that when you go through the gate, you're soon walking amidst pine trees. About a quarter mile into the forest is a hill—that's where Bruce and Vicki have often performed other kinds of ceremonies, and that's where we were going to perform this renewal ceremony.

There were about 30 of us gathered at Bruce and Vicki's home that afternoon. It had been raining all morning, and the ceremony was scheduled for 2:00 P.M. As you might imagine, we were concerned as to whether the rain would disrupt our plans, and in fact, Bruce had cleared the garage as a contingency plan. But somehow, it just wasn't as romantic or meaningful to have the renewal ceremony in their garage, so I suggested to those who had gathered that we pray for a clearing that would last until the end of the ceremony. Most everyone joined in a brief appeal to the weather gods, asking that the rain stop. Maybe the gods didn't hear us, or else they were just being a little slow, but it kept raining. We kept improvising, though, trying to figure out how to move everyone from the house to the garage so we could start the ceremony.

The First Miracle

Amazingly, it abruptly stopped raining. This was the first miracle of the day.

A cheer went up from the group. The sky was clearing, and five minutes later, we were all making the trek to the hill. Once we arrived, Bruce and Vicki stood at the very peak with their daughter, Kim, nearby, and myself next to them, as the rest of the friends and family made a circle to enclose the couple at the center. A bamboo arch had already been set up, with flowers layered upon it. After our prayers about stopping the rain were answered, there was a sense of magic and anticipation in the air as we began the ceremony. In fact, the rain stopping and the sun emerging was a perfect nature symbol for a renewal ceremony.

Another friend, Will, lit the sage and smudged the perimeter of the circle of people, then smudged each person. I proceeded with the invocation, and especially thanked God and the spirits for ceasing the rain. It looked very much like a marriage ceremony, but with a slightly different focus. I welcomed everyone and addressed the couple. I checked with them to be sure they were choosing to renew their vows and their marriage, and of course, they agreed.

Somewhat nervously, but still within the celebratory spirit of the event, Bruce and Vicki stated their vows to each other. In addition, they each made promises to their daughter (Bruce's stepdaughter), Kim. She, in turn, verbalized her promises to each of them, as well as her gratitude. She particularly thanked Bruce for being a good stepfather.

Then came the second miracle.

The Second Miracle

I'm looking at a photograph taken just about the time that I proclaimed their relationship renewed and regenerated in the eyes of our Creator. Bruce is kissing Vicki, and as I recall, it was a particularly lengthy and passionate kiss. There, just above their heads and to the right is a rainbow. It arcs down from the sky, and the pot of gold seems to be just behind the newly re-wedded couple! It was an astounding, magical synchronicity, the sort that so often happens when the sacred context for ceremony is clearly and firmly established.

Following the proclamation and the beautiful celestial art that appeared, the couple turned back to back, facing the community of friends and family that were present in order to signify their connection to the people who witnessed the ceremony. The couple then walked down the hill to where the guests had formed two lines opposite one another, then strolled through this corridor of friends and family while everyone tossed flower petals at them.

After many hugs and handshakes, we returned to the house, where there was now a rose bush with a couple of small buds of red roses. Prior to the ceremony, some friends had dug a hole in the ground just outside Bruce and Vicki's back door in preparation for the planting. Bruce set the young rosebush in the hole, and together the couple shoveled a spade full of earth into it. Then, each guest was invited to put some of the earth into the hole, to fill up the area around the bush. When everyone had done so, we gathered once more around this powerful symbol of the couple's renewed and continuing love. Bruce and Vicki thanked everyone once more, and Bruce led us in a prayer of gratitude for the assistance and guidance of Spirit in the ceremony.

Then we all shared in a sumptuous feast.

Remembrance

While we don't usually think of the anniversary of a loved one's passing as a celebration, it really should be. An important focus for such a remembrance is to honor the person's life, not their death. Sometimes this type of anniversary can be performed with a quiet ceremony in solace; other times, it can be shared. Whatever the choice of ceremony, the primary focus should be on gratitude, expression, and enthusiasm. Other emotions may surface as well, particularly sadness or grief. These and other emotions are welcomed in the context of the celebration.

Journey to My Father's Gravesite

My father had been dead three years, and my mother had died 18 months prior to his passing. They were buried in a memorial park in our hometown of Cedar Rapids, Iowa. I had returned to Iowa for my nephew's wedding, and stayed on for a couple more days to visit with my family there. My father had died on September 13, 1992, and it just happened to be close to the anniversary of his passing.

While staying at my sister's, one night just before I went to sleep I received a strong message to visit my parents' gravesite.

Although I had done other ceremonies related to my father's passing (which I described previously), I heeded the prompting to do yet another, this one near the ground in which his ashes had been buried. The next day I did just that. I took some sage, tobacco, a rattle, my ceremonial bandanna, and although I rarely wear any jewelry, I put on a simple beaded choker—my "medicine man" necklace—that had been gifted to me by Hank Wesselman, a fellow shamanic practitioner.

I set out on my journey to the cemetery. I recall being curious about what my sister and brother-in-law, as well as others in the family, might think about my doing this, but when I announced my intentions, they didn't say a thing. As I've noted, I've always been a bit different—to my family I had always been "the quiet one"—and had kept my spiritual and shamanic practices private. At the time of this occurrence, however, I was clearly emerging from the spiritual closet.

I arrived at the gravesite shortly after noon, having stopped along the way for two flowers, one for my mother and one for my father. Although both my parents were buried there, I was more strongly called to perform a ceremony for my father, most likely because it was the anniversary of his death. I sat down in front of my father's grave, and placed a white rock on the east end of it and a dark rock on the west. I put on my bandanna, lit up some sage, and prayed. Then I slowly began rattling. As I did so, I softly sang a song of remembrance, one that had come to me a few months ago.

I'm sure I was quite a sight to the handful of others who were visiting their deceased loved ones' gravesites. I was on a mission, so any initial self-consciousness melted away into the arms of those spirit guides and helpers who were there to support me. My intention and focus was very clear. Tears came to my eyes as I touched on the grief of my father's physical absence. I missed him terribly.

I continued to sing and rattle, then paused, listening to the stillness. I picked up the dark rock, sitting on the west end. The west is a symbol of death, release, and surrender. I asked Spirit to gently remove those characteristics, so reminiscent of my father, that were no longer useful, such as rage, shame, and low self-regard. Then I took a deep breath, focusing on these specific traits, and blew them into the dark rock, returning it to the west end of the grave. I then placed my hands upon the earth, palm down, sending as much as possible of any of these unwanted qualities down into the welcoming bosom of the Mother.

I then picked up the white stone and asked the spirit of my father to instill and support other qualities into me through this rock. I asked for reinforcement of such qualities as directness, dedication, and commitment to spirituality, and more freely expressing my love to family and friends. I breathed these traits into the white rock, and once they were settled, put it into my pocket for safekeeping. It still rests on my altar today.

The Messages

Then something remarkable and unexpected happened. My father, or my father's spirit, communicated with me, as he had when I performed the ceremony in the woods sometime ago. He told me to deliver messages to various family members. I took out the only paper I had with me, some written directions to my sister's house, and on the back wrote down his messages.

I returned to my sister's house and proceeded to deliver some of these messages. Each one struck me as being completely appropriate. These messages were as follows:

Steven—"Take your dark glasses off. Let the world look into the eyes of truth."

Ron (my oldest brother; my father's stepson)—"The darkness prevails. You need to let the light in and learn about love and true understanding."

Wally (my next oldest brother; my father's stepson)—"I have loved you as my own. Your integrity must now become king."

Nancy (my father's stepdaughter)—"My beloved Nancy. I am sorry I was not a better father for you. Your tears and your laughter must be seen and heard."

(When I relayed this message to Nancy, she was deeply touched, and tears welled up in her eyes. She knew that this message really did come from my dad.)

Nicole (my oldest daughter, 12 years old at the time)—"My precious granddaughter. Your 'yes' must always be stronger than your 'no.' Your softness and beauty are my delight."

Catherine (my youngest daughter, ten years old at the time)—"In the betwixt and between, you will never be seen, come out, come out, wherever you are, and show the world your precious star."

Jim (my brother-in-law; Nancy's husband)—"Thank you for loving my daughter so steadfastly. You're a man among men."

(I wasn't sure how Jim would take this, but when I passed this along, he got wide-eyed and teary, something I had never seen him do before).

Needless to say, it was a powerful ceremony, one of celebration that was certainly healing for me, and I suspect, for the others who had received these messages from across the veil.

Grandma Pearl

My wife, Doreen, tells how she honored the anniversary of her beloved Grandma Pearl:

My Grandma Pearl passed away in November of 1994, and I was grief-stricken. But then I felt her spirit come to me and comfort me. Her frequent "visits" helped heal my grief. Over the course of the year following her death, I actually grew to feel closer to her than I had while she was living. Perhaps her physical death allowed us to spend more time together, spiritually.

Grandma Pearl had always had an interest in metaphysics and psychic phenomena. Her frequent visits helped to instigate my renewed passion in spirituality. I feel like Grandma encouraged me in this area, as a way of helping other people, through me.

I decided to express the deep gratitude and love I felt for Grandma Pearl by holding a celebration on the one-year anniversary of her passing. By then, I realized that her spirit was more alive than ever, so it didn't feel morbid or sad to hold this celebration. It was more of a celebration of the continuity of her life, and of our bond following death.

Since Grandma Pearl's favorite flower was the gladiola, I bought 12 in various colors, representing the 12 months since her passing. I arranged them in a large, beautiful vase and put them on the center of my dining-room table.

Then, all alone with just Grandma Pearl and myself, I had an afternoon tea party. I talked with her and played music, just as if she was physically in the room with me. My heart swelled with gratitude for this beautiful, powerful woman who was (and still is) my grandmother. I told her aloud all the things I was grateful for about her. Tears ran down my face as I told her how much I loved her. I felt her presence with me more strongly than ever that day. It was clear that Grandma Pearl and I were both grateful for each other.

The ceremony was a beautiful physical expression of our mutual love and appreciation. I know that Grandma Pearl appreciated being remembered in a positive, uplifting way—after all, that was how she had lived her physical life.

Wedding Receptions

This isn't about the actual marriage ceremony, but the festivities that follow. Once the couple has been officially married and presented to the community as husband and wife, then the party starts! The stage of incorporation in the marriage ceremony—where the newly wedded couple now reenters the community with a new identity—signals the end of the *transition*, opening the way for the wedding *celebration*, typically called the wedding reception.

Just as in marriage ceremonies, there's no "correct" way to create a wedding reception. The more contemporary traditions call for a party, with food, music, and dancing, and these have their roots in many ancient traditions and indigenous tribal celebrations.

Certain elements in modern weddings prevail, such as the newly wedded couple dancing the first dance together, then doing so with one another's opposite-sex parent, followed by all the guests joining in. Tossing the wedding bouquet, the best man giving the couple a toast, and generally eating and drinking a lot all are aspects of this type of ceremony, too.

You can add other elements to a contemporary type of ceremony, or you can choose to create an entirely different type of festivity. Couples from different religious traditions can incorporate key elements from their own cultural or religious traditions. I officiated a ceremony where the groom was Iranian-American and the bride was Jewish. The service was translated into Farsi (the native language of Iran), and we incorporated traditional elements from each culture, both in the marriage ceremony and the reception. If the couple prefers a more contemporary wedding reception, they can choose to weave in other alternative elements. You might consider the following:

— Ask the attendees not to bring gifts, but instead, either suggest that they give a gift of money to one or two of your favorite charities, or perhaps arrange for envelopes to be availabe so that guests have the option of donating to one of those charities. This works particularly well for two people who bring plenty of household goods into the marriage and don't need any more.

— Arrange to have your attendees sit in a circle and have them tell a story about something they know about the two of you, or else recite a poem, offer a blessing, or make some other presentation.

— Burn incense throughout the reception, using one of your favorites.

— Plan a nature hike as part of the ceremony.

— Hold the ceremony outdoors.

— Pass around a goblet, and as each guest pours a splash of wine into it, they offer a blessing. When they've all done so, the couple each takes a drink from the goblet.

— Ask them to bring a gift that symbolizes their wish for you as a couple. For instance, an acorn can symbolize the seed of the strength of the oak tree.

— As a group, take a nature hike. Perhaps go to a high point near the place where you're holding the reception, ask the group to circle the bride and groom, and have the guests offer their symbolic gifts or their blessings.

. . . And the list could go on and on. Turn on your imagination. Remember, it's a celebration. Do something fun, maybe out of the ordinary.

❋ ❋ ❋

I recall a wedding celebration I attended on the Hawaiian island of Molokai. The bride and groom were longtime residents of that island, which has a relatively small population. Everyone knew everybody else.

The entire process went on for a whole week—seven days. I was told that it was being done in the ancient Hawaiian way. The families and guests joined in from start to finish, making fresh flower leis, setting up the yard, preparing the food, and so on. It was truly a community event, and one of the most festive weddings I've ever attended. There was drumming and dancing. The bride performed the hula that she used to first entice her man. A luau followed the actual marriage ceremony, and we feasted and drank for the entire afternoon and evening, some staying until dawn.

When Doreen and I were married, we opted to hold off on the reception until we returned from our honeymoon. We invited many friends and family and specified that we didn't want any gifts, but if they would like, they could offer a blessing in the form of a prayer, song, or simply good wishes. The day came, and there were lots of guests. As the evening went on, some people left, and as the revelry subsided somewhat, we gathered in the living room.

There, both Doreen and I spoke of our gratitude for those friends and family present, for our ancestors who could not be physically with us, and to God. We expressed thanks to all who'd supported us throughout the courtship. We said a prayer together as a group, and since it was quite soon after the horror of 9/11/01, we prayed for peace, for guidance for those who had lost loved ones, and for solace for those who had died.

Once that was complete, we invited people to approach us throughout the remainder of the evening if they had some blessing to offer us. As this subsided and the party banter began again, I quietly pulled out the drums and rattles that were sitting in the corner of the room. As people saw this, some helped themselves to a drum or rattle, and I began a steady, rhythmic beat.

The ancient percussive rhythms began to blend as more people started to play. We drummed for about the next half hour. Some got up and danced, while others would hum or chant to the rhythm. It was very spontaneous and organic, truly a joyous, exuberant expression through sound and movement. This type of improvisational music and dance with a group is one of the passions of my life.

And a good time was had by all.

Chapter 29

Earth Seasons and Celestial Cycles

For everything there is a season,
And a time for every purpose under heaven:
a time to be born, and a time to die;
a time to sow, and a time to reap . . .

— Ecclesiastes 3:1-2

Throughout history, we human beings have honored seasonal and celestial cycles through ceremonial celebrations. These seasonal changes are the naturally occurring signals from Mother Earth that tell us when it's time to plant and harvest, and when it's time to carry out various other activities in our lives. For our ancestors, life often depended on harmonizing with these cycles and appealing to the spirits of the land and sky to bestow their blessings on the community.

For those of us in the modern world, it's hard to imagine how closely interwoven our ancestors' lives were with the seasons and celestial cycles. For nomadic cultures, seasonal changes dictated the movements of the tribe. As we evolved into agrarian societies, settling in particular geographical areas and establishing our communities there, watching the changes in seasons and climate became critical to food production. Spirituality, especially an Earth-honoring variety, was integrated into daily life as a matter of survival, rather than merely a philosophical abstraction or something to be randomly attended to. Sacred ceremonies were a way to bring the community together, to pay homage to the forces of nature, and to ask those natural forces for assistance in sustaining life.

We were much more intimate with the spirits of the land and sky. We had to be.

Contrast this with much of our current Western society, where the flick of a switch produces light, food is readily available at the nearby grocery store, and stories are told by the moving images on our television screens. If it's too hot, we turn on the air conditioning, jump in the swimming pool, or drive our cars to the seashore. If it's too cold, we turn up the thermostat, buy a bunch of blankets and warm clothes, or else light the fire in the fireplace with the gas lighter.

In our contemporary societies, the level of dependency has shifted considerably. We now rely much more on artificial products designed to make life easier, more efficient, and more comfortable than on the harmonious cooperation between one another and the spirits of the land. As we become increasingly subservient to the technological and corporate matrix that governs our world, this then becomes the "god" to be worshipped and prayed to (or cursed!). In this misdirected focus of our spiritual hunger, among other things we sacrifice more leisurely and beneficial cooperation with others in our community.

Invasion from Outer Space

This is vividly illustrated by the story of what happened when television was introduced into a remote Inuit tribe, the Dene people, in northwestern Canada in the '70s. As told by Jerry Mander in *In the Absence of the Sacred*, most of the residents were happy when TV was first introduced, thinking that it would provide a quicker and more effective means of communication between the various Dene communities, some of which are hundreds of miles from one another. These communities had been self-sufficient for centuries, but at the time, the government was making a lot of changes in their areas, and everyone wanted to keep abreast of what was going on.

Television seemed to provide the answer, but it didn't.

Only one hour per week was dedicated to local community programs, with very little of it focused on the Inuits, even though they were the majority population. In addition, 60 percent of the programs originated from the United States. The effect on the lifestyle was insidious.

In Mander's book, Dene woman Cindy Gilday described what happened:

> . . . People are sitting in their log houses, alongside frozen lakes with dog teams tied up outside, watching a bunch of white people in Dallas standing around their swimming pools, drinking martinis, and plotting to destroy each other or steal from each other, or to get their friend's wives into bed [*Dallas*]. Then after that they see a show that is about a man turning into a machine [*The Six Million Dollar Man*].
>
> The effect has been to glamorize behaviors and values that are poisonous to life up here. Our traditions have a lot to do with survival. Cooperation, sharing, and nonmaterialism are the only ways that people can live here. . . . TV always seems to present values opposite to those. . . .
>
> You have to realize that most people still live in extended families here. Ten people might live in a one- or two-room house. The TV is going all the time, and the little kids and the old people and everyone are all sitting there together watching it. . . . It's like some kind of invasion from outer space or something.

After a meeting with members of the Native Women's Association, Mander notes, "One of the most intense discussions of the day concerned TV's impact on traditional storytelling practices. For centuries it had been part of Dene family life for the grandparents to tell tales to the kids for several hours each night before bedtime. With television, storytelling has virtually stopped. Meanwhile, many storytellers are dying off without passing along their skills."

Unlike the Dene people, we who have been raised in Western societies have assimilated modern technology, perhaps without having a clue as to what has been the cost. One major cost is that we no longer live our daily lives in a dynamic, intimate relationship with the earth, with her waters and with her land. Another price we've paid is that we dismiss a deeper stratum of knowledge, one that springs from the innermost well of imagination and spiritual awareness, one that allows you to *know* in your heart of hearts that there truly is a living, breathing Spirit that animates all of this, and that we're an integral aspect of this web of life.

The demonstration of this Power that is behind everything, and especially the expression of that Power in all its various and wondrous manifestations of life here on Earth, can best be experienced when we ceremonially honor the seasons of our planet and the celestial events that govern our lives. These types of ceremonies remind us that in this existence, we're profoundly bonded to the earth and her cycles.

Sacred celebrations help us navigate through the various rhythms of death and rebirth, decay and renewal, and dark and light that are forever unfolding around us and inside us. When we cooperate with these seasonal and celestial changes with our own dance of letting go and receiving, releasing and restoring, and dying and being born anew, life becomes easier. When we coordinate our own internal rhythms with these cycles, we learn acceptance and appreciation. Honoring these seasons through appropriate ceremony helps restore congruency between our spiritual awareness and our instinctual selves.

As we increase in this awareness, we naturally develop greater motivation to take very practical steps to honor the earth, such as recycling, conserving energy, and generally being a good guest. I urge you to explore and experiment with creating ceremony in the name of the true Mother and the true Father. Your great-grandchildren will thank you.

"In every deliberation, we must consider the
impact of our decisions on the next seven generations."
— from the Great Law of the Iroquois Confederacy

❈ ❈ ❈   ❈ ❈ ❈

Chapter 30

Seasonal Holidays

M ost of us are introduced to seasonal celebrations through cultural and religious occasions, such as Christmas, Halloween, and Easter. Rarely, however, are we taught how these holidays (or *holy-days*) are related to seasonal festivities that have been practiced for thousands of years. Yet many of these festivities have their foundations in the Earth-honoring practices of our ancestors. The legends, music, and symbols vary somewhat depending on cultural mythos and religious or spiritual practices, yet the substructure of these types of holidays are strongly embedded in these ancient festivals, where the ever-changing cycles of light and dark were honored.

The seasonal festivals that most of us are at least somewhat familiar with are called the *cross-quarter days*. These are represented by the summer and winter solstice, and the spring and autumn equinox. In the Northern Hemisphere, the summer solstice is the longest day of the year, the winter solstice the shortest (in the Southern Hemisphere *December 21* is the summer solstice; *June 21* is the winter solstice). The equinox days are the crossover points, where dark and light, and day and night are equal in length. We know from the equinox onward that the daylight will either be increasing or decreasing, with a complementary shift in the length of the nighttime.

In the Northern Hemisphere, solstices and equinoxes occur on approximately the following dates:

Cross-Quarter Days

Winter Solstice	December 21
Spring Equinox	March 21
Summer Solstice	June 21
Autumn Equinox	September 21

It's commonly held that these calendar dates mark the beginning of one of the four major seasons: winter, spring, summer, or autumn. However, these are more accurately called cross-quarter days because they mark the *middle* of their particular season, each season comprising one-quarter of the year. A more accurate way of describing these holidays would be to call them *mid-winter, mid-spring, mid-summer,* or *mid-autumn.* By the middle of spring (March 21) in all but the most northerly vicinities, it's clear that winter is completely over, and you have only a few weeks until summer begins to show its full force. Also, most of us think that June 21 is the beginning of summer; however that's not the case. In fact, consider that Shakespeare, who was keenly aware of natural cycles, set his play *A Midsummer Night's Dream* on June 23—right next to the solstice, June 21, or the middle of summer!

For our ancestors, these cross-quarter days were important, but not quite as significant as the actual beginnings and endings of any particular season. The transition points for each season are called *quarter* days, since they divide the year into four distinct seasons. These quarter days were also called fire festivals, since early peoples lit huge bonfires to celebrate the light, the movement of the sun, and to welcome the start of the next season. Since these celebrations were communal events where everyone feasted, the fires were used for cooking as well.

The quarter days were a time of festivities, just as the cross-quarter days were. These festivities allowed the community to pause, congregate, and prepare for the coming season, while at the same time acknowledging the passing of the previous season.

These quarter days are often known by their ancient Celtic or Greco-Roman names as follows:

Quarter Days (Northern Hemisphere)

Imbolc, also known as *Candlemas*	January 31/February 1
Beltane, also known as *May Day*	April 30/May 1st
Lammas or *Lughnasad* (pronounced LOO-na-sa)	July 31/August 1
Samhain (pronounced SOW-en), also known as *All Soul's Day, All Saints Day, Halloween*	October 31/November 1–2

Quarter Days (Southern Hemisphere)

Lammas/Lughnasad	January 31/February 1
Samhain	April 30/May 1
Imbolc/Candlemas	July 31/August 1
Beltane	October 31/November 1

(From here on, I'll describe seasonal celebrations from the perspective of those in the Northern Hemisphere, as those are the ones with which I'm most familiar. I invite readers in the Southern Hemisphere to translate these festivals into their appropriate time frames.)

Although universally celebrated by our ancestors, these quarter holidays have been largely ignored in contemporary times. Fortunately, as many more people develop a keener interest in reconnecting with their ancestral roots and honoring the earth, these quarter, and especially the cross-quarter seasonal celebrations, are being revived and renewed.

When put together in sequence for the year, from the growing light to the fading light, we have eight phases, or seasonal markers, with some of the holidays or events that take place on or near those dates:

Quarter and Cross-Quarter Days	Secular and Religious Holidays	Dates
Imbolc/Candlemas	Groundhog Day	January 31 February 1–2
Spring Equinox/Ostara	Easter, Passover, "Spring Break"	March 21*
Beltane	Labor Day, May Day, Mother's Day	April 30/May 1st
Summer Solstice/Litha	Graduation, Father's Day	June 21*
Lammas/Lughnasad	(No common secular holiday)	July 31/August 1
Autumn Equinox/Mabon	Harvest, Rosh Hoshanah, Yom Kippur	September 21*
Samhain	Halloween, All Saints Day, All Soul's Day	October 31/ November 1–2
Winter Solstice/Yule	Christmas, New Year's Day, Hanukah, Kwanzaa	December 21*

These dates are approximate

By creating sacred ceremony to express our gratitude and our joy for these seasonal markers, it helps us commemorate our often forgotten and neglected connection to Mother Earth. By periodically pausing, taking time out to stage sacred celebrations in honor of these Earth rhythms, we become more keenly aware of how these seasonal cycles are very much reflected in our own internal rhythms. Spring and summer are naturally more expansive and expressive, both in the natural world and in our bodies, while autumn and winter are a time of slowing down, of releasing and turning inside. Our bodies and our psyche coordinate with this cycle by our turning inward as well, spending more time in stillness and contemplation, and thus corresponding to the decreasing light.

At the onset of winter (October 31/November 1), we can greet the darkness without fear, reminded via the ceremonies appropriate to this seasonal initiation that we're inseparably bonded to these Earth rhythms, and through private and communal celebrations, that eternal life will endure the coming darkness. At the beginning of spring (February 1), in spite of any residue of winter, we're reminded with visible signs that life is renewing and the light is increasing once again. We notice in our own makeup the budding desires to become more active.

So whether you live in the Northern or Southern Hemisphere, when you watch the light shift and change, and observe other signs that tell you one season is passing away while another is making its appearance known, you can consecrate these changes through sacred celebrations. These ceremonies will annotate the seasonal shifts and allow you to move through them with greater grace and dignity.

I'm not suggesting that you forego the contemporary ways of celebrating commonly recognized holidays. In fact, I encourage you to do so, in ways that are congruent with your particular religious and/or spiritual beliefs. These contemporary holidays serve to unify us as a culture or religious group, and connect us as human beings through the symbols, songs, and stories that are representative of the archetypal Earth rhythms and seasons upon which these holidays are based.

In addition to these more familiar celebrations, I suggest that you explore and experiment with ways to create ceremonies to honor these quarter and cross-quarter days. From your creative, instinctual imagination and your knowledge of ceremony, you can devise a beautiful private or communal celebration—one that acknowledges the innate elegance of the changes in season. Doing so helps us be a better guest on this planet.

Again, your great-grandchildren will someday thank you.

❋ ❋ ❋   ❋ ❋ ❋

Chapter 31

Celebrations for
All Seasons

Any ceremonies that serve the purpose of honoring our Earth
Mother can be appropriate for any of the quarter days or cross-
quarter days. In the spring and summer, as the days lengthen,
Nature will probably beckon you outside. For the autumn and winter seasons, you may choose to do these ceremonies indoors or
outdoors, depending on where you live, how cold it is, and on any
other personal preferences.

The primary purpose of all of these sacred celebrations is to
honor the earth and honor the cycles of light.

Some of the following are best done with others, as a community, whether it's just a few people or a larger group. Others can be
done alone or with one or two friends.

Give-Away

In *Celebrate the Solstice,* Richard Heinberg describes the history and function of the give-away ceremony:

> In agricultural villages in many parts of the world, any yearly
> food surplus is distributed at seasonal festivals. In some cases, the
> surplus goes first to a headman who, acting as trustee of the peo-
> ple, gives it away at a feast. He acquires status or prestige in this
> way, and so competing headmen may vie to see, not who can
> accumulate the most wealth, but who can give the most gifts.

For the Native American nations of the plains and the Pacific Northwest, give-aways were an ancient and essential feature of tribal economy. White settlers of the nineteenth century, however, saw these festivals as a threat to the capitalist values that their own government was then seeking to instill in the Native population. The give-away and the *potlatch* (the name for the practice among the nations of the Northwest) were discouraged and even legally banned, and Indians often resorted to heroic measures to continue the custom in the face of persecution and punishment.

In many tribal societies, no prestige flowed from wealth per se; indeed, to keep a surplus while anyone else was in need was considered shameful. In most societies that practiced the give-away, the socialist maxim of "from each according to ability, to each according to need" was put into practice far more effectively than was the case in any of the failed industrialized communist nations of the twentieth century. In the tribe, communal values were neither decreed nor enforced by a centralized authority, but had deep roots in culture and were spontaneously preserved and expressed in the course of daily life in every family and village.

A give-away ceremony can be as simple as asking guests to bring very practical items, such as food, clothing, or other useful things to be exchanged. Another way is to have the guests bring an object that has personal meaning, one that might be difficult to let go of. This object will have a story that goes with it, one that says something about the owner. With this type of ceremony, the group should be relatively small, ideally about eight to twelve people, at maximum, twenty.

It's best that the object be one that symbolizes a personal triumph over a challenge, or some life transition that the person has gone through. Or it can represent a part of the person that they have outgrown, or an object that was quite useful for a time in their lives, but now has mainly sentimental value. It's critical that those invited understand and are clear about the intention of the ceremony and how to choose the appropriate item.

A give-away is *not* about giving away something that you no longer have use for, or passing along a gift someone else gave you for which you had no use anyway. Instead, it's about passing along an object that represents something significant about you, and in turn, when you give it to someone else, you're passing along that significance—and that blessing—to them.

I gave away a homemade rattle at one of these types of cere-monies. It was beautiful, one of the first I'd ever made, hand-painted with symbols that had been given to me during a journey. I initially rejected the idea of giving the rattle away, because I *really* liked it, and it signified my deepening involvement with shamanic work. I still miss that rattle sometimes; however, I also know that the per-son who received it is benefiting from owning it.

In exchange I received a small, jade Buddha figure from a woman. It continues to occupy a center place on the living room altar, and seems quite content to do so. I'm certain that its owner had some reservations about letting it go. The story associated with this Bud-dha was that someone had given it to this woman during a pro-tracted and potentially life-threatening illness. She remembers how comforting it was to see it sitting at her bedside during her recovery, and she had been well for four years at the time of this particular give-away ceremony.

When you consciously coordinate this type of ceremony with Earth's seasonal holidays, the act of giving isn't only a relinquishment; it becomes a metaphor for the release or death of the old season. The act of receiving something new in your life opens you up to whatever the next cycle brings, to a rebirth or a new beginning.

If you perform this ceremony outdoors, create the sacred space by having a physical circle within which participants may carry their gifts. If indoors, consecrate the space that will be used for the cer-emony. In either case, place a blanket or small table in the center of the circle where you and your guests will place the objects to be offered. Ask everyone to hold on to their gifts for the time being. Burn a candle in the middle of the altar, perhaps decorated with other items appropriate for the season—for instance, a bough of fir dur-ing the winter seasons, flowers during the spring, or fallen leaves dur-ing autumn.

Once everyone has gathered, open the ceremony with incense, prayer, and music. Let everyone know what the intention is, that one of the tasks is to let go of whatever they brought with them, and to do so with gratitude. This is difficult sometimes, but very possi-ble to do. Answer any questions that may come up, then proceed.

First, each person takes a couple of minutes to describe what they brought to give away, and what meaning it has for them. Then they describe what they hope the gift will bring to the recipient, who at this point is unknown. Once they have told the story of the gift, then they place it on the altar.

There are a couple of different ways to administer the giving and receiving of the items that participants brought. One way is to have someone choose the gifts to be given, and who will receive them. Designate either the youngest or oldest in the group to do so. Explain that it's best that they follow their intuition in their choices, and that they don't have to make any logical sense. They would start with one of the gifts and give it to the intuited recipient. The recipient may comment or not. The one choosing the gifts continues until all are given away.

An alternative is to have everyone place their gifts on the altar when they first arrive. When it's time to start, get everyone seated, and designate someone in the circle to initiate the process. This person chooses the gift to which they're most drawn and asks who the giver is. The giver then tells their story about the gift. Then the giver becomes the next recipient, choosing one of the other gifts. This continues until all the gifts are dispersed.

With either procedure, once the gifts are all accounted for, open the floor for sharing observations and comments. Once this is complete, then it's time for a delicious feast. Be sure to ask everyone ahead of time to bring a dish of food to share.

Sweat Lodge

Although there's evidence that similar ceremonies were performed in other cultures, a sweat lodge is most closely identified as a Native American tradition, useful for healing and purification. There are several hundred different types of sweat lodges, or *inipis*, and for those of us who aren't Native American, fortunately some of these traditional inipis are being offered for the use of peoples of all ethnicities and races.

There are commonalities to this powerful and sacred ceremony. It takes place in a closed, tentlike structure, which you enter in a particular fashion. A huge fire is started several hours before the start of the lodge, and in the fire are a number of stones being superheated by the fire.

Someone trained in the tradition of the particular sweat will give participants instructions, and guide the sweat. When it comes time to start, participants enter in a prescribed manner, then sit down in a circle around a small pit dug in the earth. Typically, seven heated rocks are brought in, the flap or door is then closed, making it completely dark but for the glowing rocks. This is the first round. The leader places some herbs on the rocks, often will say a prayer and/or sing a song, then pours water over the rocks to create steam, which also carries with it the aroma and the effects of the particular herbs used.

After the first round, in which prayers and songs are offered, the flap is opened, and an equal number of heated rocks are brought in. This is repeated three times more in most lodges, for a total of four rounds, with each of the four rounds having a different theme and emphasis. The challenge isn't to "gut it out," but to surrender any discomfort or suffering to Spirit to have it transformed, and thereby, healed. The purpose is also to send prayers outward to any person or situation in the world that needs healing.

Earth Renewal Ceremony

Jade Wah'oo Grigori, whom I've mentioned before, contributes this story of a ceremony inspired by his mentor, Juan Pena, a Native American shaman. Under "Grampa Pena's" tutelage, Jade became the keeper of "the ways," a centuries-old shamanic tradition from the Southern Ute native peoples. This ceremony in particular describes how a ceremony can, unlike a ritual, evolve over time as new information is received.

The Dance of Renewal

My Grampa Pena stood under the overhanging roof of his porch.

"Grandson," he said, "when I was young like you, these hillsides were covered in tall grass," he indicated with a gesture of his hands waist-high growth, "and wildflowers of every color grew all over these hills." Upon

hearing this statement I was shocked, for we were standing in the midst of a semi-arid desert, the hillsides barely
supporting scattered rye grass and prickly pear cactus.

"The seasons are different now," Grampa spoke. "The
winters are too long and too cold; summers are too short
and too hot. It's like this, Grandson, because nobody
cares for the earth anymore. Nobody sings the earth
awake in the spring, dances her dance of celebration in
the summer. No one sings her to sleep in the fall. There
is no one left to dream the dreams of the Earth Mother.
That is why it's so bad these days. Like a mother whose
children steal from her, spit upon her, and abuse her, even
that mother must pull herself back when she has nothing
left to give. Yes, sir! Our Earth Mother, she has pulled
herself back from the world."

This he said with sadness, drawing his arms and
clenched hands up tight to his right side. "And Grandson,
in your day it will get much, much worse." My gut felt as
clenched as his fists. A nausea spread through me as the
truth of what he spoke settled into my awareness.

Then Grampa Pena shuffled forward, arms extended
in supplication, then stepped backwards, pulling his
hands into his solar plexus. He next turned 90 degrees to
the right and shuffled forward and back again, repeating
this for each of the four directions, with great precision
and power. Returning to face the east, the old man spread
his arms wide in a circle, embracing the universe, then in
one fluid motion, moved them into position as if cradling
a newborn child. After this, he dropped his hands and
arms toward the earth, then turned to me and spoke.

"Grandson, I give this dance to you. It's the dance to
awaken the Earth Mother in the spring, celebrate her in
the summer, put her to sleep in the fall, and dream her
dreams in the winter. Grandson, I remember the dance.
There is a song that goes with this dance. But the one
who carried that song, I guess he got killed when the
invaders came and slayed our people. You're going to
carry this dance out to the people, but first you must go
find the song that goes with it."

I was stunned by the task my grandfather had just set before me. How was I to find a song that had been lost for over 100 years? I had no idea of how to do so. Regardless, with that as my dedication, I set forth upon my quest.

Never "looking" for the song, I sought to be ever more available for the song to make itself known to me. The years went by. Juan Pena died, a hearty man of 104, in 1982. With his death, the caretakership of the knowledge and ceremonies he had carried all his life, as with the grandfathers and grandmothers before him, passed to my care. Although never forgotten, the quest for the song went onto the back burner.

The Song of the Earth Mother

Spring equinox, 1986: I was spending the day in prayer and fasting from sunrise to sunset. I had chosen as the place to do this my "grandmother cedar tree," a large and beautiful red cedar located at the mouth of a steep-walled canyon deep in the Southern Colorado wilderness. Contemplating the inexplicable dying of the trees I had heard about on the radio that morning and the swift erosion of the sandstone I had seen in the canyon earlier, I asked myself what this was all about. I went into the Silence and from there asked the question, and opened myself to Spirit.

A deep and sultry woman's voice spoke from the cliffs across the way. "AIDS."

With a crescendo of awareness, I understood. I understood what Grampa had told me about the Earth Mother needing to pull herself away when she had nothing left to give. When her presence is withdrawn, there is little left to hold the physical form in coherence. The trees, without her essence in full force, were no longer able to withstand minor assaults, such as from gypsy moths or environmental difficulties. Rocks had the binding force of their crystalline structures diminished to the point where they had begun to disintegrate. Earth Mother/Form-Giver was the essence of our immune system. With her pulling back, we have become increasingly susceptible to the rampages of viruses and bacteriological infections.

I cried. I sobbed and wept, wracked dry of tears, "What can I do, Mother?" I called out. "My life belongs to you, to do with as you wish, what is it that you want me to do with this knowledge?"

As soon as I asked that question, my mind jumped back 14 years, to 1972, when I was dying of a "terminal" illness. Living in a tipi in the Colorado Rockies, far away from other humans, my life force had ebbed to the point that on one particular morning I knew, with a certitude, that this was the day I was going to die. Dragging myself outside my lodge, I pulled myself upright by grabbing onto a limb of oak brush. Standing upon wobbly legs, I spread my arms to the morning sun and breathed in the air of our Mother's breath. "Thank you. Thank you for this life. It has not been an easy life, but it has been a good life." I spoke my final words in this life, a prayer of appreciation.

Up from the ground beneath my feet, a power, vibrating and overwhelming, surged through my whole body. Life! Vigor! Vitality! I was alive, renewed, healed! "Mother," I called out, "my life belongs to you! Guide me; have me do as you wish. My life is no longer my own, but yours!"

In response to my plea, from the cliffs across the way, her voice sang forth with a song evocative of her Spirit. As she sang, I sang subvocally with her. She continued singing, and by the fourth time, she sang *through* me, my voice no longer my own, but hers!

That was the song of the Earth Mother! The very song that Grampa had instructed me to find *had already found me 14 years earlier!*

Enthralled and ecstatic, I sat beneath the red cedar tree. I went into the Silence, and sat with this gift. Then unexpectedly and spontaneously, I sent the song back to her. "Earth Mother, this song is sung in the ancient tongue that no one any longer understands. The people I work with speak English, Earth Mother. Please return this song in English." Then I sat again within the Silence.

After several moments, from the cliffs I heard her sing, in English: "Cloak of Water, Cloak of Fire, Cloak of Air, Cloak of Earth, We bring you Birth! Water Flowing, Fire Burning, Air Blowing, Earth Growing, We bring you Birth!"

The Ceremony Evolves

The dance, which my Grampa Pena had passed to me, now had the song to go with it. Of course, a dance and a song in and of themselves do not make a ceremony, yet now the work could begin. Spirit had placed these two primal ingredients in my care. Now it was up to me to build on these ingredients. With continued meditation from within the Silence, a vision of the earth-renewal ceremony and its component structures emerged. Each time I worked the ceremony, adjusting it here and there, it came into greater alignment with natural law, allowing the ceremony to evolve into its current expression.

Originally, I simply placed a stone upon the ground, and while drumming and singing the song, danced the dance to each of the four directions. The buildup of power was palpable. While immersed in this power, I had a vision of a dance pole around which I was to dance. With further meditation and consultation with Spirit, I was shown details of the vision, including the manner of construction of the dance pole. I then built the dance pole given to me in vision.

The pole itself is about 12 feet tall, with seven notches evenly spaced up the west side. This notched pole is a "ladder" of Mongolian origin, which is my ancestral heritage. About one-third of the way from the top is a hoop woven of 13 boughs of evergreen, placed perpendicular to the pole. The hoop is connected to the pole via a four-directional cross of stout sticks. From each of the ends of these sticks, ribbons are hung for each of the respective directions: red for the east, yellow for the south, black in the west, and white hung from the north. The entire construct is referred to as a *Yupa*. The Yupa is placed into a receiving hole in the earth so that it stands upright.

Once the Yupa, or central dance pole, was established, refinements in the ceremony began to flow forth. As more and more people participated in the dance, two major developments came into being. The first was a *moon circle*, a ring of dancers moving moon-wise, or counterclockwise, around the perimeter of the dance grounds. The persons dancing in the moon circle are maidens and grandmothers. These women hold an amplified "lunar force field."

The second addition was to place a large *dance drum* in the northeastern quadrant. Although incorporating the moon circle had tangibly intensified the power, after a few weeks with the drum in the northeastern quadrant, it became apparent that something was off. Upon further investigation and contemplation, it became glaringly apparent what was wrong. Since the participants dancing to the four directions from the Yupa represented the earth, the women dancing around the perimeter represented the moon, and the drum was the heartbeat of the sun, we realized that the sun was positioned *between* the earth and the moon! So we placed the drum outside the circle of moon dancers, which brought an immediate feeling of rightness and harmony.

As time went on, there was still a sense of something being slightly askew. There were times of the year when the ceremony seemed more balanced and powerful, particularly in late spring and late summer, when the drum was aligned with the rising sun. From the moment of this realization, the drum has been placed in position with the rising of that day's morning sun. Since then, the power of the earth renewal ceremony has increased exponentially.

The alterations introduced to this ceremony were not mine alone. Individuals who had become dedicated dancers of this ceremony inputted their own visions and inputs, and these refinements were incorporated as appropriate to the intent of the earth renewal ceremony.

Fire Ceremony

Fire played an important role for early humans in the celebrations that took place during these seasonal markers, particularly (though not exclusively) on the quarter days. Since these seasonal marker days were determined by the characteristics of the light, fire was a powerful symbol and expression of that light. Also, it served a practical function of cooking food for the feasts that were an integral part of these festivities. Fire represented not only the heat and fullness of the sun in mid-summer, but also the warmth and promise of its eventual return in the middle of the darkest days of winter.

If you live in a place where you can safely and legally do so, I'd suggest making a bonfire or even a campfire, and let it be the focal point of the ceremony. Another option is to build a fire in the fireplace. The only limitation with a fireplace is that you can't form a circle around it, but in that instance, a half-circle will do. If these aren't possible, use candles as the centerpiece.

You can adapt other ceremonial proceedings to these seasonal festivities, such as a healing ceremony, or you can keep this purely a quarter day or cross-quarter day celebration as fits the needs. In either event, the idea of the fire festival is to feast and have fun.

Ask everyone attending to bring an item of food. Of course, if you do this outdoors, people can bring food to cook in the fire. Ask them to bring drums, rattles and any other percussion instruments (didgeridoos and flutes are nice additions). Once you've welcomed everyone, established the ceremonial space, called in the spirits, and offered prayers, then set the intention for the drumming.

You can drum for healing, for peace, or simply to honor Mother Earth. You can drum to honor the increasing light, the fullness of the light, or for the light to carry you through the periods of increasing darkness. You can even drum to welcome the darkness, as a means to honor not only the light, but also to honor the shadow. Invite people to sing or dance as they're moved to do so.

Once the intention has been set, as the organizer and facilitator of the event, start the drumming. The initial beat will establish the rhythm, so I'd suggest that the pace of the drumming match the season. For winter months, a slower, steadier beat coordinates with the season, whereas a faster rhythm works for the holidays that celebrate the increasing light.

As in many instances with drumming in groups, the rhythm takes on a life of its own. As I've noted previously, after a few minutes of drumming, people tend to go into a mild trance. As this happens, spontaneous movement and spontaneous shifts take place in the rhythm, often becoming quite magical in the expression. In some instances, there is spontaneous chanting that blends with the overall rhythms.

Once the drumming stops—and although you can cue the stopping with a signal, it often stops without any prompting—maintain the silence for a few moments. Through the drumming, you have built up considerable power within the group. Take a few moments of silence for everyone to feel and embody that power as it leads to the next step, which is to extend that power outward.

Next, offer a prayer that this power goes out to the world to those in need of its healing force. This can be for a healing for an individual, for the land, or for a world conflict or crisis. To extend it to individuals, ask people to state out loud the names and locations of those they know among their families, friends or in their community who are suffering and can use this blessing. Others in the group can then contribute to this extension of healing power by hearing these names and then conveying their blessings to the named individual.

This simple yet powerful ceremony can then be concluded with another prayer, this one of gratitude for the abundant blessings we're all privileged to have. Once the ceremony is completed, then it's time for the feast! At any time during or after the feast, the music, drumming, and dancing can be reinstigated.

If you want to add a nice touch, and if you think the group will be receptive to this, after the drumming and the healing blessings are sent forth, you can pass among the participants a simple food item, such as grapes, that you've prepared in advance. Similar to the healing ceremony and peace vigil described earlier, when everyone has an item of food, one person starts by feeding the person next to them in the circle, that person feeds the next, and so on until it comes full circle. This symbolic piece of food represents how we feed and nourish each other, emphasizing how we're all connected as a community.

✺ ✺ ✺   ✺ ✺ ✺

Chapter 32

Earth-Honoring Ceremonies for All Seasons

The main objective of any of these types of ceremonies is to honor Mother Earth, to take time out to express your gratitude for all of the gifts she gives us, and to acknowledge the passing of the seasons from one to the next through the one-year cycle it takes for the earth to move around the sun. There are multitudes of ways you can express your gratitude on these quarter days or cross-quarter days.

Some of the following suggestions can be done without creating a full ceremony, although you can certainly make any one or more of these an aspect of your holiday celebration. These are just a few of the myriad ideas that you can explore, and as always, it's the intention and sincerity with which you do them that counts.

Energy Fast

For a 24-hour period, from one sunset to the next, disconnect yourself from the electrical and technological "matrix." Unplug the phones, the computer, the television, and don't use any electrical lights or devices, not even ones powered by batteries. Light candles, build a fire in the fireplace, and definitely watch the sunset. Have dinner by candlelight. Eat only raw foods for dinner that evening, such as a salad. Go to bed early.

In addition to honoring the season, you're experimenting with the dependence we have on these sources of energy while getting a sample of what it must have been like for people in centuries past. Sometimes engaging in this type of experiment leads people to be more conscientious about their usage of electricity. Also, doing so can help you meditate on the cycles of the seasons. In fact, the sunrise and sunset perfectly encapsulate the growing light and the decreasing light in a short time span, corresponding to *Imbolc* at sunrise and *Lughnasad* at sunset. These times of the day can also be good times for ceremony, such as a healing ceremony of release at sunrise.

On a rather chilly (for Southern California) December 20 a couple of years ago, I went to the top a nearby hill just before dawn. There I did a simple ceremony, where I drummed as the sun was rising, as a gesture of welcoming the returning light. At times, I jokingly tell people that I did this so the light would return and the days would get longer, and sure enough, it worked!

Cleansing Fast

In many religious and spiritual traditions, fasting for one to several days is a discipline that's not only potentially healthy for the body, but can also be performed as a sacramental gesture to honor any particular seasonal holidays. The Druids, the pre-Christian Celtic priests, would purify and cleanse themselves by ingesting only apples and apple juice for three days prior to performing ceremonies. When you make a sacrifice of any sort, one where you give up something for a period of time, the spirits approve and smile upon you. Abstaining from any habit, craving, or addiction for a period of time will do, and one of the most basic means of abstinence relates to our usual eating habits.

Cleaning out via your diet and dedicating this action to the seasonal festivity allows you to acknowledge the letting-go process that's the hallmark of any seasonal shift. In and of itself, it's a release ceremony. By doing so at the very basic, elemental level of food and eating—that is, by foregoing your normal diet—it becomes a conscious and conscientious way to celebrate the coming of the new and the passing of the old. (An excellent resource for fasting is

The Miracle of Fasting by Patricia Bragg and Paul C. Bragg, available from Health Science Books).

Consult the appropriate health professionals in order to determine what type of cleansing diet is right for you. For some, an appropriate regimen is to abstain from all foods and drink only water. Another method is to do a juice fast using only fruit and vegetable juices. When I've done this sort of cleansing fast, I use fruit and vegetable juices with protein powder, plus psyllium seed husks, which is an intense fiber useful in cleaning out the colon. I enjoy coffee, so a sacrifice for me, albeit mild, is to give up coffee for the period of the fast.

Do this "cleansing fast" anywhere from one to seven days. Again, use good judgment and experiment in different ways. Try drinking only water for one day. Or try a version of a fast that's appropriate for you over a three-day period, building the fast around the seasonal celebration—the day before the holiday, the holiday itself, and the day following.

When I've engaged in this type of ceremony, I've linked up with other people. It helps a great deal to have at least one or two other people doing it with you, for motivation and support. Also, make it a point to check in daily, and if at all possible, meet face-to-face as a group. If it's possible to meet, open with a prayer and smudging. Have each person check in as to how they're doing with the fast, then follow with a few minutes of a reading from a spiritual text, followed by a short discussion. I'd usually suggest closing with a feast, but in this instance, your feast may consist of water or juice! Each day that you do the fast and meet as a group, a different person can bring in the text for the reading.

An alternative to meeting in person is to communicate via the Internet. Each person can take turns finding and sending spiritual readings via e-mail. Yet another way is to do this by phone, either conferencing the call, or if geographically separated, meeting in subgroups and using the speakerphone. Use your imagination to discover ways in which you can support each other.

At the conclusion of the fast, I highly recommend the fire festival ceremony, and as a part of that, a release ceremony of your choosing. See the section on Healing Ceremonies to find one that would be suitable for your group.

Recycle and Trash

If you have a garage full of stuff, you don't have to wait for spring to go through a portion of it and recycle what you can, and trash the rest. My wife, Doreen, did this recently, and we held an informal ceremony using the fireplace, burning about four grocery bags full of old papers that had been accumulating.

Any of the eight seasonal markers are great times for this sort of physical and psychic housecleaning. Trust your own intuitive sense, and as I've said, experiment. On one of the quarter days, clean out your closet, and recycle your clothes and shoes. On another, go through the boxes in your storage closet. If your city doesn't provide recycling services, take some of those items to the appropriate recycling resource, or initiate a campaign to bring recycling to your community.

Another Earth-honoring task is to pick up trash. Whenever we go to the beach, Doreen is always looking out for broken balloons, as the seagulls sometimes mistake these for food, get them caught in their throats, and die. There's a section of beach that I patrol every so often, taking a trash bag and picking up trash. The Surfrider Foundation regularly sponsors community "clean the beach" days, where volunteers gather at a particular site and collect all the refuse and recyclables. Often they sponsor these to correspond with the spring equinox or summer solstice. In your community, there are undoubtedly organizations that sponsor this sort of cleanup. If not, start one!

Anytime you pick up trash or recycle anything, you're contributing to the sustenance and beauty of Mother Earth. Every time you do something like this, you're doing her a favor, as well as all other life on this planet.

Release and Renewal

As described in the chapter on healing ceremonies, this type of ceremony can be incorporated in any Earth-honoring celebration. Any seasonal holiday can be an appropriate time for this type of ceremony; however, I would suggest experimenting with the quarter days, as these more distinctly demarcate the change of seasons, where one season is ending (release), and we see the distinct signs of the next one beginning (renewal). Another option is to coordinate this type of ceremony with the full moon (release) and the new moon (renewal).

�֎ �֎ ✖   ✖ ✖ ✖

Chapter 33

Solar Cycles
and Seasons

The Cycles of Light

"Spring is the beginning of things,
when the energy should be kept open and fluid;
summer opens up further into an exchange or
communication between internal and external energies;
in the fall it's important to conserve; finally, the winter
is dominated by the storage of energy."

— Huang Di, the ancient emperor in
The Yellow Emperor's Classic of Medicine

When we consider the eight seasonal markers, or seasonal holidays, it's useful to visualize a circle, with these markers as points along the circle. This more graphically illustrates the cyclical nature of the seasons. As noted, there are sacred celebrations and activities you can do at any of these eight seasonal markers. At the same time, there are characteristics that are particular to each of these holidays that correspond to the attributes of the light and whether it's waxing or waning.

Although somewhat arbitrary, since the cycle of seasons is a continuum, we'll start with the seasonal holiday that marks the growing light, and circle back around to it. In *A Woman's Book of Rituals and Celebrations*, author Barbara Ardinger describes this annual transit throughout the seasons, drawing direct parallels between these cycles, the daily sun cycle, and the phases of the moon:

To set out in time with the Goddess, therefore, we begin in the dawn of the year, at Candlemas, which is also the year's new moon. This is the season of the quickening light, of waking up after winter's rest; it's the season of promise, potential, and laying plans and planting seeds.

We celebrate the growth of light and outward-bound energy through the spring and into Midsummer, which is the year's noon and full moon. This is the time when the seeds we planted in the spring bloom, when our days are warm and sunny. Potential becomes actual; it's the time of full power and manifestation.

With the summer solstice, which is the longest day of the year, comes the beginning of the growth of the dark, and we celebrate growing darkness through the fall. Fall is the season of harvest, of evaluation, of reaping what we sowed last spring. It's the season of quieter, inward-bound strength. Our days still seem long, but we also look forward to the longer nights of rest that the lengthening nights will bring. It's the time to come in and rest after our efforts, to do inside work, to relax in the beauty of the year's dusk.

As the wheel of the year makes its final turn, we enter the night and winter, which is the year's dark moon. This is the time to sleep and dream, to use the powerful inner energy the dark brings to do a final harvesting and examine the leavings of our year. And just as the summer solstice tips us over into the waxing dark, so the winter solstice tips us over again into the waxing light, and the wheel of the year becomes a spiral. It's the spiral of the days and years of our personal lives, the spiral of the eternal days. . . .

And so we begin with the festival of the growing light, *Imbolc*, or *Candlemas*, with ideas and suggestions for ceremonies that are in accord with the particular season. Again, these aren't meant to replace the more familiar holidays (unless you're ready to!), but to enhance them and offer another type of festivity that's more directly associated with the earth rhythms. In addition, for readers in the Southern Hemisphere, note the holiday and the characteristics, and adjust the dates to accord with your perspective.

Please use your imagination and creativity in honoring any of these seasonal holidays. As you read about their meaning to early peoples, there will be a part of you that intuitively knows what to do in order to spiritually acknowledge and sanctify these passages.

Imbolc/Candlemas (January 31/February 1–2)

We look for the groundhog about this time of year to come out of hibernation, and as the story goes, if he sees his shadow, then we'll have six more weeks of winter. *We* also begin to come out of hibernation, though tentatively at first, looking for signs of renewed life as well as the evidence that winter's breath is still upon us. If we see our own "shadow," it may require us to examine and clear any fears of moving forward into the growing light of day.

Imbolc is the Celtic name for the womb of Mother Earth. This quarter day is also known as Oimelc, or Brigid's Day. *Oimelc* literally means "sheep's (or ewe's) milk." This was the first milk of the ewes, a few weeks before the lambing season, so the milk was a signal of the preparation for new life. *Brigid,* also called Brid (pronounced *breed*), Brigit, or Bride, is known as the Goddess of fire and fertility, of inspiration and poetry, and is a healer and protector. Often she's visualized as a pregnant young maiden carrying the young seed of the sun. At *Imbolc,* which is one of the fire festivals, she's said to wear a radiant crown of candles.

Candlemas is a derivation that grew from this fire Goddess. Christianized Celts associated Brigid with the Virgin Mary, and this festival came to be known as the "Feast of Mary of the Beginning of Spring," where candles were brought to the church to be blessed, thus a "Candle Mass."

Commemorating *Imbolc*—*Planting* and *germinating* are strong characteristics of this seasonal celebration. In southernmost latitudes, you can plant some early seeds, whereas in northernmost latitudes, you can germinate these seeds indoors and later transplant them outdoors. Do this with appreciation for the tenderness of the Earth Mother's belly and her receptiveness to the first signs of awakening life.

As the early peoples did at all the quarter days, a *fire festival* can be the basis for any other ceremonies. Perhaps planting a sapling, or some bulbs for flowers. If it's still cold outside, the indoor hearth can serve the purpose to warm everyone and be useful as a focal point for a release and renewal ceremony.

Candles, candles, candles, especially on the first night of *Imbolc.* Set up candles and meditate on the beginning seeds of this next cycle, those thoughts and desires that you had described at the winter solstice. Then quietly journal on what you see as the initial stages of manifesting those desires.

This seasonal marker is an excellent time for a *cleansing fast*. I'd suggest three days, though even 24 hours is an excellent way to greet the beginnings of the spring season. Coordinate the cleansing fast with a fire ceremony and a release and renewal ceremony, and you'll assure your own movement as you notice yourself thawing for an early internal spring.

Spring Equinox/Ostara

The spring, or vernal, equinox is the time of year when the sun crosses the plane of the earth's equator, and day and night are of equal length across the entire planet. Now there's increasing evidence that the season that was begun on February 1 is blooming much more fully. Since winter is clearly over, now crops can be sown without reservation. Mother Earth is pregnant, and plants and animals are being born everywhere. A belief among some Native American peoples is that during this time, one must walk very carefully on the earth because she's swollen and pregnant.

Another name for this seasonal quarter-day is *Ostara*, also called *Oestre* or *Eostar*. An ancient image of Ostara was of a goddess standing amid the flowers of spring, holding an egg in one hand, with birds flying all about her and a rabbit hopping around her feet. All of these images appear today during the seasonal festivities as symbols of newborn life. Ostara is also a Northern European name for *Astarte*, which means "womb," and is another name for *Venus*, the goddess of love, passion, and creativity. It was also known as "Lady Day," or *Eostre*, which took place on the first full moon after the vernal equinox.

Easter, named after this festival, is one of the Christian Church's "moveable feasts." It falls near this time, and is calculated by a combination of celestial events and the Gregorian calendar. It occurs on the first Sunday after the first full moon following the equinox, and is the celebration of Jesus Christ's resurrection, his triumph over death. Prior to this holiday, members of the Catholic Church prepare with a period of meditation and sacrifice, known as Lent. In its archetypal form, the festival of Ostara is the resurrection of the light, the triumph of the sun over winter.

So this festival is the time of renewal and rebirth, of saying a clear and definite farewell to the hibernation that was a central theme of winter, and welcoming the increasing light. We notice the obvious signs on the face of the earth, and also feel them inside us. Often we start to experience a familiar feeling of restlessness, which sometimes has been called "spring fever," especially if your work requires you to be inside for long periods of time. It's nature's call to be outside, to renew, to be active and creatively expressive. You'll find that you want to sleep less and feel the urge to get up at dawn to enjoy the day.

Commemorating the spring equinox—*Get outdoors!* That's the simplest and best way to honor this season. Do so as often as you can. Decorate your altar and your home with flowers, colored eggs, and anything else that reminds you of spring.

Planting, now, more than at any other time, becomes a way to connect with the earth and with the season. Again, although we think of this time as the beginning of spring, it really is mid-spring. Create a ceremony around the planting. Pray, meditate, and communicate with the earth spirits (or if you prefer, the *fairies* and *plant devas*), and ask their help in growing your flowers or your vegetables. Plant a tree, whether in your own backyard or somewhere in the woods. Toss the seeds from any fruit or vegetables you eat along the roadside, in your backyard, or anywhere this would be appropriate and environmentally compatible.

Letting go of the old and unwanted is also a theme, also known as "spring housecleaning." Ideally, if you can find an old oak tree near a stream, act out a ceremony of release and renewal. During this season, this is clearly representational of what Mother Nature is doing. She has cleared out winter, and is now birthing anew. Create the ceremony around this theme. Use a biodegradable symbol of the old, and bury it. Find a symbol, something from the natural world, which represents what is showing the buds of manifestation at this time. Visualize what is growing within you, and write it down in your journal.

This is one of the best seasonal holidays to do an Earth renewal ceremony. It's a remarkable community event, so persuade some of your friends and family to join in.

Get out at night, somewhere away from city lights, and look at the stars. Learn about some of the springtime constellations, and the movement of the planets. Soak in the nighttime coolness that tells you that it's not yet summer. The next seasonal celebration is the one that will herald the beginning of summer.

Beltane/May Day (May 1–2)

The flowers are in full bloom, passions are running high, the heavenly energy descends, and the Earthly energy rises. Abundant life is all around as the light gets brighter and the days get warmer and longer. Spring is melting into summer and the name *Beltane*, which means "brilliant fire," accurately describes the increasing presence of the light. The nights are shorter, so you'll typically be sleeping less and spending more time awake during the longer days. If you're not already doing so, make it a point to spend some time outdoors each and every day.

It's the season of Mother's Day and the sacred marriage of the May King and the May Queen. The fertility of the king and queen is reflected in the land, crops, animals, and people. It's also another one of those quarter days where the early peoples lit a bonfire, which served the purpose of not only cooking the feasts and providing light and warmth, but also for blessings, healings, fertility, and preventing diseases. A Celtic tradition was to "leap the *Beltane* fires," which was for good luck and the fulfillment of wishes. It also served to heat up one's loins and carnal desires, since this was also an intensely erotic time.

It's the season for the Maypole and for May baskets. The dance around the Maypole honors the life-giving fertility of the earth. In days gone by, men and women would dance in a spiral while holding colorful ribbons, moving ever closer to the middle, where not only the ribbons intertwined, but their bodies would mingle as well. This rite was also an elaborate form of foreplay during this season where lusty passion was unabashedly expressed.

Commemorating *Beltane*—*Passion* is the strongest theme of this seasonal festivity. Not only sexual passion, but also sensual passion—aromas, sights, and sensations of the earth's flourishing bounty.

As the Yellow Emperor, Huang Di, said about this season, "It's important to be happy and easygoing and not hold grudges, so that the energy can flow freely and communicate between the external and the internal." Take it easy and don't get stressed! If you do, just go outside and soak in the warmth of the expanding summer.

If you perform only one or two more elaborate seasonal celebrations, make this one of them. Hold a *May Day* celebration, with a Maypole dance and plenty of flowers to decorate the May baskets. Devise and produce games, perhaps borrowing from your childhood memories of family picnics. The women and the girls can make crowns of flowers for their hair, and for the men, garland necklaces from the spring grasses.

And music, music, music! Flutes, guitars, harps, drums—instruments and music that express playfulness and passion. In your Maypole dance, the participants can hold brightly colored ribbons that are tied to the pole as they do a spiral dance, wrapping the ribbons around the Maypole. Most of all, have fun!

Build a *bonfire*. For the early Celts, bonfires were essential for each of the quarter days, most especially for *Beltane*. Hold a fire ceremony, and find a place where you can safely do it outdoors. Have a feast with it, and if possible, build the fire as the night falls, following your May Day celebration. You may even want to "leap the *Beltane* fires," if you can do so safely.

A *drumming circle*, whether as part of the larger ceremony, or independent of it, can be a great way to celebrate and honor this season. Get some friends together, ask them to bring percussion instruments of any kind, and provide whatever instruments you have. Gather in a circle. One drum starts the beat, and others join in as they feel like it. Encourage people to get up and *dance*, as they feel so moved. In fact, take every opportunity you have to dance.

With passion being the primary theme, if you're in a relationship, set aside some time during *Beltane* for *lovemaking*. If you can, make love outdoors, and augment the setting with your own touches, such as candles, additional flowers, blankets, and essential oils. If you prefer, do this inside, and prepare the room in such a way that it will provoke the senses, such as spreading rose petals on the bed. Start the ceremony by taking a ritual bath together, washing one another's bodies, anointing them with oils of your favorite aromas. Some of my favorites are jasmine, lavender, cinnamon, patchouli, and frankincense. Take your time, and spend a lot of time caressing and kissing.

I'm sure you'll know what to do from there.

Summer Solstice/Litha (June 20–23)

"School's out!" is perhaps the most memorable way of marking this time of year for many of us. And it's very much a seasonal marker of completion. The summer solstice is the day when the light is at its fullest, and paradoxically, it's also the start of its waning. Even so, the days are long and full, the nights hot and dry. In spite of the onset of the sun's dying strength, it's a season of abundance. The festivities are much like *Beltane*, but whereas *Beltane* celebrations had a playful and carefree feeling about them, the hot midsummer season lent itself more to a fiery, sweaty, breathless sort of passion.

Litha, another name for midsummer, is from the name of a goddess of fertility, power, and abundance. This name accurately describes the characteristics of the season, and also reflects what's going on inside us. We take off from work during this season and go on vacation. The land around us is reaching its peak of fertility. We connect with that sense of power around us and inside us. It's an erotic, sexual, and sensual time of year. Even our clothing is looser and lighter, and will be more frequently absent from our bodies.

Shakespeare's play *A Midsummer Night's Dream*, a romantic farce that takes place on June 23, expresses well the tone of this season. Like *Beltane*, it's a time to enjoy the playful and sensual fullness of the season, with the exception that you're also aware that the daylight will soon be decreasing. And so it should be, as the seasons continue to fold into one another.

Commemorating the summer solstice—Just as you may welcome the dawn at the winter solstice, so you may say farewell to the sun at dusk of the summer solstice. Take a drum, rattle, or flute with you to a high point where you can witness the sunset, and meditate for a few minutes as the sun heads for the horizon. Then, as it settles in for the night, say farewell in your own way—singing, playing an instrument, or in stillness and silence, knowing that even though the days will still be long and hot for a while longer, the light will be decreasing steadily.

These are still days of fire, so once more a *fire ceremony*, much like our predecessors enjoyed, is a fitting celebration. This is a time to reflect back on the cycle of the growing light, from *Imbolc* to now, and see what's manifesting from the seeds that were germinated at that time. Did you finish that project that was instigated at *Imbolc?* If so, dance around the fire and drum and play music to celebrate. If not, do a release ceremony, using the fire to transform that which is holding you back from finishing it, represented in written or other symbolic form.

When the sun is directly overhead, a simple gesture is to stand with feet wide apart, arms open wide, with the palms facing up to the sky, head tilted back with eyes closed, and in this position, embrace the warmth of the sun. It's a very honoring gesture, aside from feeling good, and one that can be repeated several times during the period of the solstice.

Lammas/Lughnasad (July 31–August 1)

You can still feel the summer heat, and in fact, you can now feel it even more intensely than at the solstice. These are known as the "dog days," because the "dog star" Sirius (the brightest star in the sky) is now rising and setting with the sun, and will do so from mid-July to September. With the heat comes slightly shorter days and longer nights, as well as the time of the first grain harvest.

Lammas means "loaf mass." It's a celebration of the bread made from the first grains to be harvested, and signals the initiation of the harvest season. *Lughnasad* (pronounced LOO-na-sa) comes from the Irish god Lugh, who is both a sun god and a god of grain. His name means "bright or shining one." His name and association with the harvest reflects the two strongest elements of this season. He loved games and competitive sports to keep up the physical strength and vitality of his followers, so the festivities in his honor included these kinds of activities.

This also marks the death of Bel, the corn king. During the festivals, corncakes were made in the shape of the corn king's body, and consumed along with ale made from the first crop of corn. This was a ceremony to honor the king who gave his life so that the people could have food—an early Communion ritual.

There are no secular holidays during this seasonal shift that we have in common, so the field is wide open as to how to honor and celebrate this holiday. It seems that the main way to celebrate this seasonal marker is to take a vacation, which may be the remnants of this festival.

Regardless, what's called for is to celebrate the themes of the first harvest, coupled with the intensity of the sun's light and heat. It's a playful time, so a vacation during this season is congruent with the theme of ancient festivals. The key here is to get outdoors and be active, since we're still enjoying the residual heat of summer in spite of the barely discernible shorter days.

Commemorating *Lughnasad/Lammas*—Bake some *bread* and break some bread with friends and family. Although bread is generally available throughout the year, you can create a ceremony around its baking and sharing. Bake it from scratch if you're so inclined, or you can purchase it premade, ready to bake. Either way, invite a few friends and family over, perhaps in the late afternoon when it cools down. Let the smell of bread offer its enticement to your guests. Once it's done, set it out with great flair, and have butter, honey, and jams available. Create a feast with the fresh-baked bread. Ask your guests to bring fresh foods, such as organic fruits and salads, ones that preferably are grown locally and are in season. Include these along with fresh grains and nuts as part of the table. Let this fresh food feast be dedicated to the bounty of Mother Earth, the nourishment that she provides for us all.

An appropriate alternative is to have a *picnic,* one where you bring these items to share in a feast. Let the centerpiece be these representations of the early harvest, as this is truly the central theme of this holiday.

You can include in the ceremony a *ritual feeding* of one another, as I described previously. Before the full meal takes place, each person takes some grapes, wedges of apple, or slices of fresh bread. You create the sacred circle, and the host explains the purpose of this part of the ceremony, that the joy in giving and receiving are the same. Sharing food is the most elemental and basic way of giving and receiving.

The guests are then asked to close their eyes and imagine that they haven't eaten for a couple of days. As this idea sets in, the host turns to the person on their left and feeds them, slowly and deliberately. The task of the recipient is to receive very slowly and chew very slowly, savoring each bite with gratitude. The person who first received the food then turns to the person on their left and does the same. This proceeds around the circle until everyone has had a chance to experience it.

Autumn Equinox/Mabon (September 20–23)

Once again the time of light and dark are in balance on this day as the sun crosses the equator, making this the counterpoint to the spring equinox. This time, however, it's evident that the days are continuing to get shorter and we're headed for a greater increase in the darkness. It's the time of the fall harvest, when the earth has given us its all. It's a time to begin food storage. I remember when I was young how my grandmother spent this time of year pickling foods and making jams and jellies, to be used throughout the coming period of the darkening light.

In one version, *Mabon* comes from Queen Mab of the fairies; in another version *Mabon* means "son of the mother," as well as the "Son of Light," the mother being the Goddess Modron, Guardian of the Otherworld. The legend is that Mabon was taken from his mother at only three days old, and for some time dwelt in the Otherwold, invisible for a period of time, even from his mother, only to be reborn at a later time.

The *harvest* is the dominant theme here. For this harvest, whether of food or of projects completed and things achieved, the focus is on *gratitude*. This is possibly a better time for a national thanksgiving celebration, aside from the more traditional one.

It's also a time of preparation for the decreasing light, time to gather the nuts and store them, time to put into the dark of the Otherworld any ideas or projects that need to gestate.

Commemorating the autumn equinox—This is the season of full harvest, so one way to commemorate it is to sponsor a *shared feast*, one where everyone brings a dish. Along with the feast, incorporate a sharing of gratitude. This can be done simply, during or following the feast.

Another ceremony is to gather representations of all of those things you've harvested, the *fruits of your labor,* the end result of things that were planted earlier in the year. Bring those together, and put them on your altar, or create a special one just for this ceremony. These "fruits" can be earned diplomas or certificates, projects that have been completed or are near completion, photos of new friends or of newly born children or grandchildren, marriage or divorce papers, and any other symbols of completion. Put them all together on the altar, or in front of it, and spend a few minutes meditating on them. Feel what goes on in your body as you look at these altogether. Consciously breathe while you're doing so. Feel the pride, or any other feeling, as you meditate on these. Express your gratitude through prayer, especially to the spirit guides who helped you.

Performing a *community ceremony* of any sort confirms those relationships that can continue to be active during the coming season. This is a great time to do a *sweat lodge,* if one is available. Through this type of ceremony, we purify and heal ourselves from anything that may be carried over from the days of greater light.

A private ceremony you can do is one of *transmutation.* Find a representational object, such as a crystal or a stone. Consider what undesirable personal characteristic(s) you want transmuted, or transformed. This can be fear, doubt, anger, shame, and so on. Set up in front of your altar, and prepare for a ceremony in your usual way. Take the object, and using your breath, blow into it those characteristics that you want transformed. Name what you want them to transform into—for instance, anger into calmness, or turmoil into peace.

When this is completed, take the object and bury it in a place that's accessible, such as near a tree in your backyard, or in a park. Leave it there for six months, until the sun crosses the equator one more time, to confidently assert the growing light at the spring equinox. Your task is to dig it up on that day, then leave the object in direct sunlight for several hours once you've done so.

I performed this ceremony recently, blowing into a quartz crystal doubt and skepticism, asking that it be transformed via the crystal and the assistance of the spirits, especially the Earth Mother, into faith and discernment. I buried the crystal close to the roots of a tree in a nearby park. At the spring equinox, I retrieved it, feeling certain that it had not been disturbed. I know that my faith and my discernment strengthened over the six-month period, and attribute this growth to this ceremony.

Samhain/Halloween (October 31–November 1)

This is the time of year when the veil between the world of the living and the world of the dead is at its thinnest, the night when the dead return to visit us, to feast, and communicate with us. The seeds from the dying plants fall to the earth, and there they wait until the proper mixture of heat and light once again stirs the life within. *Samhain* (pronounced SOW-en) is the most important, but also the least understood of the ancient Celtic festivals. *Samhain* means "summer's end," and it's clearly the initiation of the darkest time of the year.

The secular holiday of Halloween, as well as the Christian holidays of All Saints Day (November 1) and All Soul's Day (November 2), all have their roots in ancient Pagan or Celtic festivals. Halloween in contemporary times contains some of the elements of the original festivities, but has been distorted in its meaning and expression.

In *A Woman's Book of Rituals and Celebrations*, Barbara Ardinger articulates the deeper meanings of this holiday:

> How many of the kids who put on their (Halloween) costumes and thrust plastic bags at us for candy know what "trick or treat" really means? Do they know that Halloween is our most sacred holiday? Do they know why they dress as ghosts and witches and carry plastic jack-o'-lanterns?
>
> Today, alas, it's only party time.
>
> But it hasn't always been so.
>
> Hallows, Hallowmas, All Hallows Eve—the "hallow" in all three names comes from the Middle English word that means "holy." When something is hallowed, it's sanctified and consecrated. Even when the Christian Church took over our holiday (holy day), it kept the name, for "Halloween" means "hallowed evening." Not only that, they also made November 1 All Saints Day and November 2 All Souls Day.

On All Souls Day, the barriers between this world and the Otherworld are removed, and the dead are able to rise from their own graves. In our culture, death is dealt with poorly, as something to be denied and to be feared, so instead of honoring our ancestors and deceased loved ones on this holiday, it's taken on an entirely different kind of spin. Trick or treat had an entirely different meaning. Originally, you would leave food for the ancestors and the fairies. If you didn't, then they'd play tricks on you, perhaps for the entire year.

However, these ancestors that were portrayed as ghouls, ghosts, and goblins actually visited us to help us. They weren't scary at all. The treats left for them were to welcome them, to let them enjoy memories of their time while on Earth. Psychic powers are highest on each of the quarter days, but are at the strongest at *Samhain*. The communication between the living and the world of the dead is at an all-time high, with messages being exchanged both ways.

Commemorating *Samhain*/Halloween—One of the most elegant ceremonies you can do on this day is one celebrated in Mexico and other Latin American countries, called *El Día de los Muertos*, or *Day of the Dead*, celebrated on November 2.

As described by a friend, Martha Granados, it's a holiday set aside to honor your deceased loved ones. Technically, it's two days, as November 1 is the day to honor any children who have died, while November 2 is to honor the adults who have passed on. Of the two, November 2 is the most important, and is thought of as the actual holiday.

To commemorate this day, you set up an altar specifically to honor those ancestors. You spread rose petals across the altar, then add a candle or candles, a glass of water, some flowers, and photos of loved ones. In addition, you set on the altar an *ofrenda*, or offering, of small bits of food, preferably the types of food your deceased loved ones enjoyed. As Martha says, "Of course the spirits can't eat the food, but they enjoy the sight and smell of it." And they're no doubt honored that you devoted this day to their memory.

That night you light the candle and say a prayer of gratitude and invitation, and ideally leave the candle lit all night. Practically, leaving it lit for a few hours still pays homage to your deceased loved ones. It will undoubtedly bring up some emotion, so it's an opportunity to yield to any unfinished grief or sorrow.

Martha described her experience:

> I was very close to my *abuela* (grandmother), who died in 1994. Many times she came to me in my dreams, and I would cry. Then one time in a dream she told me, "I'm with you always," and after that, I didn't feel so sad. After her death, on *El Día de los Muertos*, I would put rose petals on the altar, a picture of her, a candle, a glass of water, and light the candle. Then I would put some of her favorite foods—tortillas, garlic, chili peppers, salt, pepper, pumpkin seeds—these were the kinds of things she used to cook with. I'd put some flowers there also, and light the candle and leave it burning for a few hours at night.
>
> I loved my *abuela* so much. Ever since that dream, I know she is always with me. Doing this makes me feel even closer to her.

Once the children have stopped knocking at the door, and all the treats are gone, I can think of no better way to celebrate the deeper meaning of this very special quarter day than the ceremony for *El Día de los Muertos*.

Winter Solstice/Yule (December 18–January 6)

This is the season of religious and cultural celebrations worldwide, including Christmas, New Year, Hanukah, and Kwanzaa. It's the darkest day of the year, around December 21, yet with that darkness comes the promise of the returning light. Celebrations and stories abound across cultures, telling of the birth of a sun god at this time of year. In the fourth century, by decree, this time of year became the official birthday of Jesus (the Christian "sun god"), and was moved to coincide with more familiar solstice festivals and holidays.

Many of the better-known practices of this season have their roots in the practices of ancient peoples. One of these is the ancient Roman festival, *Saturnalia*, named after the god Saturn, which took place at this time of the year. It was considered to be the greatest festival of the year in imperial Rome. A weeklong celebration starting on December 18 and lasting until December 25, it was a time of revelry and the upheaval of social norms, where society was turned upside down. Distinctions between servants and masters were temporarily abolished, schools were out, courts were closed, and even wars were delayed. Evergreens were used for decoration, feasts were held, and sexual liberties were indulged. It was all-out party time, a time for pranks and practical jokes, time to revel and rejoice.

Yule was another term for this season. In *Celebrate the Solstice*, Richard Heinberg describes how we came to call this seasonal celebration *Yule.*

> The Scandinavian word *Yule* (Danish *Jul*) long ago came to denote Christmas, and is so used today in English-speaking and northern European countries. Its derivation is uncertain, though it may come from the Anglo-Saxon word *hweol*, or "wheel," referring perhaps to the course of the Sun through the Solstices and Equinoxes. In any case, many historians have suggested that the term originally may have designated a Teutonic Solstice festival. Perhaps the twelve nights of Yule festivities coincided with the twelve days when the Sun's rising and setting points seemed to "stand still" at the southern extreme on the horizon.
>
> The Germanic peoples had marked their seasonal festivals with fires, dancing, and sacrifices. The fires of the winter Solstice were thought to promote the return of the Sun, to burn away the accumulated misdeeds of the community, and to ward off evil spirits. The tradition of the burning of a special log (the Yule log) on Christmas Eve was practiced throughout Europe, from Scandinavia to Italy. Indeed, the words for Christmas among the Lithuanians and Letts literally signify "Log Evening." The Yule log was in some places considered the Fire Mother of the Sun god.

Heinberg goes on to suggest possible origins of the Christmas tree:

> Though it's somewhat futile to search back in history for the "first Christmas tree," it's possible to trace notable turning points in the evolution of the ceremonial evergreen—in seventeenth century Germany, with the first written descriptions of "fir trees set up in the rooms of Strasbourg and hung with roses cut from paper of many colors, apples, wafers, spangle-gold, sugar, etc."; in England in 1840, when the German Prince Albert set up a tree in the palace for his wife, Queen Victoria; and across the Atlantic in

1845, when a children's book, *Kriss Kringle's Christmas Tree*, which has been described as the most influential Christmas book in the United States, spread the fashion throughout America.

Heinberg cites legends and historical clues about the foundations for our modern-day Santa Claus. There are legends about the fourth-century bishop of Myra, Nicholas—robed, gray-bearded, wearing the pointed bishop's cap—famous for his anonymous generosity, especially to children. In Germany, legend tells of a man named Knecht Ruprecht, who traveled from town to town, testing children's knowledge of their prayers. If they passed the test, he gave them treats, and if not, he gave them a stick. Christmas plays in England from the Middle Ages on often featured "Father Christmas," a jolly, white-bearded old man who wore a wreath of holly.

Washington Irving, in *Father Knickerbocker's History of New York*, published in 1809, is credited with a description of our modern Santa Claus, with his sleigh and magical reindeer who brought gifts to good children. This magical figure may even have more ancient roots in shamanism, as he has many attributes of the shaman. He flies through the air, talks with the animals, lives at the edge of village Earth (North Pole), moves from one realm to another (via the chimney), and has a magical bag that always has surprises in it (much like the "medicine bag" of the shaman).

The strongest component of this season is *light*. Throughout the year, there is the dance of light and dark, and at the winter solstice, this dance is at its most intense and pronounced, with the longest period of darkness and the shortest period of light. Our ancestors, without the advantages of electric lights and central heating, were no doubt apprehensive about whether the winter's coldness and darkness would ever come to an end, and whether their family or tribe would survive the harshness of the season.

The fire that heated the home, candles placed about, and a great faith in the eternal cycles of light and dark, heat and cold, death and rebirth, were what kept up their spirits. The various solstice festivities kept up their hope. The symbols of light, such as the bonfire, hearthfire, and candles, reminded them that the light would return as it had for every year. Other symbols, such as a tree that was brought in, an "ever-green," helped them to remember that even in the harshest of times, life continues onward.

Commemorating the winter solstice—*Slow down!* That's perhaps the best way to commemorate these times. It's the time of year when life is dormant, when the seeds that are in the ground will be there for a while, until the proper amount of light and heat beckon them to germinate and sprout. It's time for us to rest and recuperate, to settle down for "a long winter's nap," to go to bed earlier and to sleep later. This is quite a challenge in these hectic, hurry-up times, but with such an intention, you can do it.

Everyone tends to rush around during the holidays, frantically trying to fulfill the Christmas wish list and prepare for the feasts. If our inner nature is in step with the season, then to override this with such tremendous forced activity can't help but contribute to stress. When our organic self is stressed, it compromises the immune system, and voilà!—illnesses, such as colds and flus, beat down the door of our natural defenses.

One effective ceremony to remind us of this is an *energy fast,* which I described earlier. This is perhaps the best cross-quarter day to do so. Let yourself surrender to the darkness. Light candles, then go to bed very early. An addition to this would be a *day of silence,* to couple this with the energy fast. If you want to round it out, at the same time as these do a *cleansing fast.*

On the morning of the return of the light—that is, after the longest night of the year—I like to go up on a mountain and greet the sunrise. It's possible to do various ceremonies in connection with this time. As I mentioned, one year I danced and drummed as the sun rose.

Needless to say, *feasts* and *festivities* with friends allow us that time for pause and appreciation. These kinds of activities remind us that we're part of a clan, tribe, or family, and that we need not suffer the dark times alone. Make time in your schedule for such gatherings, and create ones that fit your needs and desires. Some of these can be formats for a sacred ceremony.

Another powerful ceremony augmented by this season of darkness and light is a *manifestation* ceremony, similar to a release and renewal ceremony but with a slight twist. This past season, some friends of ours, Chris and Becky, had a few of us over for a New Year's Eve ceremony. We all brought a dish to share, and there were snacks as we sat around the warm fireplace, socializing, with flute music or some drumming occasionally being played on one side of the room. On the steps leading to the house, they had constructed lamps made from paper bags folded halfway down, with sand in the bottom and a lit candle on top of that.

We started the ceremony rather informally, when our hosts brought out a whole bunch of crayons and paper and, not so subtly, placed them in the center of the living room. They explained that on one sheet of paper, we were to write or draw the stuff we wanted to leave behind (release), and on another, those attributes and attitudes we wanted to have expand (manifestation).

We all set to work. On the release piece of paper, I wrote such things as "shame," "fear of disapproval," and "self-doubt." On the manifestation paper, I wrote "faith," "purpose," and "courage." On both papers, the words were stylized and multicolored. We all had fun doing this activity, yet there was serious intent.

Whenever any of us finished, each person took the release list to the fire, and with a prayer threw it in. Once everyone had done this, then we walked together to the backyard. There we found lanterns similar to those in front outlining a path to a small plateau of dirt. We followed the path, and circled around a hole that was dug in the center of the mound.

We prayed together, then chanted "Om" three times. Chris explained that we were to bury the manifestation paper when we were ready. Each of us in turn did so, and once we all finished, everyone then added a handful of earth. The purpose of this was so that Mother Earth could take these requests into her bosom and nurture them through the darkness of the winter into warmth and light of the coming sun days, such that these items would manifest.

We circled together once more and sang a couple of songs, then closed with a prayer. There was a tremendous sense of camaraderie and support. It was a beautiful solstice ceremony, designated to welcome not only the coming new year, but also the return of the light.

❋ ❋ ❋   ❋ ❋ ❋

Chapter 34

Lunar Cycles
and Seasons

The moon and its cycles are strongly associated with the feminine, and for millennia it has been seen as a symbol of the goddess. Its light is considered to be powerful and magical. This powerful association with the feminine shows itself not only in various cultures' mythos, but also supported by science. The Swedish scientist Svante Arrhenius has statistically confirmed that the sidereal month—the 27.3 days it takes for the Moon to move through all 12 Zodiac signs—coincides with the period of human [female] ovulation. Also, the ocean's tides ebb and flow according to the relative positions of the moon and sun, yet the strongest influence comes from the pull of the moon's gravity.

In many cultures the moon goddess and Creator were one and the same. Polynesians called the Creator *Hina*, which means "moon." She was the first woman, and her name continues on in the Polynesian word for woman, *Wahine*, "made in the image of Hina." The Lakota Indians called the moon "The Old Woman Who Never Dies." In the Basque language, the words for *deity* and *moon* are the same.

The moon was commonly believed to rule life and death, as well as the tides. Many people living near the ocean were convinced that a baby could only be born on an incoming tide, and a person couldn't die until the tide went out. Birth at full tide or full moon meant a full and charmed life. As we'll see, the moon's cycles of light and dark continue to represent metaphorical births and deaths.

The moon has a tremendous influence on our bodies and minds. A full moon is very energizing, stimulating both our sexual and aggressive energies. More babies are conceived or born at the full moon than at any other phase, and almost any police officer will tell you stories about how the "crazies" come out and commit weird crimes during this time (it's also when the werewolves come out!). In contrast, during the New Moon phase, people feel generally calmer, sometimes even depressed. It's more a time of quiet, self-reflection, and release, a time of contemplation and preparation.

Four Quarters, Eight Phases

The four quarter-phases of the moon are well known and marked on most calendars. Most of us are familiar with the new moon, first quarter, full moon, and last quarter. Another perspective is to account for the "in-between" phases, and in so doing, we find that there are actually eight phases. These eight phases correspond directly to the eight seasonal markers, and in these cycles of the moon, we see the same movement from growing light to fullness to diminishing light to darkness as we do in the annual cycle:

Imbolc/Candlemas (February 1)	New moon
Spring Equinox/Ostara (March 21)	First quarter
Beltane/May Day (May 1)	Waxing crescent
Summer Solstice/	
Midsummer (June 21)	Full moon
Lammas/Lughnasad (August 1)	Waning crescent
Autumn Equinox/Mabon	
(September 21)	Third quarter
Samhain/Halloween (October 31)	Dark crescent
Winter Solstice/Yule (December 21)	Dark moon

We'll stick with the four most familiar phases and plot the primary attributes of these. In describing them in this way, you'll get a feeling for the cyclical nature of dark and light, as well as a sense of how the characteristics attributed to these phases are reflective of your own inner process at any given time:

New moon—Rebirth, personal growth, initiating projects, blessing and energizing ongoing projects, healing (the beginning of the next breath)

Waxing moon—Nurturing projects along, growth and gain, attraction (breathing in)

Full moon—Fulfillment, climax, abundance, release, protection, divination—very powerful! (the fullness of breath)

Waning moon—Letting go, rest, cleansing, clearing negative emotions, completion (breathing out)

Although ceremonies can be performed at any of these four phases, the most powerful and dramatic ones will be those done to honor the new moon and the full moon. Ceremonies generated for the new moon represent new beginnings and are the initial stages of increasing light, just as they are at *Imbolc*. Ceremonies similar to the ones you created to celebrate the summer solstice can be performed at the Full moon, where the light is at its maximum. Passions run high both at midsummer and at the full moon, although like the moon's softer light, these passions are more subtle and beguiling.

You can use this understanding and your creative imagination to design ceremonies appropriate for any of the other phases; however, the focus here will be on ceremonies for the new moon and the full moon.

New Moon Manifestation Ceremony

Manifestation is the theme here, in that the silvery, thin crescent hints of things to come. This is a time to plant seeds, to set your intention on getting things started and to reenergize and bless projects that are under way, a time to manifest healing and well-being.

You can do this simple ceremony either alone or in a group. I'll describe the ceremony to be done by yourself; if you do it in a group, you can modify it accordingly. Check the date of the new moon on your calendar. Note that on many calendars, the new moon is, in actuality, the dark moon (no visible moon), so set your ceremony for two days past the date marked on the calendar. The new moon is the first sign of return, when there is a slight but noticeable crescent of light in the western sky.

In addition to the usual supplies for ceremony, keep a notebook and pen handy, a small packet of seeds, and a container for the seeds. Any kind of seed will do, from birdseed to wildflower seeds. Set your sacred space and your altar. Smudge to clear your sacreds, the room, and yourself. If it's warm enough, you can do this outside. Set the container on the altar and fill it with the seeds. Open with a prayer, and let yourself settle into the ceremonial space you've created.

When you're ready, open your notebook, date it, and at the top of the page, write down the following sentence: "I now choose and accept these things into my life, or something better for the highest good of all concerned." Below this statement, list any desires, no matter how few or many. Be as detailed and as specific as possible, and be careful what you ask for—you will more than likely get it!

List as many desires as you wish, and don't limit yourself. It's important to put down small things, such as getting tickets to the new play that's opening, or dinner with a friend; as well as larger things that may take more than a month to manifest. These smaller manifestations help to create movement, to give life to this list.

When you've completed the list, close your eyes and visualize these items going into those seeds on the altar, each one into a separate seed. Then see and feel those seeds growing, and as they do, see the items on the list growing, coming into form. Imagine what it will be like once these items are full and active in your life. See the process of growth and the end result. Take your time doing this, perhaps with a favorite piece of music playing in the background.

When this process is complete, take the container of seeds and put them outside in the light of the new moon. The next day either germinate them, plant them, or spread them out for the birds. Do so with gratitude.

Throughout the month, when an item on your new moon list manifests, don't just cross it off the list. Instead, rewrite the entire list, leaving out the item or items that have now appeared in your life. As you're doing so, you may think of other things to add. When you repeat this ceremony at the next new moon, check your list carefully to see if you need to eliminate anything, especially things that just aren't "soul food."

You need not do this every new moon, unless you so desire. However, doing so periodically allows you to review your desires, to eliminate those on the list that *seemed* desirable, but simply don't connect once you've lived with the idea. If you're growing the seeds, during each new moon ceremony, spend some time simply "being" with the new growth.

If you seem to have some trouble manifesting, then have I got a ceremony for you! Only this one you'll have to do during the full moon, the period just before the light starts to wane.

Full Moon Ceremony

Fulfillment and *release* are the themes for ceremonies during this lunar cycle. As I mentioned, this is a very powerful time to make use of this goddess's generous power. There has been a period of buildup; now the moon is at its brightest, softly lighting the way at night. It's preparing to move into a cycle of decreasing light and corresponding release. There are two types of ceremonies that fit with the themes, the first being *fulfillment* and the second being *release.*

Moon Bath

This is a simple yet very powerful ceremony. One or two days before the full moon, preferably when it's at its highest point in the sky, go outside. Stand fully in the light of the moon, feet shoulder-width apart, elbows bent and arms outstretched, with palms open and facing up. Your arms can be in front or to your side, but don't strain. Find a posture that will be comfortable for a few minutes.

Once you find a suitable position, close your eyes, tilt your head as if you were looking at the moon, and see if you can actually *feel* the moonlight on your face. Bring your head back so that you're facing forward again. Now feel the moonlight, starting at the crown of your head, slowly cascading down your body, eventually covering every square inch of your skin, even through your clothing (if you're wearing any!). Enjoy the sensuality of this. Perhaps you can smell it or taste it, or even with eyes closed, see the light being absorbed by your body.

At the same time, imagine that the same moonlight is gently penetrating the crown of your head. Let its nurturing, healing, powerful substance merge with every bone, muscle, and tissue—every cell in your body. Feel its gentle radiance filling you and healing you. If there are areas of your body that need extra attention, focus on them, and see the moonlight being more concentrated in those areas. Enjoy this experience as much as you possibly can.

After about five to ten minutes, rest your arms at your side and be still for just a few moments. Simply notice how your body feels. Thank the goddess for her gifts, and then journal about this experience.

An alternative, once you've taken your moon bath, is to use the power that's now filling your body. You can do so in a couple of ways. If you have some sacred object that you want to "recharge," once you're filled with moonlight, take that object in your right hand (which is the giving hand), and hold it for a few minutes. That's all you have to do.

Similarly, if there's someone with you who needs a healing, once you've gathered the power of the moonlight, place your right hand on the area that needs assistance. If it's a more general kind of malaise or an emotional condition, place it on those areas of their body that seem to most need the touch. If you're not sure, start with the person lying down, with one hand on their heart and one on their belly. Trust your guidance or intuition as to where the touch is most needed. Taking a moon bath enhances intuition and psychic abilities, so be confident that you'll know what to do.

Full Moon Release

This is a version of a release ceremony using the power of the full moon. I would suggest that you do this at the peak of the cycle, just before the moon starts to wane. Use fire for the release, and preferably do this ceremony outdoors in the full moonlight. It can be done alone, although I like these types of ceremonies in small groups, even if it only involves two or three people. I'll describe the process for a group, and if you're doing this alone, you can modify it accordingly.

Prepare the space as you would do with any sacred ceremony. On *separate* slips of paper, write down all the things you want to release. These can be personal characteristics, such as those you discovered in the new moon ceremony that may be holding you back from manifesting your desires. They can be addictions to food, drugs, alcohol, or sex; or suffering over a loss—particularly a relationship—or any physical or emotional pain from which you desire relief.

Gather together around the fire, smudge everyone, and then invoke any helping spirits or guides. Take a few moments to enjoy the sky, to breathe in the night air. As a group, focus your intention by praying for support together. Each person then reads what they've written on each individual slip of paper, one at a time. After they've read each item, toss the piece of paper into the fire.

One person at a time can engage in this process with all of their items, then move to the next person; or people can randomly release one item at a time, as they're moved to do so. When you put each slip of paper in the fire, say aloud, "Begone!" or "I release you!" with conviction and power. If you're so moved, go ahead and howl at the moon, dance, drum, sing, and chant once you've released all of the items!

When you're all done, close with a prayer of thanks. Although not always necessary, a shared feast is always a nice touch with which to follow this ceremony, as it is with others.

Even simpler yet, notice the moon regularly. Observe its phases and its changes. If you live near the ocean, start tracing the tidal changes and their relation to the moon. Notice how you feel at the various phases, especially the full moon and the new moon. For women, track your menstrual cycle, and see if you can trace how that rhythm aligns with the lunar cycles. Men, of course, have no obvious physical signs of these lunar cycles, so it requires us to be more attentive to our moods and how they may be affected.

❀ ❀ ❀   ❀ ❀ ❀

Afterword

Thus concludes *Sacred Ceremony*. If there's one thing I want you to take with you when you put this book down, it's the confidence that you have the power within you to cooperate with the spirits, guides, angels, God—whatever you call that mysterious Force of Life that animates, guides, and directs all of us—in creating sacred ceremony. By your willingness to be courageous and experiment and explore with ceremonies, putting your egotistic concerns and your apprehensions aside, you're honoring something ancient and primal—founded in the stars, moon, and sun—and you're especially honoring our beautiful and precious planet Earth.

It's crucial at this time in human evolution that we turn to this ancient wisdom that resides within every one of us, a wisdom that's being retrieved and revived on many fronts. It's a profound *knowing* that embodies universal truths, one that recognizes that as long as we're guests on this planet, our intention must be to be *really* good guests.

Our job while we're guests isn't to dominate the earth, but to be *compassionate stewards*. This means accessing and using the wisdom that comes both from the heavens and from our humanity to nurture and care for *all* life while we're here—plant, animal, and human. One of the best ways to help us remember this God-given assignment is through creating sacred ceremony. Through the powerful and magical experiences that emerge as we honor the holiness in everyday life via ceremony, we experience the truth of who we are and the reality of our collective and sacred legacy.

Blessings to all of you. May Love and Light always be the guiding force in your life. May your heart, mind, and soul always be open, and may each of us revere the earth and all her children with every breath we take.

✖ ✖ ✖   ✖ ✖ ✖

I Am Not I

I am not I
I am this one
Walking beside me whom I do not see,
Whom at times I manage to visit,
And whom at other times I forget;
Who remains calm and silent while I talk,
And forgives, gently, when I hate,
Who walks where I am not,
Who will remain standing when I die.

— from *Lorca and Jiménez: Selected Poems* by
Juan Ramón Jiménez, translated by Robert Bly

Recommended Reading

You'll find the following books useful in further exploring the art of ceremony:

Healing

Healing Ceremonies: Creating Personal Rituals for Spiritual, Emotional, Physical and Mental Health, Carl Hammerschlag and Howard D. Silverman. New York: Perigee Books, 1997.

Healing Words: The Power of Prayer and the Practice of Medicine, Larry Dossey. San Francisco: Harper San Francisco, 1993.

Rituals of Healing: Using Imagery for Health and Wellness, Jeanne Achterberg, Barbara Dossey, and Leslie Kolkmeier. New York: Bantam New Age Books, 1994.

Spiritual Dimensions of Healing: From Native Shamanism to Contemporary Health Care, Stanley Krippner and Patrick Welch. New York: Irvington Publishers, Inc., 1992.

Trauma and Recovery: The Aftermath of Violence—from Domestic Abuse to Political Terror, Judith Herman. New York: Basic Books, 1997.

Traumatic Stress: The Effects of Overwhelming Experience on Mind, Body, and Society, Bessel A. van der Kolk, Alexander C. McFarlane, and Lars Weisaeth, Eds. New York: The Guilford Press, 1996.

Waking the Tiger: Healing Trauma, Peter Levine, with Ann Frederick. Berkeley, CA: North Atlantic Books, 1997.

Transitions

A Healing Divorce: Transforming the End of Your Relationship with Ritual and Ceremony, Phil Penningroth & Barbara Penningroth. www.1stbooks.com: 1st Books Library, 2001.

A Practical Guide to Alternative Baptism and Baby Naming, Kate Gordon. London: Constable and Company Limited, 1998.

A Sense of the Sacred: Finding Our Spiritual Lives Through Ceremony, Adele Getty. Dallas: Taylor Publishing Co., 1997.

A Woman's Book of Rituals and Celebrations, Barbara Ardinger. Novato, CA: New World Library, 1995.

Crossroads: The Quest for Contemporary Rites of Passage, Louise Carus Mahdi, Nancy Geyer Christopher, and Michael Meade, Eds. Chicago: Open Court Publishing Company, 1996.

From Beginning to End: The Rituals of Our Lives, Robert Fulghum. New York: Ballantine Books, 1997.

I Do: A Guide to Creating Your Own Unique Wedding Ceremony, Sydney Barbara Metrick. Berkeley, CA: Celestial Arts, 1992.

Rites of Passage: Celebrating Life's Changes, Kathleen Wall, Ph.D., and Gary Ferguson. Hillsboro, Oregon: Beyond Words Publishing, Inc., 1998.

Shamanic Guide to Death and Dying, Kristin Madden. St. Paul, MN: Llewellyn Publications, 1999.

Weddings from the Heart: Contemporary and Traditional Ceremonies for an Unforgettable Wedding, Daphne Rose Kingma. Berkeley, CA: Conari Press, 1995.

Celebrations

Celebrate the Earth: A Year of Holidays in the Pagan Tradition, Laurie Cabot, with Jean Mills. New York: Delta Trade Paperbacks, 1994.

Celebrate the Solstice: Honoring the Earth's Seasonal Rhythms through Festival and Ceremony, Richard Heinberg. Wheaton, IL: Quest Books, 1993.

Celestially Auspicious Occasions: Seasons, Cycles & Celebrations, Donna Henes. New York: A Perigee Book, 1996.

Shamanism and Spirituality

In the Absence of the Sacred: The Failure of Technology & the Survival of the Indian Nations, Jerry Mander. San Francisco: Sierra Club Books, 1991.

Messages from Your Angels, Doreen Virtue, Ph.D., Carlsbad, CA: Hay House, Inc., 2002.

Sacred Legacies: Healing Your Past and Creating a Positive Future, Denise Linn. New York: Random House, 1999.

Shamanism as a Spiritual Practice for Daily Life, Tom Cowan. Freedom, CA: The Crossing Press, 1996.

Soul Retrieval: Mending the Fragmented Self, Sandra Ingerman. San Francisco: Harper San Francisco, 1991.

The Four-Fold Way: Walking the Paths of the Warrior, Teacher, Healer, and Visionary, Angeles Arrien, Ph.D. San Francisco: Harper San Francisco, 1993.

The Spell of the Sensuous, David Abram. New York: Vintage Books, 1997.

The Spirit of Shamanism, Roger Walsh. New York: Jeremy P. Tarcher, 1990.

The Way of the Shaman, Michael Harner. San Francisco: Harper San Francisco, 1990.

Urban Shaman: A Handbook for Personal and Planetary Transformation Based on the Hawaiian Way of the Adventurer, Serge Kahili King. New York: Simon and Schuster, 1990.

Visionseeker: Shared Wisdom from the Place of Refuge, Hank Wesselman. Carlsbad, CA: Hay House, Inc., 2001.

Music

Fortunately, there's an abundance of good music available for meditation, journeying, and for use during ceremony. Below are just a few titles that I've enjoyed and found useful.

Ambient 1: Music for Airports, Brian Eno. New York: Caroline Records, Inc. • www.caroline.com, 1978.

Chakra Suite, Steven Halpern. San Anselmo, CA: Inner Peace Music www.stevenhalpern.com, 2001.

Following the Circle, Dik Darnell. Littleton, CO: Etherean Music, 1988

In Beauty I Walk: The Best of Coyote Oldman, Coyote Oldman. San Francisco: Hearts of Space, 1997.

Liquid Mind III: Balance, Chuck Wild. Hollywood, CA: Chuck Wild Records • Liquidmindmusic.com, 1999.

Lunar Reflections, Ian Cameron Smith. Sydney, Australia: Rhythmist Productions • www.iancameronsmith.com.au, 2000.

Sacred Spirits: Yeha-Noha, Beverly Hills, CA: Virgin Records, Ltd., 1995.

Shamanic Dream, Anugama. Kihei, Hawaii: Open Sky Music • www.openskymusic.com, 2000.

Shamanic Journey: Didjeridu, Stephen McDonnell. Mill Valley, California: Foundation for Shamanic Studies • www.shamanism.org, 1997.

Shamanic Journey: Multiple Drumming, Bridgewalker Drummers. Mill Valley, California: Foundation for Shamanic Studies • www.shamanism.org, 1993.

The Book of Secrets, Loreena McKennitt. Stratford, Ontario, Canada: Quinlan Road Music, Ltd. • www.quinlanroad.com, 1997.

The Eternal Om, Malibu, California: Valley of the Sun Publishing • www.sutphenpublishing.com, 1991.

The Silent Path, Robert Haig Coxon. Westmount, Quebec: R.H.C. Productions, 1995.

Trance, Gabrielle Roth and the Mirrors. New York: Raven Recording • www.ravenrecording.com, 1993.

Waves and *Waves II*, Angel Earth. Detroit, Michigan: Angel Earth Music • www.angelearth.org, 2002.

Ministerial Licensing

Universal Life Church • www.ulc.org, (520) 721-2882.

Circle of Sacred Earth Church, Inc. • www.circleofthesacredearth.org

Ceremonialists and Shamanic Practitioners

These organizations and individuals offer workshops and referrals. Some do individual consultations, but not all. Check the Websites for further information.

Angeles Arrien, Ph.D. • www.angelesarrien.com • (415) 331-5050 (workshops and training programs)

Foundation for Shamanic Studies • www.shamanism.org • (415) 380-8282 (workshops and referralsto shamanic practitioners)

Jade Wah'oo Grigori • www.shamanic.net; or write jadewahoo@shamanic.net (contemporary shamanism and ceremonials)

Larry G. Peters, Ph.D. • www.tibetanshaman.com • (310) 455-2713 (Tibetan shamanism)

Serge Kahili King, Ph.D. • www.huna.org • (808) 827-8383 (Hawaiian shamanism)

Tom Cowan, Ph.D. • www.riverdrum.com (Celtic shamanism)

Wilbert Alix • www.trancedance.com • (512) 708-8888 (contemporary shamanism and trance dancing)

Spiritual and Ceremonial Resources on the Internet

Ceremonies and Rituals—www.celestialhealing.com. Gives some new twists on ceremony.

Ceremonies and Rituals—www.ritualarts.com. Lots of examples of ceremonies and rituals.

Drumming—www.remo.com. Lots of information on drumming, especially the health benefits.

First Moon—www.celebrategirls.com/history.html. Information on ceremonies for a girl's first menstruation.

Herbs and Ceremonies—www.create.org/Elchai. Recommendations for herbal treatments plus ideas for ceremonies.

Holidays—www.holidays.net. Just about everything you'd want to know about any holiday.

Lunar Phases—www.mooncalendar.co.uk. Order a calendar based on the moon's phases.

Seasonal and Holiday Calendars—www.earthcalendar.net. Shows seasonal and religious holidays throughout the world.

Starcrafts—www.starcraftsob.com. Resource for information and sacred objects.

Vision Quests—www.schooloflostborders.com. This school comes highly recommended.

Weddings, Blessings, and Ceremonies—www.kuhina.com. Hawaiian ceremonials and blessings.

※ ※ ※   ※ ※ ※

About the Author

Steven D. Farmer, Ph.D., is a spiritual psychotherapist, hypnotherapist, minister, professional speaker, shamanic practitioner, and author of several articles and books, including the bestselling *Adult Children of Abusive Parents* and *The Wounded Male*. Steven has appeared on numerous radio and television shows and offers lectures and seminars on sacred ceremony, spiritual healing, trauma recovery, and men's issues. He makes his home with his wife, Doreen Virtue, in Laguna Beach, California. Between them they have two daughters and two sons.

✼ ✼ ✼

Dr. Farmer welcomes your letters and inquiries about presenting workshops. You can contact him by calling or writing Hay House, or by visiting his Website at: **www.StevenDFarmer.com**.

✼ ✼ ✼

Steven says, "I welcome any stories about experiences you have had with sacred ceremonies for possible inclusion in future publications. Please include your permission to edit and reprint these stories." Send them to: **SacredCeremonyStories@StevenDFarmer.com**.

Hay House Titles of Related Interest

Books

Aromatherapy A–Z,
by Connie and Alan Higley and Pat Leatham

Secrets & Mysteries:
The Glory and Pleasure of Being a Woman, by Denise Linn

Spellbinding:
Spells and Rituals That Will Empower Your Life, by Claudia Blaxell

Visionseeker:
Shared Wisdom from the Place of Refuge,
by Hank Wesselman, Ph.D.

Wokini:
A Lakota Journey to Happiness and Self-Understanding,
by Billy Mills, with Nicholas Sparks

Audio Programs

Journeys into Past Lives,
by Denise Linn

Karma Releasing,
by Doreen Virtue, Ph.D.

Your Journey to Enlightenment,
by Dr. Wayne W. Dyer

Card Decks

The Four Agreements Cards,
by DON Miguel Ruiz

Healing Cards,
by Caroline Myss and Peter Occhiogrosso
(50-card deck and booklet)

Magical Spell Cards,
by Lucy Cavendish
(44-card deck and booklet)

Messages from Your Angels Oracle Cards,
by Doreen Virtue, Ph.D.
(44-card deck and booklet)

※ ※ ※

All of the above are available at your local bookstore,
or may be ordered through Hay House, Inc.:

(800) 654-5126 or (760) 431-7695
(800) 650-5115 (fax) or (760) 431-6948 (fax)
www.hayhouse.com

❋ NOTES ❋

✖ NOTES ✖

� NOTES ✖

❀ ❀ ❀

We hope you enjoyed this Hay House book. If you would like to receive a free catalog featuring additional Hay House books and products, or if you would like information about the Hay Foundation, please contact:

Hay House, Inc.
P.O. Box 5100
Carlsbad, CA 92018-5100

(760) 431-7695 or (800) 654-5126
(760) 431-6948 (fax) or (800) 650-5115 (fax)
www.hayhouse.com®

Published and distributed in Australia by:
Hay House Australia Pty. Ltd., 18/36 Ralph St., Alexandria NSW 2015
Phone: 612-9669-4299 • *Fax:* 612-9669-4144 • www.hayhouse.com.au

Published and distributed in the United Kingdom by:
Hay House UK, Ltd., 292B Kensal Rd., London W10 5BE
Phone: 44-20-8962-1230 • *Fax:* 44-20-8962-1239 • www.hayhouse.co.uk

Published and distributed in the Republic of South Africa by:
Hay House SA (Pty), Ltd., P.O. Box 990, Witkoppen 2068
Phone/Fax: 27-11-706-6612 • orders@psdprom.co.za

Published in India by:
Hay House Publications (India) Pvt. Ltd., Muskaan Complex,
Plot No. 3, B-2, Vasant Kunj, New Delhi 110 070 • *Phone:* 91-11-4176-1620
Fax. 91-11-4176-1630 • www.hayhouseindia.co.in

Distributed in Canada by:
Raincoast , 9050 Shaughnessy St., Vancouver, B.C. V6P 6E5
Phone: (604) 323-7100 • *Fax:* (604) 323-2600 • www.raincoast.com

❀ ❀ ❀

Tune in to **HayHouseRadio.com®** for the best in inspirational talk radio featuring top Hay House authors! And, sign up via the Hay House USA Website to receive the Hay House online newsletter and stay informed about what's going on with your favorite authors. You'll receive bimonthly announcements about: Discounts and Offers, Special Events, Product Highlights, Free Excerpts, Giveaways, and more!
www.hayhouse.com®